I TOOK
A HAMMER
IN MY HAND

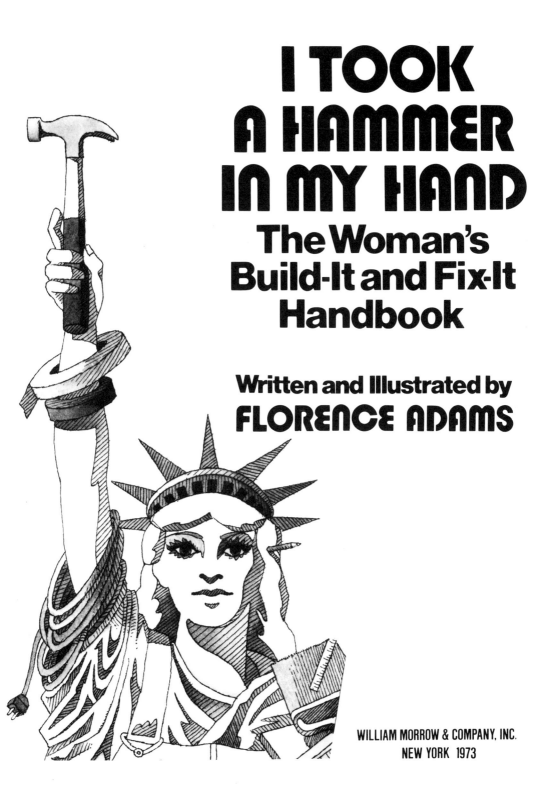

I TOOK A HAMMER IN MY HAND

The Woman's Build-It and Fix-It Handbook

Written and Illustrated by
FLORENCE ADAMS

WILLIAM MORROW & COMPANY, INC.
NEW YORK 1973

Copyright © 1973 by Florence Adams

All rights reserved. No part of this book may be reproduced
or utilized in any form or by any means, electronic or
mechanical, including photocopying, recording or by any
information storage and retrieval system, without
permission in writing from the Publisher. Inquiries should
be addressed to William Morrow and Company, Inc., 105
Madison Ave., New York, N.Y. 10016.

Printed in the United States of America.

1 2 3 4 5 77 76 75 74 73

Library of Congress Cataloging in Publication Data

Adams, Florence.
    I took a hammer in my hand.

    Bibliography: p.
    1. Repairing—Amateurs' manuals.   2. Dwellings—
Maintenance and repair.   3. Woodwork—Amateurs'
manuals.   4. Automobiles—Maintenance and repair.
I. Title.
TT151.A3   643'.7   73-10347
ISBN 0-688-00165-3

CONTENTS

walls, concrete and cinder block walls, wood walls . . . and the proper hanging hardware to use for each type, toggle bolts, molly bolts, expansion plugs, lead plugs, masonry nails

ACKNOWLEDGMENTS

Because my most frequent approach to solving a build-it, fix-it problem has been to ask questions, I must first thank just about all the friends I have, for their contributions to my growth in this area are the largest.

Very special thanks for criticism, encouragement, suggestions and professional knowledge and appraisal to: Joan Balaguer, Nancy Carter, Donna Barkman, Trudie Lamb, Brett Vuolo, Mimi Anderson, Judy Brown, Alice Harrall, Barbara Harrison, Mary Lou O'Neill Haggerty, James Berry, Frank Dailey, Jim Hughes, John Mortimer, James O'Neill, Toni and Bill Valk, Vigilante Plumbers (Michael P. Vigilante, Michael J. Mazzeo, Anthony Vigilante), Court Sash and Door Lumber (Tony Biondo), Pat's Auto Repairs (Pat Granato), and Anthony Pellegrino (electrician).

Also, particular thanks to my editor, Hillel Black, a special person, who asked for more . . . and more . . . and more, so he too could know.

I must thank my children, who patiently waited for their mommy to have more time for them again, and who were bought off by the promise that I would build that jungle bedroom as soon as the book was finished.

Last, but not least, I must thank my parents, my mother, who, in spite of the "unladylike" talents I've developed, has always had encouraging words for me. (I suspect she thinks my father is giving me the know-how nudge from heaven.) And my father, for his tools, for having encouraged my talents . . . and for the nudge.

"The widening of woman's sphere is to improve her lot. Let us do it, and if the world scoff, let it scoff—if it sneer, let it sneer. . . ."

LUCY STONE
National Women's Rights
Convention, Cincinnati, 1855

AUTHOR TO READER

"In the beginning," the Bible tells us, God created water (among other things). After that it proceeds to illustrate the significance of water in various biblical stories. Thus, we are introduced to water, before we see it in action.

However, in the handyperson area, the "in the beginning" information is frequently absent. This is so true, so often, that it contributes heavily to our intimidation whenever we go seeking a how-to method. ("Before you change the washer in the faucet, turn off the water"— a well-illustrated lesson in changing a washer, with its underlined warning, but not a word about how one turns off the water! This is the type of problem we face most of the time.) References to unknowns hang us up and stop the progress we aim for, and continued searching doesn't always alleviate the situation. This is the criticism frequently made about how-to books and magazines, and it's true. Thus one of my objectives, when I decided to attempt a book like this, was to start at the beginning. As a matter of fact, there is a great deal more emphasis on the beginning than on the end. There is no end! Where you go from the beginnings will become the end.

Another reason for this book is that I would like to change the handy*man* image to handy*person,* to shatter the mystique. Whenever we open home-repair books and magazines we are confronted with pictures of a man doing it—his thing! If a woman is in the picture, she is holding the ladder or a piece of wood. She's the "helper" on the job. Those women who have crossed the line and picked up a hammer to do a job themselves have discovered how simple many tasks are. (So much for the mystique of the handy*man.*) Some of us feel obliged to hide our accomplishments from our husbands, or lovers, or brothers, or fathers. (Maybe we can do something they can't do; best to leave well enough alone.) Some of us show off the product of our efforts and are patted on the head, or elsewhere, with a "Pretty good job for a woman. . . ." Others build in private so some man won't butt in and ruin it. (Once I was outside, sawing a 4-by-8-foot piece of plywood in half, when a male neighbor came along, took the saw out of my hand and said, "Here, let me do that for you, that's no job for a woman!" He cut it so unevenly that the wood was useless and I had to buy more. My distress about the wood was coupled with the frustration of knowing I couldn't tell him he messed up the job. That was then; now I wouldn't give him the saw.)

Another lack in our growth is that our female birthright doesn't include the freedom to expose ourselves to the "watch and learn" information. Construction sites are not comfortable places for women to hang around. When a repairman comes to your house, he's not too happy if you watch, to see what's behind that plaster wall, or what section of the toilet tank he replaced. Or, if he doesn't mind your hanging around, it's usually because he thinks you want to sleep with him! We all know how delicate this watching situation is, and how it frequently forces us to another room, another task, when we'd really like to stay and learn. Thus we are not exposed to many of the basics that men acquire without difficulty. Their questions are honored—they are men. Ours are usually answered by another question—"What do you want to know that for, lady?"—and left unanswered.

The questions need to be answered. This book is my attempt to share what I have discovered with those of you who want to begin to learn. I haven't learned it all yet, and some of my methods are unorthodox, but I'm no longer helpless around the house. In fact, I'm "that woman down the block who builds." I'm not unique, nor do I have any special talent. (A master carpenter I'm not!) What is true is that I am no longer in awe of a hammer or a power drill. I'm not afraid of being a "lady builder," and there's no lumberyard salesman, anywhere, who can ever intimidate me again! (And that's something we'll talk about later.) Two other things: I've saved one passel of money by doing it myself, and I've almost completely eliminated the frustration of waiting for him (the husband, lover, landlord) to fix it.

I'd like to tell you why I learned to fix it, make it. It was necessity, the mother of education. Six years ago, I was divorced, with two small boys to raise. The apartment rent scene, always gruesome, began to frighten me. I became convinced that I would be moving every two years or so because of rent increases, and that kind of hassle wouldn't be any good for the boys, or for me. So I took my savings, added to it borrowed money and bought a small and inexpensive brownstone house. Its selection was based on the fact that the plumbing and electricity were functioning and that it was habitable. However, the house was so narrow (13½ feet wide) that I decided we would have to occupy the lower two floors of the house. Unfortunately, there was no interior staircase joining these floors. The house originally had a staircase joining these two floors. This I knew because a friend lived in a twin house next door. What I had was a closet on each floor, the staircase long gone. That closet was the *only* closet on the floor. The tasks before me were obvious: Remove the walls of the closet on the lower floor; remove the floor of the closet above; build a staircase; build a closet somewhere else for each floor. Many other projects followed, like ripping down walls to expose the bricks (which cost nothing but backbreaking sticktoitiveness), and doing tricks with paint here and there, and as it all happened, I added modestly to my tool collection and my experience—and for me, the handy*man* mystique was over.

I think it's necessary to explain why I attempted so early in the game to build a staircase—naiveté. Later, when I casually asked a carpenter, "How much?" and he said, "Six hundred dollars"(!), it was necessity. In earlier years I'd built a few simple bookcases, so, I told myself simply (simplemindedly!), how much harder could a staircase be? It's just a bookcase with slanted sides, right?! And off I went to the library to read about staircases. (I settled for "steps.") It wasn't an easy concept, and I played with various approaches for weeks, but when at last I came up with the final plan, it took just two hours to build and attach—and it cost only sixty dollars. Naiveté! (Yes, the plan . . . and the search . . . for the staircase is included in a later section.) Allow yourself naiveté, for usually it will work the miracle.

You may already know some of what follows. Skip it. Hopefully there will be enough to launch you into a whole new dimension. And maybe, when there are enough of us, there will be books and magazines for the handy*person,* women and men doing tasks, women no longer the helper but the doer.

A postscript: Before you start any projects, be sure to have on hand the following things:

Two sturdy chairs or wooden milk boxes, to use when sawing.
One of those good mushy brooms, not the straw kind, for sweeping up the sawdust.
A medium-sized cardboard carton for saving wood scraps.
A sacred place to keep *your* tools and supplies.
A Sears, Roebuck catalog—it will be your dictionary and encyclopedia for tools and materials.
. . . And get a tetanus shot.

BUILDING

TOOLS

MY ATTITUDES

I do not necessarily want to inspire a "feminine mystique" with my attitude about tools. But I'm afraid I do have some strong feelings about which tools to use—and which to avoid if you are, like me, of limited strength, patience, and time. However, my beliefs are based, I hope, not just on my abilities, but also on good sense.

First, a few words about the history of my tool collection. When my husband and I split, he moved temporarily to a hotel and took only clothes and other absolute necessities, not, of course, his tools. Within a few months, when he had found an apartment, I had to find a cheaper apartment for myself and the boys, to ease the overall financial burden. Much tool work was involved to make this new place habitable for us. And then a year later I had bought the brownstone and was using the tools almost daily. At some point during all this moving, my ex-husband told me I could keep the tools, which included a power saw and a power drill. He borrowed the tools whenever he needed them, until eventually he bought new ones for himself. Furthermore, during the month before we moved into the brownstone, I was building the sections for a closet (8 feet by 8 feet) to replace the only one there, which was to be removed for the staircase. Every weekend, when he came to pick up the children, I was occupied in this task. The most back-breaking part of the job was screwing in the screws, millions of them, it seemed. When we finally moved into the brownstone, my ex-husband gave me a housewarming present, an electric screwdriver.

Thus, as a result of inheriting my tools, I became accustomed to some degree of ease, using what I had. Perhaps it encouraged my building ventures, not always struggling with tools that demanded strength and power I didn't possess. My point is to persuade you, if you can afford it, to buy (if you can't afford to, to borrow) some power (electric) tools for even your early projects. It may be the difference that keeps you going.

There is, as you may well know, a whole mystique involved with a man's tool collection and his use of tools. He often reads about them, browses among them and finally buys "the best." (Five years ago I was buying tools in the five-and-ten.) I have to say right now—good tools do good jobs (one point for men). The best example of this mystique involving the use of tools by men is the saw. I have often watched men saw—with a handsaw, nonelectric—something which could easily have been cut with a small power saw. I do not understand why they did not use the power saw they had—and all the men I have watched have had them. I have asked about it and the response has always been the same: "It's easier." In some instances when I questioned further, "Why is it easier?" they responded, "You get a straighter cut." Others responded, "I don't know, it just is, that's all." I can only assume that it's easier than getting out the electric saw, putting in the blade and plugging it in. Certainly the labor of cutting is easier and faster with a power saw. As far as cutting straight is concerned, only some experience is necessary to keep the saw on target. So, WHY? (That same mystery applies to drilling holes with those wretched hand drills—which, for me at least, wobble, stick, everything!)

I don't agree. I refuse to join the cursing building scene, cursing because it's hard or time-consuming. It doesn't have to be. A labor of love doesn't have to end up in a mess of mangled nerves.

Perhaps there are some jobs that a power saw or drill simply can't do. Well, I haven't found one yet. And I haven't ruined either my drill or saw, and each is about ten years old. I take that back, sorry. Once I ruined a hacksaw, which I borrowed from my son's tool kit and had to replace. It was necessary to cut the steel bars on one of my windows so that I could install an air conditioner. The job took three or four hours. It was a miserable task, and I was sore for a week, and I'll never be so stupid again. As a matter of fact, at the time I bought two air conditioners (at a great sale, and they are the very simple kind, one knob: on–off). I installed only one. The other is still in the box, unopened. No more hacksawing for me! So . . . I'm not perfect.

TOOLS TO BEG, BORROW OR STEAL

Hammer

This type of hammer is called a "claw hammer." The double purpose of this tool is interesting; the blunt end, the face, hammers nails in, and the two-pronged end, the claw, pulls nails out—the mistakes, the crooked ones. It may seem easier to hit the nail by grasping the hammer in the middle—and according to my philosophy, any way is

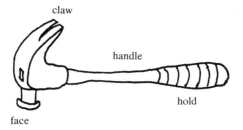

OK if it works—but you ought to know that there is more power to the thrust (the nail goes in farther each hit) if you hold the handle at the end. If you are considering buying a new hammer, try to find one with a rubber-handled end, for grip, about 14 or 16 ounces. (There are other styles of hammers—for other purposes, I guess—but this is the only kind I have, and so far it has been all I've needed.)

Screwdriver

If everything could be built with nails, what fun building would be. Alas, sometimes holding strength is required and screws are necessary, and thus the screwdriver. The most important thing to know

about this tool, to save some aggravation (it's never all fun!) is to use the proper-sized tip—in width and thickness—in the screw slot, or the metal around the slot of the screw can bend, almost shred.

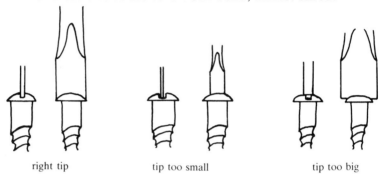

right tip   tip too small   tip too big

Sometimes you will see screwheads with cross-type slots: Usually, your screwdriver, the kind pictured above, will be fine on these screws. Someday you can buy yourself a Phillips screwdriver, which

Phillips screwdriver

has a tip that fits this cross slot. Better still, if you are about to buy some screwdrivers, Sears has a good set with three sizes of the flat tip, two Phillips sizes, a flat-tipped one with a short stem and chunky handle, and a bonus: a little round disk with four screwdriver tips that you can hang on your keychain. (The first Christmas after our separation, my ex-husband bought one of these sets for the children to give me. The other gifts he helped them select were a bottle of Réplique perfume and a book about the Beatles! I've always thought, looking back, that that might well be the best description of who I am.)

A tip: Hold the tip of the screwdriver with the forefinger and thumb of your free hand, loosely, as a guide to keep the tip in the screw slot.

Another tip: Keep a cake of soap with your tools. When driving screws, soap the threads first and the job becomes infinitely easier.

Pliers

The type pictured here are called "slip joint" pliers. (I have no idea what a slip joint is—wait a minute. That probably means that the pin

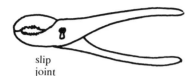

slip
joint

that holds the two pieces together can "slip" around into different positions. Clever! And the grabby ends of the pliers—claws? —can "slip" around variably sized things.)

They are also called mechanics' pliers. You are probably as familiar with this tool as with the hammer and screwdriver. It does jobs that other tools do better, perhaps, but so what? Nuts (of nuts and bolts) are best dealt with by using the proper-sized socket wrench, open-end wrench; but pliers are fine, it's just a little more work holding them closed. A frequent use is to pull out the nails that have no heads, or that have sqwooshed heads that hammer claws can't grab.

Saw

As I said earlier, my experience with nonelectric saws is almost nonexistent, so I did a little research, in case these are all you have and can't afford an electric one.

HANDSAW   The handsaw is used for general cutting (so is the electric saber saw). The trick to getting a start with a saw: Pull the saw toward you lightly, to establish the cut line, then shove it down. If that works, just keep going, heavier on the downstroke. Drudgery! (For all handsawing, saw at an angle, not vertically up and down.)

KEYHOLE OR COMPASS SAW   The keyhole saw, also called the compass saw, is best for cutting lines that are not straight—curves at a corner, little holes, circles. This is so because the blade is strong but not too wide. You will notice that cutting curves, for instance, is a bit rough, but the saber saw has a blade even thinner than the end tip of the keyhole saw.

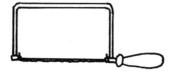

COPING SAW   The coping saw is especially good for cutting designs out of wood, because the blade is thin and can twist. Different kinds of blades are available, for different woods and purposes. Once I found a type of blade for the coping saw which would cut glass. (A saber saw will also cut designs well, because it has a thin blade.)

miter box

Wood to be sawed at an angle goes in box, blade of backsaw goes in one of the slots.

BACKSAW   The backsaw might be handy, because it is the type of saw needed to cut angles with a miter box, and, yes, I did use one of these saws once, to cut a piece of molding. Also use this kind of saw to cut corner angles for picture frames.

Left and right slots are for cutting 45° angles.   The center slot is for right angles (90°).

SABER SAW   The price of all these saws will surely be as much as or more than a decent electric saber saw. (Later for the miter box and backsaw scene. That's for fancy work.) So if you can, buy or borrow a saber saw. If you already have one and know how to use it, skip this part; if you're not sure, read on. The best kind of electric saw (or electric anything) has an on–off switch you can reach with the thumb of the hand holding the saw. You are then able to stop and start without jiggling it and groping with your other hand, which is busy holding the wood.

Also your saw should have a two-pronged claw, not one; you will

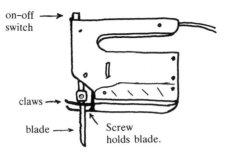

on–off switch

claws →

blade → Screw holds blade.

be able to cut a straight line by keeping the penciled cut line between the claws. If yours has only one prong, practice cutting, to learn how to guide it for straight cutting. Buy an extra package of all-purpose blades and you'll be stocked for almost everything. Keep the saw stored *without* the blade in. Insert the blade *before* you plug in the saw. Make sure the screw holding the blade is tight or the blade may come out while sawing. Then plug the saw in.

You will notice that the saw has a three-pronged plug, which will not fit into the regular two-slot outlets. If you have a three-pronged outlet (see Electricity, page 213) convenient to where you are sawing, use it. If not, get a three-prong adapter from the hardware store. The saw's three prongs plug into the three slots of the adapter and the adapter's two prongs plug into the wall outlet. Wait! Don't plug it in yet. You will notice a wire with a little U-shaped piece of metal at the end of it. This is the ground. (Read Electricity to learn about grounds, if you need to know). The round, third prong on the saw plug is the ground for that, and this little wire on the adapter continues the function. Unscrew the screw holding the switchplate against the wall, just a bit. Slip under the U-shaped metal end of the wire and screw it tight again. And for added safety against shock, wear sneakers and stand on a piece of wood.

OK, now plug in. Hold the saw a speck away from the start of the cut line, laying the claws on the wood with the line centered between the claws. Switch on and go forward, slowly and carefully. If you turn on the switch while the blade is touching the wood, you'll scare the life out of yourself, because the saw will jump and jiggle all over the place.

In case you are unfamiliar with the physical process of arranging and sawing the wood, I'll give you some tips.

Place the wood, if a board, on two milk boxes or two chairs of the

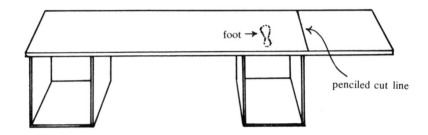

penciled cut line

same height, with the penciled cut line to the right of the boxes if you are right-handed, to the left if you are left-handed. The longest length should be on the boxes. If the free end is very long, a third box should be used under the middle of it. If you're right-handed, put your left foot on the left side of the wood while cutting and brace it firmly. The firmer the wood is braced, the easier the cutting will be. As you near the end of the cutting, about two inches or so away, grab the edge of wood near the end on the free side *(A),* and hold it firmly, so that it won't crack or splinter off, ruining the edge, before you finish. (Yes, you have to be a bit of a contortionist!) You could also clamp the wood to the boxes for firmness, but you'll still need the foot on top, or the saw will push the whole contraption forward with it.

If the length you want to use is on the left, cut exactly right of the cut line to obtain the true length. All that sawdust is wood that the saw has chewed up, at least the thickness of the blade. Also, because of this lost wood, measure one piece at a time and cut, when you are cutting more than one piece from a board, so that the measurement will be true.

clamp

Clamps are almost a must when cutting from a very short piece of wood, because it has to be held rigid. You could lose a few fingers if you try to hold a small piece without help.

Go slow with a saber saw. Don't push too hard, especially on tough wood, like plywood or two-by-fours (which are usually fir, not pine). The motor could get too hot from hard work and burn out. Not forcing will save it. Keep your eye on the line and blow away any sawdust that builds up on the line and obscures it.

Finally, it is necessary to mention a term now so that you know it, and so that you not do the thing yourself but have it done in the lumberyard. The term is "ripping." This means sawing the wood the long

← rip line

way, making the board less wide. Always buy the correct width, or have the correct width (if not available) ripped from what is available at the lumberyard. Not only does it take forever to rip, but a long rip is bound not to be as straight as you want it, if cut by a saber saw. Now, when you're ready for a table saw (that's been on my Christmas list for a couple of years, but no, Florence, there is no Santa Claus), then it's a different story. The difficulty is the wood grain: It's easy to cut across the grain, but difficult to cut "with the grain."

I think much of one's fear of the electric saw is simply related to the noise it makes. It deafens the mind. Every morning for a few days, get up and turn on the saw for a minute or so to get used to it.

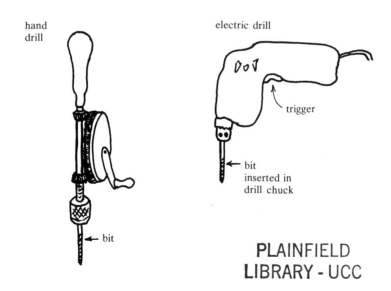

hand drill

electric drill

trigger

← bit

← bit inserted in drill chuck

Drill

This is truly the most magic tool, the one that makes you comfortable building. It is used to predrill holes before screws go in, holes slightly smaller than the screws. It is used to drill the holes for nuts and bolts and the holes for doorknob bolts. It is used to bore holes in masonry for lead plugs. And it is used to make holes in wood for the saw blade to go in when you are making inside cuts in wood, like circles, etc.

In terms of what kind of drill to use, I have to admit that I've had absolutely no success (absolutely!) with the hand drill. Maybe I'm holding it wrong. It wobbles, I can't get a good grip, and I've given up trying. I can't give you one tip about them.

A ¼-inch electric drill is all I am able to tell you about. Beg, borrow (or steal) the money to buy one, or locate a friend who will lend you one. (Sears has them starting at nine dollars or so. Watch for a sale.)

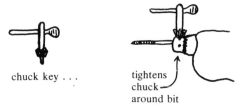

chuck key . . .   tightens
                         chuck
                         around bit

All kinds of bits are available, for wood, metal and masonry. They come in diameters from very, very tiny (and very, very breakable—

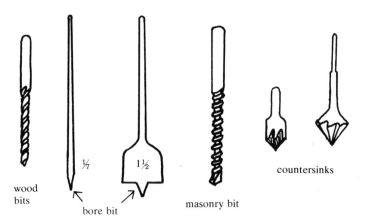

wood bits   ¼   1½   countersinks

bore bit   masonry bit

don't wobble the drill with a tiny one) to 1½ to 2 inches. A good investment is a box of assorted bits. Buy the larger-diameter sizes as you
need them, or buy a set of various sizes, or borrow the larger sizes—
people have less difficulty lending bits than drills.

If you are predrilling a hole before screwing, drill a hole slightly
smaller in diameter than the thickest threads of the screw, so there
will be some wood left inside the hole to grab onto. Don't drill the
whole length of the screw, either; leave some real stuff for the screw
to grab onto at the end. Besides making the screwdriving easier, predrilling helps prevent cracking of the wood by removing some wood
ahead of time.

Sometimes the screw seems to get stuck and screwing becomes
very difficult. When this happens, tap the head of the screw lightly
with a hammer—not too hard or you'll ruin the threads (see illustration A)—and you may just be able to nudge it past a tough spot in the
wood. If this doesn't work, perhaps the predrilled hole was too small;
remove the screw and use the next-sized bit and drill again (see illustration B); or use the same bit and drill a little deeper; or, if you think
the next size will be too big, use the same bit you used and drill into
the hole again, jiggling the drill slightly. This will make a slightly bigger
hole.

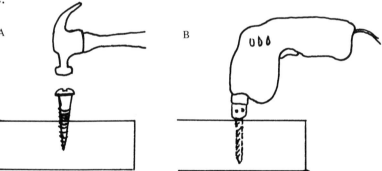

An easy way to find out which size drill bit to use with a screw (or
nail) is to place together between your finger and thumb the screw and
the bit you think appropriate. Roll them. You will be able to tell if the
bit is right, for it will feel slightly smaller than the screw.

Another way of determining the right size bit is to hold the bit
behind the screw. The bit should be only as thick as the stem around
which the screw threads wind. Thus, if you look at these two together

(bit behind screw) you shouldn't see the bit . . . but not too small a bit! If you see some of the bit in the thread area, you can see that it's too big; it will eat away too much wood that the threads of the screw are supposed to grab onto.

Practice drilling holes in some old wood to see if you are getting straight cuts. Practice drilling horizontally and also vertically. There will be times when you'll have to do it each way. If you discover you have a tendency to drill crookedly, work on it, so that eventually you can eye it straight.

In order to get the hole exactly where you want it, hammer the tip of a nail into the center mark (dot), or push the point of the pencil deep into the wood as you make the dot, or make a dent with the tip of the drill bit, right before you turn the drill on. (This last is what I do, not always successfully.)

"Countersinking" is a term referring to driving a screw or nail so deeply into the wood that its head is below the surface; it can be hidden by applying wood putty over it flush to the surface.

Predrilling a hole for a screw to be countersunk is done in two steps. (Three if you count preparing the wood for the bit so that it goes in dead center.)

1) Make a dent in the wood—at dead center—by tapping a nail into the mark with a hammer.

2) Drill the screw hole, using the selected, proper-sized drill bit for the screw.

3) Remove the screw-hole bit and put the countersink bit into the drill. Drill into the hole already made until you think the head of the screw will sink into this cone-shaped hole. A good test is to hold the screw upside down and see if the diameter of the head of the screw is slightly less than the diameter of the top of the hole.

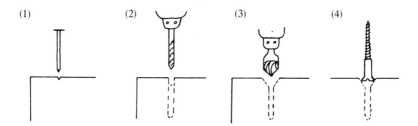

(1)   (2)   (3)   (4)

One final word about the *chuck key,* if you have an electric drill. It has a way of getting misplaced. There is a great gadget available, a rubber or plastic thing, which will hold the chuck key attached to the cord of the drill. It's a good idea to pick up one if it doesn't come with your saw.

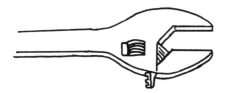

Wrench

As an all-purpose wrench, this adjustable, open-ended wrench is perhaps the best kind to have. Also, this type usually is thin and fits into tight places. Because it is adjustable, it sometimes needs readjusting to tighten it, and eventually you may want to invest in a set of open-ended wrenches, to be done with the hassle. Five or six come in a set, each end a different size, to cope with many variations.

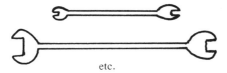

etc.

Level

This tool is a necessity when you have to know if what you are doing will be perfectly horizontal (use level as in Figure 1; the bubble to watch is *A*, the one in the center tube). For vertical use, level as

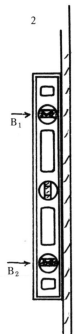

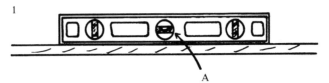

in Figure 2; the bubbles to watch are B_1 and B_2 in the outer circles. The bubbles to watch, in all cases, are in tubes which are horizontal. (Watch the bottom tube when there are two tubes in the circle.) The level pictured is similar to mine, which is made of metal, about 18 inches long and 2½ inches wide. Although it is not as big as levels can come, it is about the best size to get, rather than a smaller one.

Measuring Devices

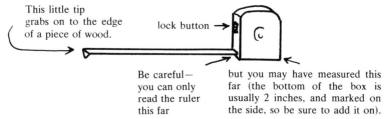

This little tip grabs on to the edge of a piece of wood.

lock button →

| Be careful— you can only read the ruler this far | but you may have measured this far (the bottom of the box is usually 2 inches, and marked on the side, so be sure to add it on). |

NOTE: Absolutely forbidden for measuring are cloth sewing tape measures. They stretch.

STEEL TAPE MEASURE   This measure is one that winds up in a circle within a small metal box. It is suggested that you get one that has the extra feature of a lock button, a button which will allow you to lock the open ruler at the measurement position it's extended to. These steel tape measures usually extend to 12 feet. This is the type of ruler I use to measure for the cut lines when sawing.

WOODEN FOLDING RULER   A neat gadget because it folds up to only 6 or 7 inches, which is handy for storage—or your back pocket. When

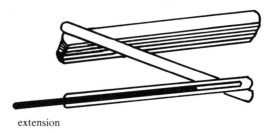

extension

opened it can extend to 6 feet and has a ruler on both sides. However, it extends only in multiples of the length of one of the pieces—mine folds to 7 inches, therefore it extends to 7 inches, 14 inches, 21 inches, etc. Until very recently, I almost exclusively used my steel tape measure to measure—often awkwardly—things for which a wooden folding ruler would have been better, the height of walls being the best example. Then one day, while browsing in the hardware store, I discovered a wooden ruler with a special gismo. Through the center of the wood in the first section slid a thin metal strip, which could come out as far as 6 inches—it was a little ruler. The multiples problem was eliminated. Yes, I bought one right away, and I recommend it to you.

THREE-FOOT STEEL RULER   A must for drawing straight lines longer than 12 or 18 inches, the usual ruler lengths we have at home. I waited too long in my building career to buy one of these and drew some pretty crooked lines in the meantime, so I recommend that you buy one now. Don't buy a wooden yardstick; they can warp, get nicks and affect the line you draw—and we want that almighty line to be perfect when we saw, so we have to concentrate only on following it!

TWELVE-INCH OR EIGHTEEN-INCH RULER (WOOD)   Perhaps this should be first, you think, but actually it isn't used that often. I am recommending it for the purpose of drawing circles. If you have one with little holes in it, you can put a pin or nail through one hole and a pencil through another. Using the nail as a pivot, you can push the ruler around and draw a circle. It isn't necessary to go out and buy one of these rulers with holes if you don't already have one; you can

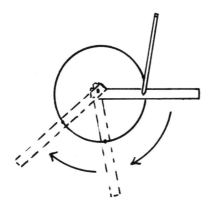

drill holes as you need them in the wooden one you have, or even in an old piece of ¼-inch x 1-inch wood.

FRAMING SQUARE OR "TRY SQUARE"   A tool you really should have, in order to guarantee a perpendicular cut line for sawing. Lay one edge of the angle along the edge of the wood and brace it against a higher piece of wood than the one on which the line is being drawn. The bracing block of wood helps keep the angle flush with the board.

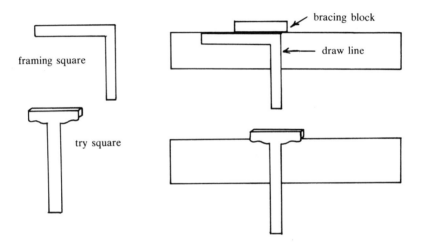

And here's a trick, if you haven't an angle ruler or a try square: Mark one edge at the desired length. The shortest line you can draw will be perpendicular to the side.

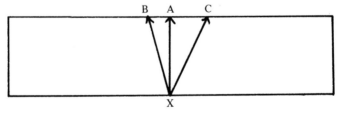

$X{\to}A$ is shorter than $X{\to}B$ or $X{\to}C$.

Sandpaper

Sandpaper comes in variable grades: coarse, medium, fine, extra fine. It's inexpensive and a package of mixed variety will last a while and be available when you need it, if you keep a stock of it in the house. Coarse gives a very heavy sanding and also a very visible one, and thus it should be the first grade used to get the hard work done. The finishing sanding should be done with fine or extra fine, a grade using finer and denser sand, which provides the smoothing quality.

Your fingertips and hands don't last too long when sanding, so it is advisable to wrap a piece of sandpaper around a block of wood. The wood does the heavy work of applying even pressure; you supply the push pressure.

When sanding a flat surface, try to go with the grain of wood, not across it, or you may leave scratchlike marks.

When sanding an edge of wood just sawed, be careful at the corners; they can easily become rounded in the sanding process. Sandpaper wrapped around a piece of wood and applied evenly back and forth along the edge prevents this.

Graph Paper

A pad of graph paper, ten squares to the inch, is a good investment. When you are planning a project, graph paper is a quick way to see the relationships of the dimensions you are planning, faster and better than all kinds of ruling and measuring on blank paper.

Pencils

No matter how often I try to duplicate my exciting desk supplies for my children, there are always some items mysteriously lost. One of these is scissors. We must have ten pairs, adult and children's varieties, tucked in nooks—scissors that will never show up until we move, if ever. And another item, of course, is the pencil! When a pencil is used by children, it becomes vastly useful in areas totally unrelated to writing. It's a building prop, an arrow; two can be used to make a stretcher for the Ken doll. When a pencil is actually used for writing and drawing, mine perhaps disappear because they still have erasers! So keep a few with your tools. Also, try to use a sharp-pointed pencil when drawing lines for sawing, etc. A dull point could mean a $\frac{1}{8}$- or $\frac{1}{16}$-inch error when it's vital not to have such a mistake.

TOOLS TO BUY WHEN YOU NEED

There are some tools that you may need some time after you feel comfortable making and doing, tools for which there are no substitutes, homemade or otherwise. Some of these have already been mentioned, like the backsaw and miter box, and some will be mentioned later. I'd like to talk now about these tools to buy when you need them.

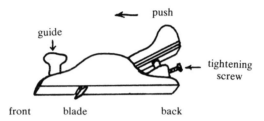

Plane

Because I'm still at the "cellar construction" level of my building career—I have used a plane only for very minor jobs, like taking a little wood off the top of a sticking door. And I have only one plane, the kind pictured above, which I discovered in research to be a block plane. There are other types of planes for the master carpenters.

The blade sticks out of the bottom, and the amount it sticks out is adjustable. It should never stick out too much; it isn't a saw and really can't be pushed to cut very deeply in one stroke. A deep cut should be made with a saw and smoothed with a plane. The cutting edge of the plane has a beveled edge and should be in position as shown here *(a):*

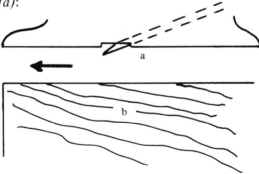

The plane should go in the same direction as the grain of wood *(b)*. This means it should go the same way that the wood grain is traveling —up, toward the edge you are planing. The plane direction in *a* is correct in relation to *b*. Going in the direction illustrated, you will only be slicing off the tips of the grain ends, but planing in the opposite direction will cause the blade to get caught in the grain and may start a crack.

Clamps

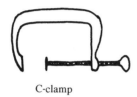

C-clamp

A clamp is a device that hold two things together. It comes in all sizes and shapes, very big and very little. It is particularly helpful when you are gluing two pieces of wood together. Another sometimes necessary use for clamps is as a brace to hold wood steady when you are sawing or drilling holes. You can clamp the piece of wood to the milk boxes or to a chair or table to steady it.

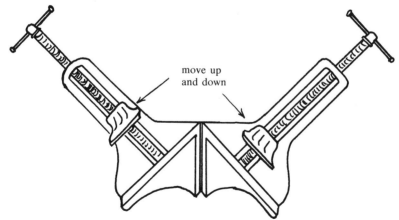

move up
and down

The most worthwhile clamps I ever discovered (and purchased right away) were corner clamps. If you can find them, buy four. Boxes, cubes, bookcases, etc. can be cornered together and tested, before you put in a nail or screw, and held together while the actual work is being done. This device is particularly helpful when you are predrilling a hole for a screw that goes through one piece of wood to another at a corner.

Another good feature is that different wood thicknesses may be held with this gadget.

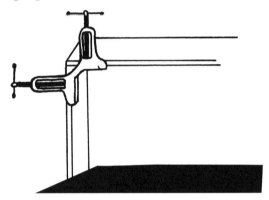

Backsaw and Miter Box

When corner joinings of this nature are desirable, you'll need a backsaw and miter box. Picture-frame corners are the best example of this joint.

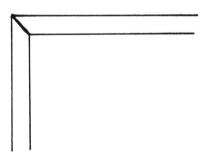

These tools are pictured earlier, in the sawing section. I would like to mention here, as we just mentioned clamps, that when you don't have a corner clamp, a good way to hold the corners together for fastening this type of corner is to place a small, flat piece of wood on each side and clamp them together over the corner. This actually creates the same effect you would get from a vise.

A vise is a tool very much like the clamping device we devised here,

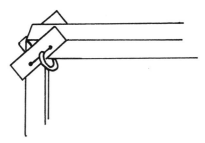

except that it's all combined into one unit. It has flat side pieces for bracing, which are separable for wide or narrow widths by a screwing mechanism.

Nail Set

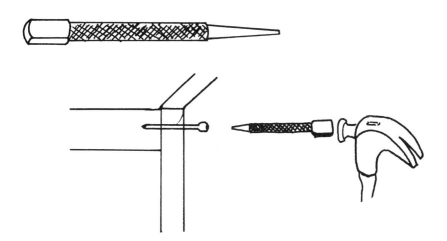

A nail set is used to make finishing nails disappear below the surface of the wood. Drive in the nail about ⅛ inch and fill the remaining hole with wood putty. Finishing nails have a slight indentation in the head for the nail set to sit in. The term for making nails disappear is *countersinking*.

Protractor

When an exact angle is required, a protractor can be the tool to use.

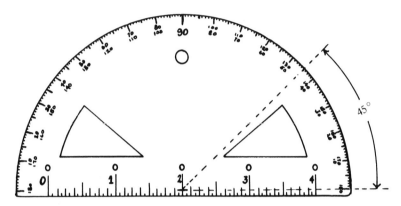

The most frequent angle needed is a 90° angle. There are 360° in a circle, 180° in a half circle, 90° in a quarter circle, etc.

Remove the arc line of a quarter circle and you have a right angle— a 90° angle.

The term "perpendicular" describes the relationship between two lines meeting at right angles, like lines *a* and *b* in the diagram.

(The term "parallel" describes the relationship between two lines traveling beside each other that are the same distance apart at all points.)

Chisel

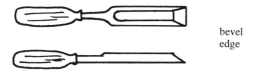

bevel
edge

Some illustrations of this tool's usefulness may persuade you not to wait until you need it, for the illustrations may solve the mystery of how some tasks are accomplished.

To notch out a piece of two-by-four so that it may join another piece:

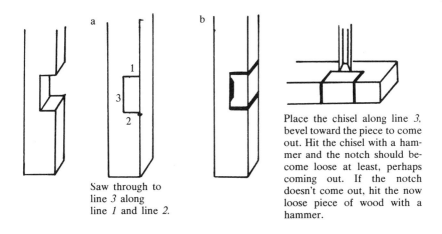

a

b

1

3

2

Saw through to
line *3* along
line *1* and line *2.*

Place the chisel along line *3,* bevel toward the piece to come out. Hit the chisel with a hammer and the notch should become loose at least, perhaps coming out. If the notch doesn't come out, hit the now loose piece of wood with a hammer.

Notch for the plate of a door hinge:

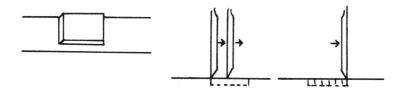

Place the chisel, bevel in toward the area to be removed, at one end and hit with a hammer. Continue this procedure to the end of area, but at the other end reverse the bevel. Clean out the area by slanting the chisel, bevel touching inside the wood, and tap it along.

WONDERFUL GIFTS TO ASK FOR

The tools that I will talk about now are the replacements for all kinds of alternate, and sometimes not quite as good, methods for doing things. In some cases, these methods have worked for me for years because I didn't know about the "real" tool; in some cases I knew about it but was too lazy to buy it and was still satisfied with the alternate; in some cases I just couldn't afford the tool/gadget. However, it's nice to know about these "real" tools, man's do-it-yourself-easier inventions. (And as more of us get out of the kitchen, where many necessary do-it-easier inventions have been designed by women, more building-ease inventions will be attributable to women.)

Awl (otherwise described as "like an ice pick")

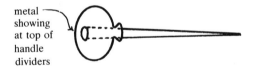

metal
showing
at top of
handle
dividers

Predrilling isn't always required for screws, especially when the screws are small. However, it's always a good idea to have a bit of a hole to start with, to put the screw into and start screwing. A nail, hammered in a bit and pulled out, will accomplish this nicely.

The awl is the tool that eliminates the step of reversing the hammer and applying the claw end to pull out the nail. (You've already got the head of the awl in your fist and can easily pull it out after you've hammered the hole.) Apply the hammer to the metal surface at the top of the head of the awl, which is the end of the metal opposite the point. Don't get an awl which does not have the metal end showing, or sooner or later you may crack the wood handle by hitting it.

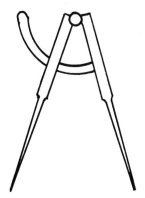

Calipers and Dividers

Either tool allows you to measure exactly something that is difficult to measure with a ruler, because the ruler is too big or whatever. You measure using the two points and hold the points along the edge of a ruler to read the distance between them; or on the calipers themselves you may use the curved guide, which also gives a reading of the distance. Dividers have points on legs, calipers do not.

Because the entire gadget is metal, you can also transfer the measurement directly by applying pressure, onto, let's say, a piece of wood. (Remember your compass in grammar school?) You can also scribe a circle on wood by using dividers.

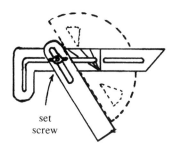

set
screw

T Bevel

The diagram illustrates one obvious use of the T bevel, measurement of an angle on the protractor, for transfer to a piece of wood or whatever.

The wing nut of the setscrew may be loosened so that any angle can be reached, and the positioning of the two pieces held together by the screw is variable. My T bevel, an inexpensive one, has four angles—30°, 45°, 60° and 90°—etched into the metal, and I suppose more expensive ones have more angles, a convenience which could eliminate the step of measuring from a protractor.

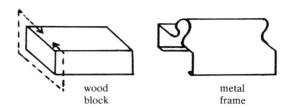

wood
block

metal
frame

Metal Sandpaper Block

Wrap a piece of sandpaper around the wood block; the frame holds both snugly. (Without this gadget, the frame is your hand.)

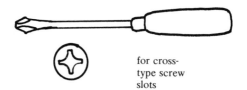

for cross-
type screw
slots

Phillips Screwdriver

Sooner or later you are going to want to attack that phonograph that doesn't work or a sink faucet. A set of these screwdrivers, with various head sizes, will come in handy.

Electric, Electric, Electric

Earlier, I extolled the joys (necessities) of an *electric drill* and an *electric saw*. If you don't have both or either, ask, beg, plead for one or both; or—if you have a mother like mine, who asks what I want and ends up sending a check—"You better pick it up yourself, dear"—add some savings to it (if you have to) and have yourself a merry, merry Christmas.

If you already have both an electric drill and an electric saw, consider next (my opinion) an *electric screwdriver*. Screwing time will be cut by a tenth, if your hands are as lazy and weak as mine, and you will find that that inspiration to make things involving screwing will blossom. Again my opinion: I think it best to have separate tools to drill, saw, drive screws, sand, etc., rather than one all-purpose tool with many attachments. A project becomes an unbelievable, burdensome monster of a task when you have to keep switching from drill bit and adapter to screwdriver bit and its adapter every few minutes. And . . . if the motor goes, you have nothing!

The *electric sander* is last on my list because, I guess, I've done relatively little "fine cabinetry," and I'm still satisfied with the results of manual methods. For a big sanding job, and more to come, it's really a must.

EXTRA HEAVY-DUTY EXTENSION CORD AND ADAPTERS   Unplugging the electric saw and the three-prong adapter and plugging in the electric drill, when you have only one heavy-duty cord and one adapter, gets to be an annoyance. Before you hang up your Christmas stocking, drop some hints.

One final word about electric tools:

Over and over, as I lend my saw or drill to a friend about to try her hand at building something needed, and convinced by me to try using an electric tool, there are expressions of awe and fear. I think we forget we're surrounded by motor-driven electrical gadgets in the house: the washing machine and dryer, the can opener, the vacuum, the blender and (I'm still scared of this one) the electric carving knife! So hang loose. You've already taken that one small step for *woman.*

FASTENING HARDWARE —

HOW TO GET IT

TOGETHER

One hundred and fifty years ago, there was some variety in tools, but very limited variety in fastening hardware. Chairs, tables, all sorts of furniture were made by connecting and joining wood (work called joinery). Sometimes puzzlelike cuts were made in wood corners, which were then fitted together and glued. Or two pieces of wood were joined by inserting and gluing small round pieces of wood (dowels) in holes made in each piece of wood.

Nails such as we know them today, smooth and very sharp-pointed, didn't really exist. In the old days they were cut and hammered into shape, probably by the blacksmith. The one remnant we have from this era is the cut nail, a masonry nail. Its function in many tasks has essentially never been surpassed by anything else.

Of course, life was simpler then. People did not cover their walls with lamps, paintings, posters, light switches, etc. Furniture was simple and functional, made to last; and because it lasted, it was not often replaced. Plumbing and electricity were nonexistent. So was machinery, for all intents and purposes. Ever notice, in pictures of old patent designs for machinery, how much of the machine was made of wood? (The simplicity of nature's gifts to us is often, to me, far more compelling than all this newfangled machinery, particularly when it comes to making and repairing.)

So much of what was constructed before the age of machinery is still strong and durable today that I am often envious of that way of life, which permitted one the time to build with quality. Yes, there was far more to do in those days—chopping wood, making the butter, the clothes, the thread for the clothes, etc., etc.—but making the furniture was part of what had to be done, not just the "leisure task" it is today, the "family handyman" scene. However, in the complex life we live today, when we must pick and choose our leisure activities from a long list (always decisions!), the time to achieve such quality isn't always available to us. Thus we must unfortunately avail ourselves of some of these newfangled gadgets—to make our lives easier(?).

Before I show you the hardware, I'd like you to see some of the wood- and/or screw- and/or glue-joining methods used—for reference, for when you find the time.

JOINTS

Butt Joint (easiest method—and least strong)

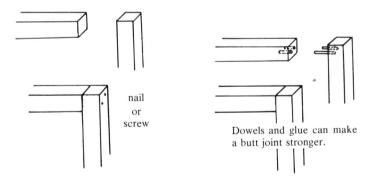

nail
or
screw

Dowels and glue can make
a butt joint stronger.

Lap Joint

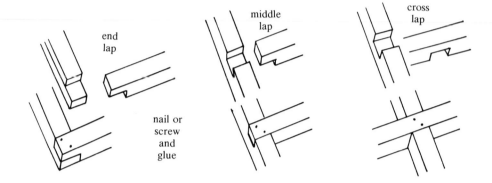

Dado Joint

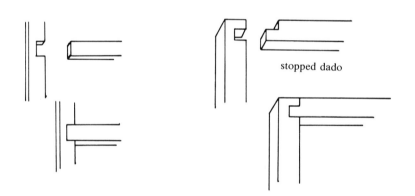

stopped dado

Dovetail Joint

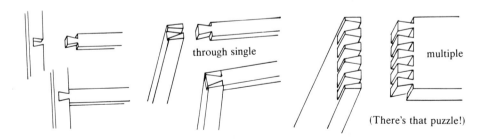

through single

multiple

(There's that puzzle!)

Miter Joint

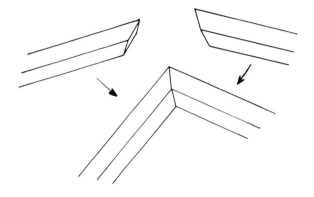

Rabbet Joint

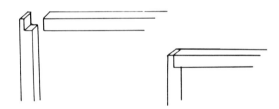

Mortise and Tenon

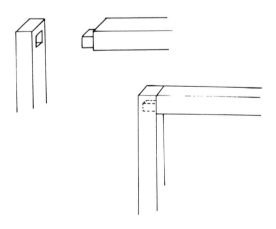

NAILS, SCREWS, NUTS AND BOLTS AND OTHER FASTENING HARDWARE

Nails and Things Hammered

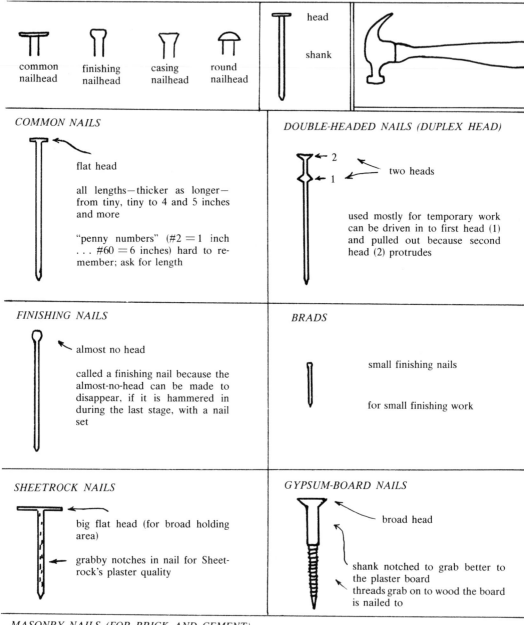

common nailhead   finishing nailhead   casing nailhead   round nailhead

head

shank

COMMON NAILS

flat head

all lengths—thicker as longer—from tiny, tiny to 4 and 5 inches and more

"penny numbers" (#2 = 1 inch ... #60 = 6 inches) hard to remember; ask for length

DOUBLE-HEADED NAILS (DUPLEX HEAD)

2

1

two heads

used mostly for temporary work can be driven in to first head (1) and pulled out because second head (2) protrudes

FINISHING NAILS

almost no head

called a finishing nail because the almost-no-head can be made to disappear, if it is hammered in during the last stage, with a nail set

BRADS

small finishing nails

for small finishing work

SHEETROCK NAILS

big flat head (for broad holding area)

grabby notches in nail for Sheet-rock's plaster quality

GYPSUM-BOARD NAILS

broad head

shank notched to grab better to the plaster board

threads grab on to wood the board is nailed to

MASONRY NAILS (FOR BRICK AND CEMENT)

ridges for holding

also called cut nails—have a very rough quality (my preference)

Masonry is cement. In a brick wall the cement holds the bricks. Nail into the *masonry,* not the brick, which holds almost nothing except a well-placed lead plug, into which a screw can be inserted.

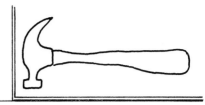

SCREW NAILS, COMMON WIRE NAILS, SPIRAL NAILS

circle or spiral threads

nonscrewable, no slot in head

Threads have excellent grabby quality for holding in wood (and hold disastrously well if you later try to take the wood apart, so be sure before you nail them).

FLOORING NAILS

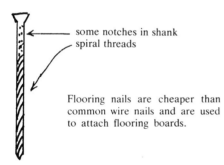

some notches in shank
spiral threads

Flooring nails are cheaper than common wire nails and are used to attach flooring boards.

SIDING NAILS

almost no shank for longer length holding

come in aluminum, bronze and stainless steel

will attach asbestos-cement shingles to sheathing (sheathing is the wood construction under siding)

thumbtack

upholstery
tack

rug
tack

staples

electrical wire staple
—used to keep wire against woodwork

Screws and Screwables

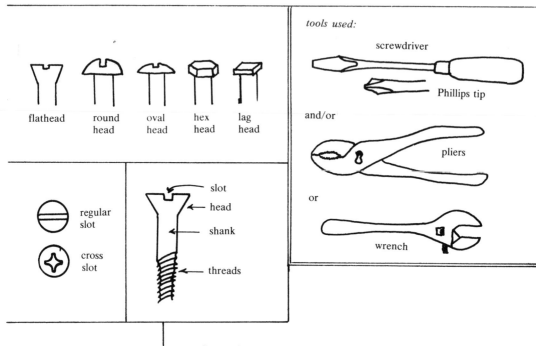

flathead   round head   oval head   hex head   lag head

tools used:

screwdriver

Phillips tip

and/or

pliers

or

wrench

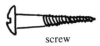
regular slot

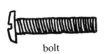
cross slot

slot
head
shank
threads

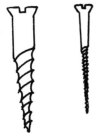

screw

bolt

Length is the measurement of the part of the screw that disappears. Screw lengths are available from ¼ to 5 inches.

length   length   length

Variable thicknesses (thickness is diameter of shank) are available for the same lengths.

Screws—all types of heads—come thick or thin, with or without shank.

Thin screws are good to use to avoid cracking wood.

wood screw

Screws are sold by length and diameter-of-shank code #.
#0 diam. = .060 inch . . . #6 diam. = 1.38 inch . . . #24 diam. = .372 inch.
(I use #6's and #8's a lot.)

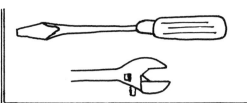

Stove bolt   **Machine bolts**   **Carriage bolt**

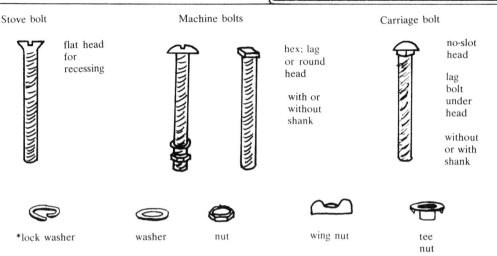

flat head
for
recessing

hex; lag
or round
head

with or
without
shank

no-slot
head

lag
bolt
under
head

without
or with
shank

*lock washer   washer   nut   wing nut   tee
nut

*A lock washer, because of its design (slit through and not flat), acts as a spring to keep a
nut from unscrewing.

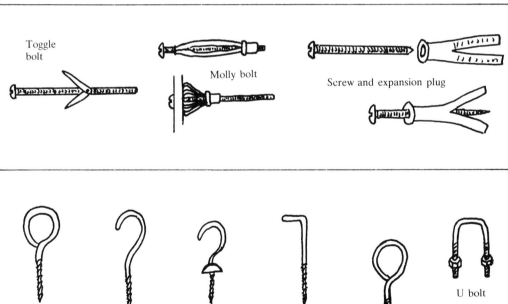

Toggle
bolt

Molly bolt

Screw and expansion plug

screw
eye   screw
hook   cup
hook   L
screw hook

U bolt

screw-eye
bolt

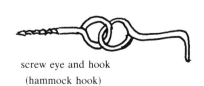

screw eye and hook
(hammock hook)

Hinges

One could easily fill many pages describing the variety of hinges available. Browsing in hardware stores will be supplemental to anything I illustrate here, for often they have their supply of hinges displayed, showing how they are used. Also, look at catalogs—Sears, Montgomery Ward, etc.

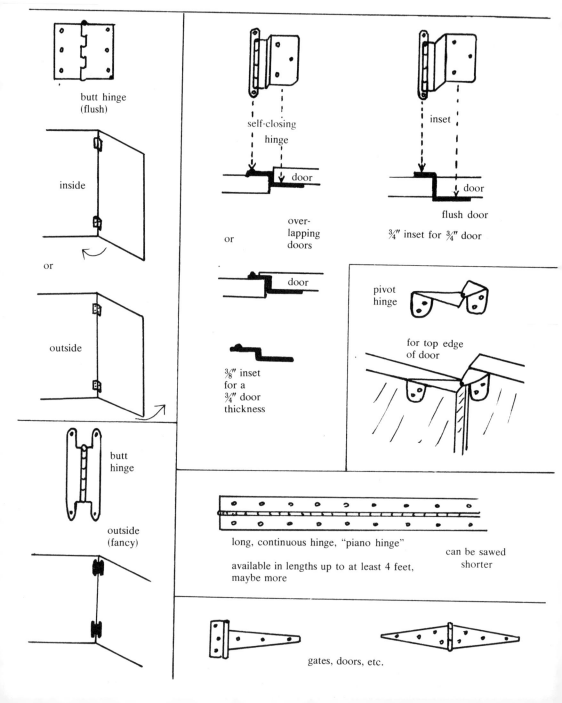

butt hinge
(flush)

inside

or

outside

butt
hinge

outside
(fancy)

self-closing
hinge

door

over-
lapping
doors

or

door

⅜″ inset
for a
¾″ door
thickness

inset

door

flush door

¾″ inset for ¾″ door

pivot
hinge

for top edge
of door

long, continuous hinge, "piano hinge"

can be sawed
shorter

available in lengths up to at least 4 feet,
maybe more

gates, doors, etc.

GLUE

Until this morning, what I knew about glues would fit on half a page, and I'll tell it now, starting with my best glue story. (1) A friend of mine, after buying a brownstone, was faced with a monumental curtain-and-drapery-making project, to cover all the windows, so she Soboed (white-glued) all the hems and trimmings. (Many of mine aren't even hemmed in any fashion yet, just neatly cut with scissors— how bad is that?) (2) White glues, like Sobo and Elmer's, are great for all kinds of things, but I didn't know you could use them for wood joints. (3) Halfway into my building-dabbling career I needed glue for wood joints, for something or other, and asked at the hardware store for the "best wood glue you have—the kind the carpenters buy." I've been using the glue they gave me ever since, Franklin glue, a kind of transparent brown glue. (4) My son uses some kind of plastic glue for his models.

It occurred to me that I should know more about glues, not just for this book, but for my own knowledge. I began a search through all the do-it-yourself books and found myself becoming terribly annoyed at the small smatterings in each section relating to glues and adhesives. Gradually I began compiling a list of names, some mentioned in other books, some lists brand new, some with information about gluing procedures, about mixing or drying or setting times— but none with consistent kinds of information about the glues mentioned. What I have gathered together I hope will be an informative chart of glues and adhesives, perhaps not all-inclusive, but as much as I could find. (I even found some conflicting information from two sources, which meant further research.)

Let me first mention some tips for good gluing:

The surfaces to be glued together should be free of any dust, grease, dirt, old glue, etc. If the old glue was water-soluble—not waterproof (see chart)—soak it off with water. Wrap a water-soaked rag around it for a bit. Or you can scrape off the glue with a knife or sand it off.

In most instances, you should let the glue on each surface become a little tacky before you press the surfaces together.

Warmth—of both the surfaces glued and the area in which the gluing is being done—is a necessary condition for many of the glues mentioned, whose directions specify 70 degrees or above.

Type of Glue	Form When Purchased	Preparation of Glue for Use	How to Set Materials and Set Time	Clamped Drying Time
NATURAL				
Animal (hide and bone mix)	a) dry sheets or strips b) flakes c) liquid	a & b) soak in water until dissolved a, b, c) heat at about 130° in glue-pot until syrup	apply glue hot, sets in 40–50 minutes	overnight
Casein (milk curd)	powder	mix with an equal part of water of ordinary temperature until paste		overnight
Vegetable (starches from plants)	powder		slow set	overnight
Fish (skin, bones)	liquid	ready to use, follow label instructions		
RESINS				
Acrylic Resin	liquid and powder	mix as directed	sets to hard in 5 minutes	quick
Aliphatic Resin		ready to use	quick set	small jobs: no clamping, big job: 45 minutes
Polyester Resin	two liquids (one of which is highly flammable)	mix just before using as directed and carefully, or it can harden		
Polyvinyl Resin	white liquid often available in squeeze type containers	ready to use	apply to both surfaces, let get tacky, press together	30 minutes to 2 hours
Resorcinol Resin	liquid and powder	mix as directed to paste	apply to both surfaces; sets more quickly at high temperatures	overnight
Urea Resin	liquid or powder	liquid: ready; powder: mix with water to get thick paste first, then add more water to heavy-cream consistency	apply to both surfaces	overnight
Epoxy (Resin and hardener)	two pasty substances	mix equal parts only as much as needed; mix with a wooden stick on a jar lid (discardables)	thin coat to both surfaces	2+ hours
Cellulose Nitrate Cement	tubed substance (flammable)	ready to use	for *porous* materials: apply to both surfaces, let dry and then press together, *nonporous:* apply to both surfaces, press together	overnight
RUBBER				
Silicone Rubber	substance in jar	ready to use	apply to both surfaces, let dry apart, apply again, press together	very fast
Rubber Base Mastic	thick paste (can)	ready to use	apply to one surface, use twisting motion when pressing together	overnight
Plastic Rubber		ready to use	apply to both surfaces, press together; quick set	overnight
Buna-N (synthetic rubber)	tubed paste	ready to use	apply to both surfaces, press together when tacky	fast
Neoprene Base	thin syrupy mixture	ready to use	TURN OFF PILOT LIGHT! DO NOT LIGHT A MATCH! apply to both surfaces, dry apart, put paper in between and remove skillfully; instant set	weight down overnight, cannot be separated
Trichloroethylene Cement	tubed substance	ready to use	apply to surfaces, place together; softens them and fuses them	fast
Sizing	diluted adhesive, like paint, canned	ready to use	paint on with brush, seals surface, also used for pregluing	no clamping; dries in hour or so
Solder	hardened in strips or liquid (jar or tube)	cut size needed; liquid: ready	extreme heat (e.g., soldering gun) applied to fuse objects	dry when cool; clamp while cooling

Best Gluing Temperature	Water: Waterproof, Resistant or No (water loosens)	Heat: Heatproof, Resistant or No (heat loosens)	Good Gap Filler	Use (bonds what to what?)	How It Dries	Some Brand Names
70°+	no	no	yes	wood to: paper, close-weave fabrics, leather, plastic laminates, wood	brittle, clear	Franklin
lower temp., 60°+	water-resistant	holds in temperatures above freezing	yes	wood to: wood, plaster, cement, leather, heavy fabrics, plastic laminates	stains; brittle, clearish	Elmer's casein glue
70°+	no	no	no	paper, cardboard, close-weave fabrics	brittle; will stain	
	no	no	no	wood, paper close-weave fabrics	brittle, not strong	
	water-proof		yes	anything to anything	hard and strong (3 tons per sq. in.)	3-Ton Adhesive
lower temp., 50°+	water-resistant	heat-resistant	yes	wood to wood, plastic lam., leather, cloth, paper; and each to any other	strong bond	Titebond
			yes	fiber glass, marble	hard	Marfax
room temp.	moderate resistance	no	no	porous materials: wood, paper, cloth, styrofoam, Masonite, leather	flexible, clear, not strong not load-bearing	Elmer's Glue-All, Sobo
room temp.	very water-proof	very heatproof	yes	porous materials used outdoors, on boats, etc.	strong, waterproof	Elmer's waterproof glue
room temp.	strongly water-resistant if not over-exposed	not above 144°	no	porous, semiporous of nonmineral nature, primarily wood, plastic laminates, veneer*	stainfree	Weldwood or Elmer's plastic resin glue *Woodworkers' cascamite
room temp.	strongly water-proof	heatproof	yes	porous and nonporous, anything to anything, wood, china, glass, tile plastics, metal, ceramics	strong (1 ton per sq. inch)	UG II (tiles) Weldwood Devon Bordens
room temp.	no	no	yes	porous and nonporous, wood, glass, china	hard, clear	Duco Cement
room temp.	water-proof	no	no	porous and nonporous, paper, books, cloth	flexible; do not paint over it	rubber cement
room temp.	water-proof	no	yes	tiles, glass, brick, concrete, metal; and nuts to bolts	hard	Miracle Adhesive, mastic cement
room temp.	water-proof	no	no	china, wood, leather, plastics	flexible	plastic mending adhesive
room temp.	water-proof	no	no	anything to anything, rubber to metal, rugs, work-pants patches, etc.	flexible	Pliobond industrial adhesive
room temp.	water-resistant	heat-resistant	no	large sheet materials to wood, wood veneering; metal to metal, rubber to rubber, leather, wood, cloth		contact cement, many brands: Weldwood, Elmer's, Devon
	water-proof	no	no	styrene plastics (you can tell if the glue softens the plastic)	hard	Styroweld
		no	no	pregluing—for materials of two different densities, if one will absorb more glue; over new plaster walls, to seal		many brands
	water-resistant		yes	to patch, seal metal	hard	many brands

In almost every case some pressure must be applied in order for the glue to dry; for the very quick-drying type, finger pressure is OK; for the slower-drying, clamped pressure* is required. Some glues set fairly fast but take a long time to dry. For a general rule, give yourself an overnight clamped or weighted drying time and you'll be safe.

Glue may be applied thinly with a brush for regular purposes; or with a syringe for thin squirts into narrow areas; or, for a large surface, with some kind of window wiper, which will help spread the glue evenly. Or some glue may be applied directly from the tube. Always wipe off immediately any excess that oozes out at the edges.

Adhesion occurs in two phases, setting and drying. The time it takes a glue to set varies with the glue, and it means the time required, after the two surfaces are placed together, for them to become un-detachable. This is the *setting* time. The materials joined should be clamped or held together with some pressure during this time. Next, it is necessary to allow the glue to dry completely in order to get the best bonding results. This amount of time also varies by type and is called the *drying* time.

Selection of glue involves consideration of what the materials will be exposed to in terms of moisture, water and heat. It is also necessary to determine the amount of stress that will be placed on the glued material.

With the glues that are flammable, great care has to be exercised. Contact cement is the most fearsome. I've always been afraid to use it. A friend of mine bought a brownstone a few years ago. Because of a careless workman who didn't turn off the pilot light, her house burned down before she even moved in!

When I made the kitchen counter for my sink, I was afraid to use contact cement and decided against Formica. I painted the surfaces with three coats of waterproof deck paint (the kind used on boats) and figured that was a smart move; it's lasted well. Just the other day some-one said, "Don't you know there's lead in that? You could be getting lead chips in your food!" Oh, God, I thought, Ignorance! thy name is Florence. Now I've got to drag us all, the children, the babysitters, the friends, the grandmothers and me, to the doctor for testing!

---

*Clamped pressure can be effected by using C-clamps, when possible, or by a rope tourniquet tightened with a small stick, or by using strapping tape—a new tape with fiber-glass threads in it—and wrapping it around as you would the rope. There are also very large clamps available. Any homemade technique you can devise which will hold the surfaces together for the prescribed drying time will do.

I don't suppose that anyone reading this is as stupid as me, after all the recent outcries about lead paint, but if you have an impatient streak like mine and don't read all the labels, start reading them now. (What are the symptoms of lead poisoning??)

THE LUMBERYARD —
AND HOW TO DEAL
WITH THE MALE
CHAUVINISTS THERE

Yesterday in the lumberyard, purchasing some wood for a new project, I heard not one but two examples of the kind of treatment that I used to get (and sometimes still get) and that you may expect, as a woman buying lumber.

The woman being waited on was trying to select about eight thin dowels (maybe a quarter inch in diameter) of manageable length so she could carry them home. Her companion, a man, was holding the dowels she had already selected; this was his entire participation in the purchase. She kept saying to the lumberman on the ladder, who was selecting lengths of 16 or 18 feet, "No, that's too long, I can't manipulate that one," which sounded reasonable to me.

"Come on, lady, I'll have to dig through this whole pile to make you happy," the salesman kept complaining.

All this time during the lumberman's abuse of the woman, her friend remained silent. As much as it delighted me to see a woman do the bit while a man dutifully held the wood, I found his silence almost unbelievable.

Finally, the lumberyard man yelled to her, "The next time, why don't stay home and send *him!*" (In other words, "Baby, this ain't your domain!")

The woman was marvelous, cool and unrelenting, and did not even answer him when he made that final remark. Instead she helped him remember how much wood she had—and helped with the arithmetic, too, so that he could do the bill. I realize now she had been to this lumberyard before and she knew the ropes, which are that "Women don't build, only men do, so women don't belong in the lumberyard." (After all, those salesmen have never seen pictures of women in handy-man books or magazines either—right?—so how could they know? And with their attitude and lack of exposure, you can be sure that their wives don't build.) And knowing this attitude, she just remained cool. Obviously she knew it would be useless to go into a long lecture or debate about women's right—and ability!—to build. Certainly, as more women become liberated, men's minds will gradually become less narrow and this (attitude), too, will pass.

Men tell me that they get hassled, too, and that may be so, but they do not have the same inner response to it for they are on their own turf, and they know they can demand their "rights."

When I first started going to the lumberyard, I think that for a long time they assumed my husband was in the middle of a building project and had sent me for more wood. Then one day, as I was buying thick, wide wood for the sides of the steps (stringer wood), the salesman asked me the typical, lumberyard, hardware-store quesion: "What are you going to do with this, lady?" Proudly I responded that I was build-ing a staircase. "You!" he exclaimed. "What's the matter with your husband?"

"My ex-husband lives in New Jersey. We're divorced," I answered. "Besides, it's cheaper to do it yourself."

"Good luck, lady," he tossed out, with an air of "Ho-ho-ho." How-ever, when he noticed that I never came in for more stringer wood but for other projects, he must have assumed that the job got done; and he has been slightly more respectful since. I still get hassled, but it's more friendly, and I know it's part of the game, which is on its way out.

The second example of discrimination happened while I was pay-ing my bill in the office. The man at the desk was on the phone and yelling, "No, lady, you better measure again, no one has thirty-feet-high ceilings! . . . Listen, lady, I'm telling you, you're wrong, it can't be thirty feet. . . ." (Pause . . . and I'm thinking of some of my friends who have two-story living rooms and begin to say, "Sure, there might be a thirty-foot ceiling height . . .") And I hear him repeat to the voice

at the other end, "A hundred and three inches, that's better, lady. . . ."
The motto of this story is, simply, Don't get caught with your head
off! (12 inches = 1 foot, 3 feet = 1 yard) I hated to hear him murmur
to himself, "Women!"

So here's how to play the scene for the first couple of times. Make
a list of what you want; make a neat one, because the salesmen often
grab it out of your hand, doubting your ability to communicate in this
area. At all times, stay cool. Tell yourself whatever kinds of fantasies
or truths that bolster your ego before you go in, like: I bet none of
these men can handle Contact, or (if it's not the very first time) the
last thing I made is still together, or, if I can cook from a recipe (which
probably none of these guys can do) then I can build from a plan, or,
I AM THE MASTER BUILDER!—anything that works for you.

Next, if the salesman asks you what you're building, answer; but
use the simplest description you can. Otherwise the purchase may
become a nightmare of confusion.

Next, if he questions your measurements or choice of wood, tell
him, "I know what I'm doing, I've been building for years." If he re-
sponds, "I've never seen you in here before," tell him you've been
using another lumberyard. Any approach is valid that will make him
concentrate so that he will cut the wood the proper size—at least,
that's how I feel. After you've become a familiar face at the lumberyard, you'll be "one of the boys."

One more word of advice: If your project fails and you have to
duplicate part or all of your original purchase, don't make the failure
obvious; go to the other lumberyard. You will be able to tell yourself
that it isn't a failure, but rather, part of the training process; but that
first lumberyard would give you the "Ho-ho-ho" treatment, and you
don't need it.

One final suggestion: If you leave an order, check the form and
make them sign it, so that if it's cut improperly, you can get them to
replace the wood.

WOOD—TRIM SIZES

Wood is the basic building material. With the exception of con-
crete-and-steel-foundation buildings, wood is what is behind every
wall and under every floor, whatever they're covered with. And wood
is basic even to concrete structures, because often wooden molds

are used to hold and form the concrete. If you don't live in a fifty-story office building or a modern apartment building, you may assume that there's wood around and under and above you.

Wood is a kind of magic stuff that may eventually spellbind you with its intricacies of internal natural design and infinite variation. Don't try always to match it, but rather enjoy its individuality. I could talk at great length about this special love affair that I have with wood, but I won't, for you will discover this joy yourself. It would be like telling you the ending of a movie and spoiling that moment of awareness, that moment when you run your hand across a piece of wood and feel your togetherness with nature. (I've said too much already.)

Wood comes in many varieties of cuts (widths and depths), as plain sliced wood (boards), and also in specially manufactured sheets of combinations of wood for special duty, for strength or paneling.

Boards

Let's talk about *boards* first. This is wood just as it's cut from the tree trunk. The most common thickness is ¾ inch, and the most common and available type of wood is pine. Pine is also the cheapest. Pure walnut or maple wood, for example, is available but much more expensive. Pine can be stained easily to look like walnut or maple or almost any other kind of wood you want. Also woods other than pine may have to be specially ordered, and that means a waiting period. For your first projects, pine is what I recommend.

I mention boards first so that you may visualize them; most bookcase shelves are boards. Besides, a board is a board is a board.

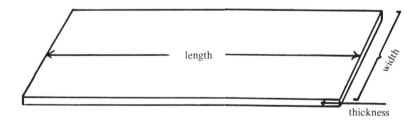

The widths of boards vary by inches and can come quite wide, but are very often difficult to get wider than 14 inches or so without special order. Now—prepare yourself—"6-inch-width wood" really comes only 5½ inches wide (or maybe 5⅝ or 5¾ inches), never 6

inches! The variety is due to the whims of the mill that cuts the lumber, or, more exactly, due to the necessity to cut just so many slices for economical reasons—who knows? (Yes, there are ways to get the exact width of wood you want—say 6 inches—and it costs! This "true size" wood is called "dimension lumber.") What you call this 5½-, 5⅝-, 5¾-inch width is "six inch"—at all times—and always bring a ruler with you in case the possible variation affects the total plan and you have to adjust other pieces. (Oh yes, I know men will argue that it's logical to be economical. But when I go to the lumberyard and one week it's 5½ inches and the next week it's 5⅝, and I can't make a final plan until I know what they have [for projects where it counts], that doesn't make sense to me!)

What I've said about 6-inch wood is true of all widths, so keep it in mind when you plan a project. By the way, this same truth applies to thicknesses; when I said ¾ inch thick before, that's give or take 1⁄16 or 1⁄32 inch—and it is called "*one inch* thick"! (I just measured the wood I bought yesterday, and it's a bit more than ¾ inch thick.) Don't give up, though; most of what you build will not demand such exactness. If you know what to expect, you'll learn to plan for the expected unexpected.

Let's talk in terms of pine from here on. Boards should be referred to as "common pine" or "clear pine" (slightly better and more expensive in looks than common) and prefixed by the thickness and width. *"One by eight, common pine, five feet long"* means a piece of wood— a board—*approximately* 7½ inches wide, *approximately* ¾ inches thick and 5 feet long—if *you* cut the length, *approximately* if cut at the lumberyard.

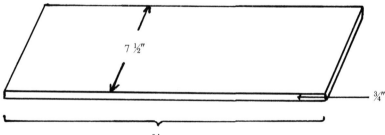

(This is perhaps the best time to mention the shorthand method of noting inches and feet. Inches may be expressed as " and feet may be expressed as '; 6" = 6 inches, 5' = 5 feet.)

I mention the option of cutting the lengths yourself, because it may be necessary for a number of reasons. You may want to wait until you get the wood home before you are sure of the cut size, or you may want to be absolutely certain of having perpendicular corners, 90° angles at the corners.

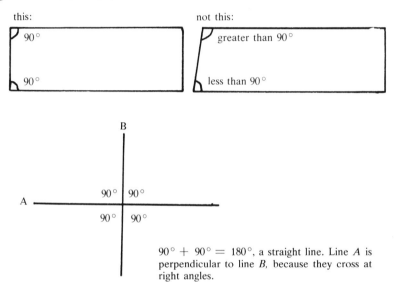

90° + 90° = 180°, a straight line. Line *A* is perpendicular to line *B*, because they cross at right angles.

I often cut my own lengths from longer pieces because often— no, always—I shop for wood on Saturdays, when the lumberyard is crowded and the cutting is sloppy.

The important thing to determine is the name of the wood you want and the length. The name is "*thickness* by *width, type of wood* (pine, walnut or whatever), the *length* desired"—"One by seven, pine, three feet long, please," and the *number of pieces* of each size. (This is how you say it at the lumberyard so that you'll get that approximate-size board.)

I want to mention, before we go on to the other wood available besides boards, that boards are available in thinner thicknesses, ¼ inch and ½ inch, and they are less strong and they bend more easily than ¾ inch, but there are many uses for these thicknesses.

Structural Wood

For *structural strength,* there are available sizes of wood that can best be described as posts. They come 2″ x 2″, (called "two-by-twos"), 2″ x 3″, 2″ x 4″, 3″ x 3″, 3″ x 4″, 4″ x 4″, etc. Two-by-fours are most commonly used and are thick and strong; they are what you may expect to find behind your walls, creating the framework. They are available in foot lengths from about 8 to 16 or 18 feet and in some places more, I guess.

For *hidden framework,* where strength is not a requirement (as in paneling), another type of cut is commonly used. Called "furring strip," it is wood approximately ¾ inch thick by 1¾ inch wide with rough, unsanded sides, and it also comes in long lengths. It is much cheaper than "one by two, pine," which is smooth and finished. Furring comes in one-by-twos and one-by-threes.

Another variety of rough wood strips is called lath. It comes approximately ¼ inch by 1¾ inch (very thin) and is used in the inside framework in some walls as a rough surface for plaster, as discussed in the next section.

For outside visible edge finishing, smooth, finished wood cuts are available. Sometimes called lattice—so-called from one of its uses, I guess—it comes in strips similar to the lath sizes and in smaller widths. It can also just be called strips.

Molding

One final cut of pure wood to mention is molding, so called because a side is shaped and molded to a particular design. It is usually triangular in form. Molding is available in many, many shapes (most

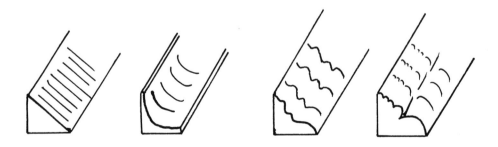

lumberyards have a picture chart of what they carry, along with the price per foot) and also comes in very long lengths.

About all this pure cut wood one thing can be said—it can warp. Thus its use is limited. When it is very important that the wood we want to use not be able to warp, and there is a possibility that it could, then we must use specially manufactured combinations like plywood and Novoply. Also, there are times when we do not need the strength of even thin pure cut wood, and for those times there is a nice cheap substitute, Masonite. And when you've painted and repainted forever, it seems, you may want to end it all, and for that there's paneling— thin sheets, fakes, that look like real wood walls; or you can do the real wood walls, using, perhaps tongue-and-groove cut wood. What are all these like?

Plywood

This is a sheet (commonly available at 4 feet by 8 feet) composed of thin layers of wood laminated (glued) together. It is available in varying thicknesses, $\frac{1}{4}''$, $\frac{1}{2}''$, $\frac{3}{4}''$, $1''$, etc. Larger thicknesses are available in "marine plywood." Plywood comes as "interior," "exterior" and "marine"; exterior and marine plywood has been laminated with waterproof glue. For all projects outdoors, be sure to use exterior or marine plywood, or you may expect the layers to begin to separate within a year. I tell you this from vivid personal experience. I built a kind of ship in the backyard for the boys last year, an object which looks also like a platform, the floor of which is plywood—*was* plywood. Every time I look out the window I am reminded of how little I knew— and of the job I'm in for next summer when I have to replace the floor! The floor is unfurling in all directions. (It was indoor plywood.)

In addition, each side, or surface, carries a grade: A, B, C or D. Grade A is best. The surfaces of each side may be of different grades. One side may have a lot of knotholes and not be very pretty and will be graded D, while the other side may have no knotholes and be un- marred and will be graded A. For the projects in which only one sur- face will show and should be good looking, A-D plywood should be used. (You could take a look at some B-D to see if it might be accept- able, for it will be cheaper than A-D.) Prices vary from high to low, for best to worst, from A-A to D-D.

Plywood is very strong (and very heavy!) and often the only alternative when the surface of something you are making must be very wide and when boards won't do and might warp anyway. The edges are rough and should be covered if they will be exposed, not just because of the possibility of splinters, but for looks. The strips or lattice mentioned earlier will do the covering; buy the width equal to the plywood thickness. It can be glued and/or nailed on.

One useful fact to know and remember about plywood: its non-warping quality has to do with the fact that it has an uneven number of layers. If you glue another layer to it, it will warp. An example of this would be gluing Formica to plywood—which I've also done and learned about too late! There is a layer sold which may be glued between the Formica and plywood and which will thus prevent warping.

However, there is a far better option available for the Formica scene and other uses; it has many names.

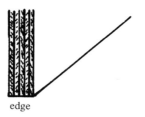

edge

Novoply, Chipboard, Particle Board

This is a sheet (also commonly available in 4 feet by 8 feet) composed of tiny chips of wood glued together to form a strong, hard surface. (If you have a Ping-Pong table, take a look at the top; it is probably chipboard.) Both surfaces look like mashed wood chips, and its use is thus limited by its looks. Counter tops covered with Formica are a common use. Things that are to be painted are often constructed with chipboard. Often free-standing closets, store-bought, are made with chipboard. By gluing veneer on the surface, you can give it a more real-wood look. (Veneer is very, very thin wood, as thin as cardboard.) However, chipboard will take a wood stain and have an interesting effect, so it, by itself, should not be ruled out. I have read that because there is no grain, only chips, screws will not hold in it; but

I have used screws in it and the things are still together. (Maybe it's only a question of time?)

Chipboard is available in variable thicknesses, like plywood, and is very heavy. It is cheaper than plywood for same-sized sheets, and is easier to saw.

Masonite, Hardboard

This is something you are surely familiar with if you have used pegboard, for that is what pegboard is—Masonite with holes in it. Masonite comes in 4- by 8-foot sheets, in variable thicknesses—$\frac{1}{4}''$, $\frac{1}{2}''$, etc. It looks as if it were made of mashed cardboard rather than wood; and it is very malleable—and easily cracks. (If you drag it along the floor you'll lose the edges.) Always think of it as hard cardboard when you use it or consider using it, so that you won't overestimate its strength. One surface is smooth and the other is rough, and I've seen it only in a brown color. It may be painted on the smooth side, but the surface is slippery as you paint, and great care and patience must be exercised. Some common uses of Masonite are: backs of bookcases, drawer bottoms where bottom strength is not necessary, and often under floor coverings like tile and linoleum to create a smooth undersurface.

Paneling

These are sheets of very thin—about $\frac{1}{4}$ inch—wood, with one surface made to look like boards of wood meeting, and when put up giving the effect of wood-paneled walls. Paneling, too, comes in 4- by 8-foot sheets and an almost infinite variety of wood grains and colors. Paneling is put up by nailing it to furring strips which have been vertically nailed to the walls 16 inches apart, center to center. Paneling can also be glued to walls if the walls are flat and smooth.

Tongue-and-Groove Wood

To get more than the effect of the real wood-paneled walls, tongue-and-groove boards are the best type to use. Their edges are cut in such a way that they fit into each other:

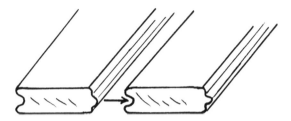

A Little More About Wood

The price guide following is included to give you some idea of what a project might cost you; and to help you decide, when you have a choice, whether to use pine boards or plywood, for example, or whether you really want to use "select" wood, wood with fewer flaws than the "garbage" wood. No, it isn't actually garbage, but often the flaws are obvious, like knots fallen out along the edge, cracks, etc. As you can see from the price list, "common," the garbage wood, is about half the price of "clear," the more select wood.

I always use common wood, but I also stand by the salesperson as he pulls out boards, and say yes or no to each board. In order to accomplish this, you have to establish a rapport in your lumberyard, or they'll hassle you. ("Come on, lady, I don't have all day to wait on you! There are other customers waiting.") Stand your ground. It gets easier the longer you are a customer.

Earlier I mentioned that many lumberyards do not carry much of a stock in woods other than pine boards; for other types you have to place an order. However, it might be helpful to know which woods are soft and which are hard. *Soft woods* (used for shelving and structural work) are pine, spruce, cedar, redwood, fir and hemlock. *Hard woods* (used for furniture, floors and trim) are oak, walnut, cherry, birch, teak, maple and mahogany.

A suggestion: Write to Albert Constantine & Son, Inc., 2050 Eastchester Road, Bronx, New York, for one of their catalogs. (It costs fifty cents.) They are nationally known for their fine selection of cabinet lumber to shop for by mail, fine cabinetmaking tools, furniture plans, etc. They will also send you a sample of twenty kinds of wood with the catalog if you send a dollar.

Pine boards (prices per linear foot:
linear = how long the board)

	common	clear
½" x 2"	6¢	13¢
½ x 3	8	20
½ x 4	10	22
1 x 2	6	14
1 x 3	8	16
1 x 4	12	20
1 x 6	18	38
1 x 8	26	48
1 x 10	32	58
1 x 12	36	68

2 x 8, used for staircase
   stringer, is 50¢/ft

An example of *redwood*
price for comparison:
1 x 4 costs 24¢/ft

2 x 4 (structural)
costs 19¢/ft

furring strip (1 x 3)
(structural)
costs 5¢/ft

Plywood (price for sheets 4' x 8')

thickness and grade	indoor	exterior	marine
¼" (A-D)	$6.33		this
(A-A)	8.81		is
½" (A-D)	$10.62		about
(A-A)	13.74		$2.00
(A-C)	$13.82	$11.55	
¾" (A-D)	16.51		more
(A-A)			than
(A-C)		$15.04	exterior
⅜"(A-C)		$7.92	

Masonite (prices by sheets of 4' x 8' and 4' x 4')

thickness	sheet	indoor	tempered (outside use)
⅛"	4 x 8	$2.56	$3.85
¼"	4 x 4	1.93	
¼"	4 x 8	3.84	6.33

Novoply (chipboard, particle board; prices by sheets
    of 4' x 8')

thickness	price
½"	$6.50
⅝"	8.60
¾"	9.60

A sample of molding:
"quarter round"

¼"	5¢/ft
½"	6¢/ft
¾"	9¢/ft

Who knows what lumber will cost years from now? Certainly not I. However, my lumberyard man tells me that in the past 3 to 4 years, he has seen a 30–40 percent increase in prices.

Go to your own lumberyard and copy onto this chart the current prices. Update the chart every year or so.

WHAT ARE WALLS?
(SOME ARE
SANDWICHES)

Here is one of the prime areas of exasperation. That wall?? How to get something to hold in, stay in, stay up, etc. For years, if the small nail I put in—on a down angle—didn't stay in, I just didn't hang anything. Then, after many questions and finally ripping down some walls, I learned what's behind all that paint. I think it will be helpful if I talk about the construction of walls, floors, ceilings and houses before I tell you how to hang the pictures.

This is the first time in my life that I've known what's behind all that paint because it's my own house and I can poke around and investigate. I'm not too sure what to advise you to do if you are a tenant and are hesitant about making holes in your walls and peeking in, but you must do some investigation if you are unsure. If it is necessary to make holes in walls, read about plastering in the Repairs and Renovation section. Then you will be able to conceal the investigation. I guess that's the best advice I can give you. You can obtain some knowledge without doing damage, however.

Interior walls first: The interior wall is most frequently a "sandwich." From ceiling to floor there are "studs." Studs are thick, strong beams (or posts), two-by-fours or four-by-fours, maybe, and they are or should be 16 inches apart from center to center. At least, it can be expected that they are 16 inches apart in construction done since pre-

fabricated wall boards came out, around World War I, I think. Prefabricated sheets come in four-by-eight-foot sizes and have to be attached to something. Four studs, center to center, are 48 inches, or
4 feet, and they are the something.

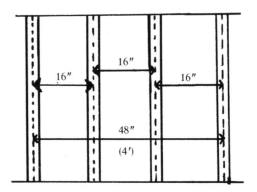

LATH METHOD

Next, attached to the studs, if plastering is the purpose, is something called lath. Lath comes in varieties, and only big poking through
your walls will tell you which kind you have.

Wood lath is made up of thin rough wood strips nailed to the studs
horizontally and fairly close together. The roughness of the wood is
necessary so that the plaster will adhere to it. Wood lath is usually

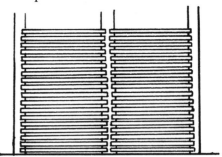

found in older houses. This is also easy to rip out. My method was to
break it at the center by hitting down with a hammer or a crowbar
and pulling off the two ends. The nails that don't come off with the
half end can be removed with the hammer claws.

Wire lath is a sheet of flat, closely meshed wire. I've never done anything with wire lath, except to rip it out—a nasty job, made worse by its rustiness; that's when you really need a tetanus shot. Having just called the lumberyard to determine the dimensions it comes in (to be sure, before I said 4 feet by 8 feet), I am suddenly thrown into confusion. It comes 26 inches by 96 inches? I have no problem about the 96 inches, which is the 8 feet, but why 26 inches?! Ten-inch overlap

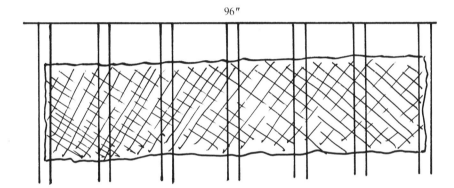

96″

on the studs? OK, another phone call straightened me out. This stuff goes on the long way, horizontally, attaching to seven studs, if the studs are 16 inches apart.

Rock lath is also called "board lath," and is made of a mined powder called gypsum, pressed into panels covered with strong paper. It has holes in it. It comes in sheet sizes from 16 inches by 32 inches to 24 inches by 64 inches. OK, no problem with that. (Any which way.)

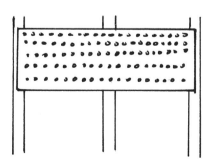

Rock lath is nailed to the studs with special nails called Sheetrock nails, which have a big, flat, round head and notches in the shank for grabbing.

Plaster: After the lath comes the plaster. What is plaster? It's some kind of powder which, when mixed with water, will get hard, adhere to rough surfaces and become itself, a smooth surface. (Hit it with a hammer and it turns back into powder, thus our picture-hanging problems!)

Actually, the powder it is made from is called gypsum, and the popularity of gypsum is probably because of its fire-retarding quality. This "cement," when mixed with water and sand, is plaster. Premixtures are very available, to which only water need be added.

I guess the lath has to have spaces or holes so that the plaster can sqwoosh through and behind and maybe catch itself in the back to hold better (?). Usually, three coats of plaster are applied; the first is called the scratch coat, the second the brown coat and the last the finish coat. The ingredients of sand and water vary in each; there is less sand in the scratch and there are probably things in the finish coat to make it look finished and smoother.

Last in the sandwich comes paint, or maybe after that comes paneling (the remodeling technique often used to cover those cracked walls).

SHEETROCK, WALLBOARD, PLASTERBOARD

An alternate to the lath method, and popular today, is the use of Sheetrock (wallboard, plasterboard—all the same) instead. Sheetrock comes in panels of 4 feet by 8 feet and is nailed directly to the studs. It is also made of gypsum and is probably the same as the rock lath just mentioned, without the holes. (I've got a lot of "probably's" throughout this book. What is nice to know but isn't vitally important to me is a "probably"; that's my philosophy. It's nice to know why things do what they do, but it's more important and necessary to know *what* they do.) The fact to know about Sheetrock, which perhaps you should call plasterboard in your head, is that it's like plaster; it cracks and crumbles easily. Don't drag it along the floor if you care about the corners; they'll break off. If you don't care, drag it, it's easier. (That's also my philosophy.)

When Sheetrock is used as a base for paint, it is necessary to make smooth somehow the places where the pieces meet. For this purpose there is a tape called plaster tape, or perforated tape. It is wide and has holes. It is applied this way: Plaster is put into the space between the two boards and along the edge of each board with a plaster-applying tool called a trowel. Then the tape is laid over this area and plaster sqwooshes through the holes in the tape. A thin layer of plaster is run over the tape and smoothed with the trowel. (Cans, small or large, of premixed plaster—nothing to add—are available for this purpose. My favorite is Dap, which is quick-drying.)

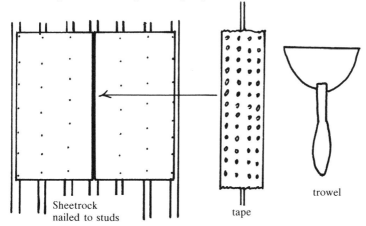

Sheetrock nailed to studs   tape   trowel

That's about it for sandwich walls, except to mention a word about paneling, which may have been nailed to the original studs or additional studding over preexisting walls. Paneling is thin, not strong enough to hold heavy things. Look for the nails to find the strips behind it and hang things through the paneling, attached to the strips.

One quick word about studs: Studs have another purpose besides holding the lath or wallboards. Some of them are "load-bearing." This means that they are helping to hold up the house. One removed could undo the house! Therefore a word of caution: Never remove a stud without checking to see if it is load-bearing. The way to determine this is to look in the cellar and see what walls and/or studs are there, besides the four walls of the outline of the house—interior walls that look as old as the house or at least were not added later. Another way to tell, if you have exposed upstairs interior walls, is to look at the studs and their relationship to the crossbeams or joists (those running under the floor horizontally). If the studs are *between* the crossbeams, they are probably structurally necessary; if they are *beside* the crossbeams, they are not.

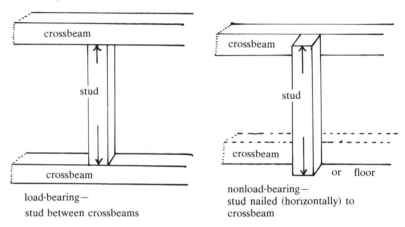

load-bearing—
stud between crossbeams

nonload-bearing—
stud nailed (horizontally) to
crossbeam

These load-bearing studs or walls are helping to distribute and carry the weight of the first floor—the studs in the cellar—and above these on each floor are similar walls, or else the floors and maybe even the house would cave in. A tiny cabin might not need additional interior support, but there are building regulations that determine when studs are necessary and how frequent they must be within a given set of dimensions. (I haven't built a house yet, and I don't know the specific rules, nor is this book going to go much beyond the interior needs. Hopefully, in a year or three, you'd like to take a crack at a cabin, as I would, and this is what we're getting prepared for here.)

So don't remove any wall without being sure of its purpose; if in doubt, don't do it—or ask an architect.

By the way, the air inside the sandwich is insulation.

Next, the "horror walls," the kind hardest to deal with, and which I have been least successful with—brick and concrete.

BRICK

Brick is usually found in exterior walls, the walls on the inner side of the outside of the house. The bricks are held together with mortar, which is composed of cement, lime and sand. Consider yourself almost as lucky as you would be having sandwich walls, if you can see the bricks inside. Any hanging job will be easier—somewhat—if you can see the bricks. When stripping the walls of my brownstone to brick, I discovered many variations separating the brick from the paint layer. One wall was covered with wire lath on studs, then plaster and paint, rusty wire lath which scared me and was a bomb to pull off. Another wall was done with wood lath on studs; and this was the easiest to remove, by the way. A third variation was something called "brownback," a form of plaster; it came off as clouds of dust—chunks or otherwise. The last and most gruesome covering was concrete—bad, bad, bad!

CONCRETE AND CINDER BLOCK

Kill yourself now! These are the worst walls to deal with. Concrete is made up of cement, gravel and other things. If you live in one of those new apartment buildings, even your floors and interior walls may be concrete or cement blocks (cinder blocks), which look like this:

This type of wall is often covered with just a thin layer of plaster and is thus deceptive. If you've tried to nail anything into it, you've seen the nail crumble and bend and make no impression, except to mess up the plaster. (However, you could be lucky and have sandwich construction over it.)

WOOD

If you happen to be lucky enough to live in a simple log cabin, count your blessings and never move! Nails and screws are all you need, with hammer and screwdriver, to hang your pictures, lamps and bookcases.

For the rest of us, more elaborate tools and nails and screw-type devices are necessary. Here they are:

SANDWICH WALL HARDWARE

Toggle bolts

The important thing about sandwich walls is the space behind the lath or wallboard, and some ingenious person invented a wonderful thing—a toggle bolt. It looks like a bolt with wings, which you can hold closed against the bolt or let spring open. (If the pieces become separated, be sure to screw the wings back on properly—see diagram.)

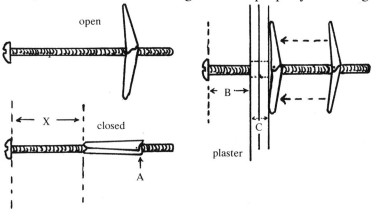

The principle of how it works may be obvious from the diagram— but how do you get it in? Drill a hole, or knock one out with a big nail, through everything, to get to the space. The hole must be as big as the biggest part of the wings, closed around the bolt, at Point A. After you have made the hole, take a piece of wire and put it into the hole to see how far in it goes; the length of the bolt may be no longer than this plus the length of the part of the bolt which will remain outside, because of what is being attached *(B)*. When you push the toggle through, wings closed, the wings must pass plaster and lath in order to spring open. If you can't tell how much space to give it on the bolt, bend the edge of a piece of wire and see how far it goes in until it grabs the inside edge. This much, *C* plus the space needed for *B* plus a bit more, is what is necessary to leave (X in "closed" diagram) to get the toggle through. Another thing you can do if it gets stuck and doesn't get far enough to spring open is unscrew the bolt a bit more and hammer it in again until the butterfly opens up and grabs. There will be leeway once the butterfly wings open; hold the bolt in your fingertips and screw it around, pulling out as you turn the bolthead with your fingers, until the wings grab at the back of the wall. Then use a screwdriver to finish the job. (Be careful not to screw it too tight, or you will crash through the wall.)

Molly Bolts

These devices are also fasteners which use the hollow space behind the wall.

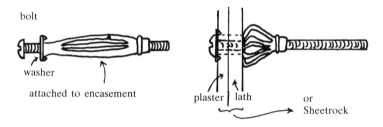

bolt

washer

attached to encasement

plaster | lath

or
Sheetrock

The molly functions similarly to the toggle. A hole is made in the wall big enough for the encasement of the screw to fit into. It should not be any bigger than the encasement, for there must be wall for the attached washer (near the head of the screw) to grab at and to keep the whole device from going right through the hole. After the hole is made, tap the molly into it, bolt and encasement. Then use a screwdriver to tighten the bolt. As you do this, the center of the encasement scrunches up against the back of the wall, thus providing the support characteristic. The difference between the molly and toggle is that you may remove the bolt of the molly and then replace it once the encasement is functional. Take a look at the diagram of the toggle again; if you remove the bolt from the wall, the butterfly wings will fall off and down into the wall.

In any instance of similar purpose, my preference is the toggle and its principle. (I'm not too happy with the molly's potential for wall smashability . . . to each her own.)

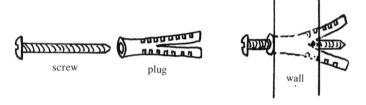

Expansion Plugs

This is a device made up of a plastic plug and a screw. A hole is
made in the wall just big enough for the plug, which is tapped lightly
into the hole without the screw. Then the screw is screwed in, and
because the plug is really too small for the screw, it expands as the
screw comes in. It is not a good idea to ask this type of fastener to
bear too much weight. (Plaster is potentially powder.)

Locate and Use the Stud

You also have the option of locating the stud and screwing directly
into that, instead of using this fancy hardware. This method will provide you with a stronger hold. However, you have to find the stud to
do this. You can knock on the walls, listening for hollow versus solid
sounds, and then test the solid sections by hammering in a long nail
here and there to position it. (Are you in the middle or at an edge?)
Or you could remove the molding along the floor and hope to see the
bottom of the studs at the edge of the plaster. Also, you have a good
chance for success if Sheetrock was used because if you look carefully
at the walls you may be able to spot the seams. Lastly, you may have
some success with a stud finder. This plastic-encased magnet is really
a finder of nails in studs. The magnet aims at metal as you move it
across the wall. (Obviously, this gadget is useless is you have wire lath.)
Test the stud finder in the store before you buy it and make sure you
have one powerful enough to do the job.

BRICK WALL HARDWARE

Lead Plugs

Along with my suggestion to think of plaster as powder and Masonite as sawdust, I'd like to tell you now to think of brick as sand and thus of its crumbly potential.

When strength is required, it is necessary to use a plug in the brick, not in the mortar holding the bricks together. (I have to qualify that by saying that I've had best results putting the plugs in the brick. My mortar seems kind of rotten and crumbly. I wonder if the whole wall will fall apart some day?) Yes, the plugs should work in good mortar, too.

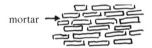

The big problem is that you need to see the bricks to know where you're at. (I think that's why I exposed my walls.)

Lead plugs are the only kind of plugs that work, when they work — three out of five times, on the average. Why lead? OK, brick is sand, right? Little grains of sand . . . that loosen. Thus, the friction of something against it and pulling weight can loosen the sand at the surface. Lead is a soft metal; it has sqwooshability. Let's look at the procedure.

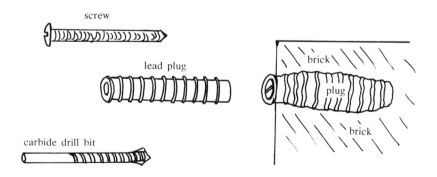

Drill a hole in the brick. Use a carbide bit, designed to bore a hole, not cut it, and one recognizable by the tip of the bit (see diagram). The proper-sized bit is necessary. The hole cannot be too big or the plug will fall out; it cannot be too small because it will ruin the plug, which will sqwoosh on the way in. (Often a package of lead plugs and screws comes with the proper-sized drill bit in the package, a good thing to look for.) The hole should be such that the plug may be tapped in. A tip: Vacuum the hole before you put the plug in. This will remove all the loose sand. After the plug is secured (and the hole should not be any longer than the plug), screw the screw in. This plug is also too small for the screw, so that as the screw enters, the plug expands. This plug is solid, not sliced like the plastic expansion plug. As the plug expands, it sqwooshes into all the nooks and crannies of the brick hole's surface, and this is why it holds, when it holds (bad bricks, bad hold). Another tip, for determining how far to drill: Lay the plug beside the carbide bit for measurement, and put a piece of masking (or other) tape on the bit. This way you will know when you've drilled far enough.

I have recently learned of another product called lead wool (looks like yarn but is thin strands of lead) bought by the pound. Jam it into the predrilled hole, which was drilled deep enough for a screw. Then put in the screw. (The woman who told me about this says this method was used to hang very heavy flowerpots from her concrete ceilings.) Be advised that this is not too easy a product to find. One place you may find it in is a plumbing-supply store. Perhaps it is in fact a plumbing material, because when I finally did find it, the hardware-store man said, "Oh, you want plumbers' lead." I took it because it looked like the sample the woman showed me.

Masonry Nails, Cut Nails

The other way to attack brick is with masonry nails. There are two varieties, cut nails and ridged nails.

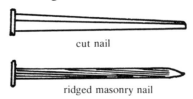

cut nail

ridged masonry nail

Cut nails look like old-fashioned hand-hammered nails and have a rough surface, and these to me are clearly preferable to the ridged nails, which feel smooth to the touch. Both these types are to be used in the mortar. (If you can't see the brick, you'll hear a clanking sound if you're hammering into the brick instead of mortar, and you also won't get anywhere!)

If in fact you can't see the brick, your dilemma may be the same as mine. On my lower floor, I have exposed the brick and have hung things. On my upper floor I have not, and have hung nothing except very lightweight pictures—a regular nail into the plaster.

CONCRETE WALL (YUK!) HARDWARE

Use lead plugs here, too.

Also, there is a gadget called a stud gun which you may rent. It will shoot a plug into the concrete wall, into which you can screw a screw. (However, I want to remind you, it is a *gun*. I have heard of ricochets. Don't use this yourself. Hire a professional.)

WOOD WALL (NOT PANELING) HARDWARE

Nails and Screws

Anyone know of a log cabin for sale?

WOOD WALL (THIN PANELING) HARDWARE

Find the stud to which it is attached, look for the seam between the panels and the nails holding the panels; that's where the stud is. Use screws or nails through the paneling into the stud.

TIPS ON USING TOOLS

AND MATERIALS

Before you start any projects, there are some tips—as many as I can think of—that I will tell you about, so that you may have the edge on the me of five or so years ago, when I was bumbling around trying to do all things without foreknowledge about how things behaved under certain conditions. For example, I always thought that you simply hammered a nail into a piece of wood, through it and into another, to connect the two pieces. Did I know that often the nail displaced so much wood that the wood cracked? (And that, of course, means buying more wood.) Or, did I know that if I drilled a hole a little too big for a screw, which would then just slip in and out, I could make the hole smaller? Yes, smaller! Lots of goodies like that I know now, and many more I don't know yet, but I'm sure of picking up some more as I keep bumbling along.

There is a right way and a wrong way to do something, and then there's my way. I cannot tell you if my ways—some or all—are right or wrong, only that they work for me. Actually, some have to be the right way, because they were learned because I was observed while doing something wrong or incompletely, and was advised of my error. If you are ever observed while using one of my methods and are told it's wrong and how to do it right, try the other way for comparison. If it is a better way for you, use it—and I'm sorry I didn't know better. (Write to me so I may also know.) But if you're more comfortable with the old way, stick to it, and don't be intimidated!

In the meantime, here's how I do it.

ABOUT CRACKED WOOD

Think about the grain of wood as almost-openings between sections of wood, and perhaps you will avoid catastrophes. Better still, think of the grain as almost-cracks. With only a little help sometimes, the "almost" disappears and the crack is a real (and only) thing!

Cracks occur when too much wood is displaced, pushed aside, when a nail or screw enters the wood. It is often difficult to tell how much, but certainly if some were displaced (removed) before the nail entered, it would be safer—right? Thus it is often wise to predrill a hole tinier than the nail and get rid of some wood. The wood being removed by the drill kind of blows back out through the grooves of the drill bit as it's being cut away, eliminating the possibility of cracking during drilling.

Cracks are almost an inevitability when you are nailing (without predrilling) near the edge of the wood, and here is where predrilling should be used when you are unsure. Try nailing and screwing in some old wood and get the feel of the problem.

Here are some illustrations to guide you:

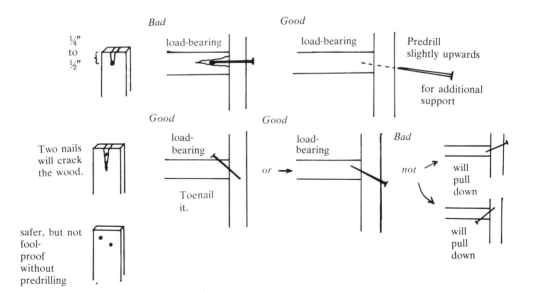

HOW FAR SHOULD A NAIL OR SCREW GO THROUGH THE SECOND PIECE OF WOOD?

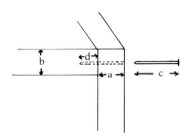

Nails and screws must go in at least two-thirds as much again as through the first piece. If *a,* the thickness of the first piece, is ¾″, then the nail must be ⅔ longer than ¾″, or 1¼″ *(c).* (⅔ of ¾ = ¾ or ½) . . . (¾ *(a)* + ½ *(d)* = 1¼) . . . *d* = ⅔ *a*

DETACHING TWO PIECES OF WOOD

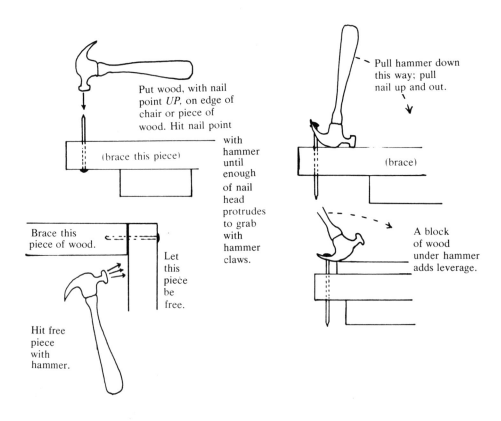

Put wood, with nail point *UP,* on edge of chair or piece of wood. Hit nail point with hammer until enough of nail head protrudes to grab with hammer claws.

(brace this piece)

Brace this piece of wood.

Let this piece be free.

Hit free piece with hammer.

Pull hammer down this way; pull nail up and out.

(brace)

A block of wood under hammer adds leverage.

DRILLING HOLES

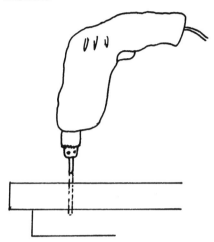

When drilling hole, place an old block of wood under the hole area and drill through to that piece. This will prevent splintering of the underside of the hole. The neatest hole edge will be where the drill enters the wood.

HOLE TOO BIG

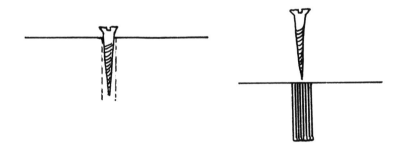

If the hole is too big, and the screw slips out or doesn't feel tight enough, stuff into the hole some wooden matches, broken off to fit and dabbed with glue, and try again.

LOOSE KNOTHOLES

Remove the knothole by hitting it out from the smaller-diameter side. Dab it with glue and reset it.

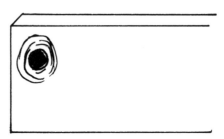

Knotholes are difficult to saw through and often fall out as a result. And they are absolutely no good to drill through, not only because they can fall out while drilling, but also because they might loosen if required to hold weight. If you have knotholes in wood you are going to use, plan carefully which way you will use the wood in order to avoid the knots.

WARPED, CURLED OR TWISTED WOOD

Wood is usually affected by dampness and improper storage. The best method of storage is to lay pieces flat, not on the floor but piled one on top of another, with the bottom piece on a series of closely placed bricks. Since dampness causes these problems, dampness is the ingredient of restoration.

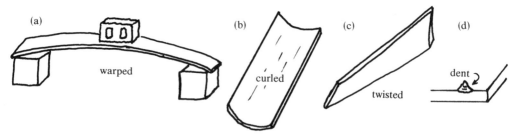

(a) Soak board, weigh down, leave overnight or longer. (b) Lay wet towel on inside of curl. In time, with new wet towels, it may un-curl (?) (c) Forget it . . . use it for scrap. (d) Dents on the surface may be removed by using a steam iron (or wet blotting paper and regular iron) aimed at the dent . . . so I hear.

SAWING CIRCLES

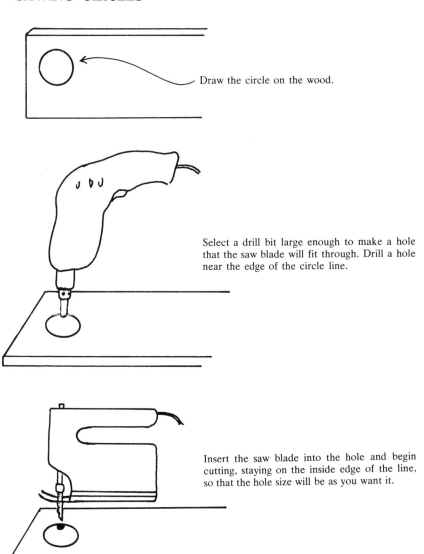

Draw the circle on the wood.

Select a drill bit large enough to make a hole that the saw blade will fit through. Drill a hole near the edge of the circle line.

Insert the saw blade into the hole and begin cutting, staying on the inside edge of the line, so that the hole size will be as you want it.

Note: Circles cut in this manner should be larger than 1½ inches in diameter. Circles smaller than this will cause too great a turning strain on the saw. For smaller circles, use the large drill bits whick look like this and which come in sizes from ¼ inch to at least 1½ inches, varying by sixteenths of an inch in size.

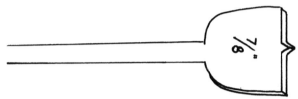

CUTTING SHEETROCK (PLASTERBOARD)

A reminder: Sheetrock is hardened gypsum powder, covered on both sides with heavy paper.

utility knife with retract- able blade

For this job you will need a utility knife, a 3-inch steel ruler and a board as long as the line to be cut. The board need only be about 4 inches wide.

1) Lay the Sheetrock flat on the floor and draw the line where the Sheetrock is to be cut.

2) Using the utility knife, score the line. You will not be cutting all the way through the gypsum, but through the paper and digging into some of the gypsum. Use the steel ruler as a guide for the knife. Don't use a piece of wood as a guide, or you'll gouge the wood as you go along, and you won't get a straight cut on the Sheetrock.

3) Place the board under the Sheetrock, one edge of the wood directly under the scored line. If the board is slightly longer than the Sheetrock, you can line it up easily from above.

4) Press down on the side without the board, hard enough to crack the gypsum within the paper. (If it doesn't crack, you haven't scored it deep enough.)

5) The paper on the other side has not yet been cut, so now you must . . . gingerly . . . turn the entire piece of Sheetrock over and lay it flat on the floor. (You may need assistance for a big piece; it's heavy stuff.) Now, cut the paper on the other side with the knife. You can

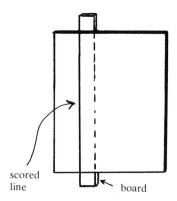

scored
line   board

mark it, top and bottom, from the crack, and draw line before you cut, or you can feel your way along the crack underneath.

If the piece you need is only a section of the whole, not as long or wide as the whole piece of Sheetrock, as is represented by X in diagram *1,* you will have to cut off an entire piece, from one side of the Sheetrock to the other, and then cut the piece needed from the smaller section.

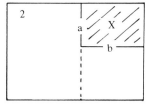
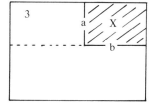

Diagram *2* illustrates one way. Cut line *a,* extended all the way to the edge; do steps 1–5, so that you have completely separated the right side. Then cut along line *b.*

Diagram *3* illustrates an alternate approach, cutting along line *b* first and separating the top section. Then cut along line *a* from the top section, to get piece X.

A marvelous gadget to look for, called a *snapper,* will make drawing those long lines much easier. Somewhat like a pulley, it operates this way: Put some crushed blue chalk in the case. Attach the hooklike device at the end of the string to one side of the Sheetrock. Pull the case to the other side, unwinding the chalk-coated string. Hold the case so that the string is taut. Take the middle section of the string between your fingers and snap it against the Sheetrock. Presto, a long blue line!

CUTTING GLASS

If you have a convenient glass store in your neighborhood, have the glass cut to the size you want. It will probably cost you less than a larger piece from which you would cut the piece you want. (And if you mess up, as I have done, it will cost you double.)

However, if you have glass available in your house, as I have (inherited with other treasures in the cellar when I bought this house), here is the way to cut the glass.

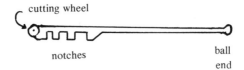

cutting wheel

notches   ball
                                                       end

You will need a glass cutter, which looks like this. (In time, if the cutting wheel gets tight, it can be loosened with some turpentine.)

Hold the cutter at an angle; *scratch* the surface of the glass, don't make a deep gouge. Lay a thin piece of wood under the line along the edge, and press down on the free side of the glass. This side, which should be the smaller, will crack off. Those little notches in the glass cutter, behind the cutting wheel, are for cracking off any remaining glass along the edge which didn't come off cleanly. The notch spaces are different sizes to accommodate different thicknesses of glass. Stick the unbroken segment into the notch and tip the cutter a bit.

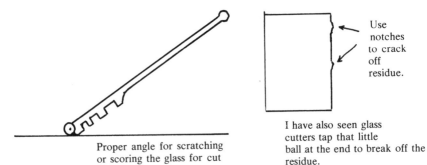

Use
notches
to crack
off
residue.

Proper angle for scratching
or scoring the glass for cut

I have also seen glass
cutters tap that little
ball at the end to break off the
residue.

CUTTING THIN METAL

Thin sheets of aluminum can be bought. I discovered this one day when I had a project in mind and asked some questions. I also learned that there are drill bits that will cut through metal. Best of all, there is a tool much like scissors which will also cut thin metal. Perhaps they are more accurately called metal snips, if you want to buy some.

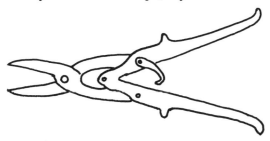

According to the box mine came in, this tool is available in different strength capacities. The strongest will cut all types of sheet metal, duct and pipe.

I might add that it's rough going, cutting metal, and your hand will be sore after a while, but it's worth it if the project is exciting enough to warrant this labor.

I'll tell you about my project, one I am still excited about. When I bought this house, most of the ceiling fixtures were those multiple-bulb types with a glass under to diffuse the light.

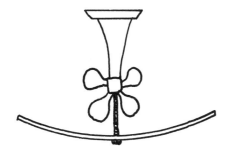

I wanted something different and eventually made a plan. This is what I did.

I cut this shape out of a sheet of aluminum and cut the circles and a small hole in the center. Then I folded it up into a box shape, like this:

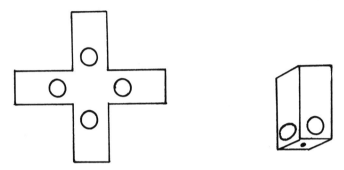

I removed the glass under the bulbs and then all the bulbs. Then I put the box up over the fixture, slipping the projection that held the glass through the hole in the bottom of the metal box, and I screwed the bolt back on, thus holding the box up against the ceiling. I replaced the bulbs of standard style with those nice, almost round kind—and the light fixture was a whole other thing!

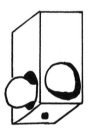

CUTTING THIN SHEET OF METAL (ANOTHER APPROACH)

Clamp the sheet of metal to be cut between two pieces of wood, or roll it around a dowel, to keep it from bending every which way when cutting. (Yes, probably a handsaw is better for this job than an electric saw.)

ONE FINAL TIP: PLAN AHEAD

(I didn't, too many times!)

Be sure that the wood lengths you order will fit into your house, through doors, halls, around curves. Determine ahead of time if you are going to have a problem.

Thin widths are always easier to maneuver around in tight areas than thick widths.

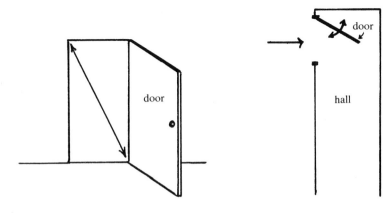

If you think there might be a possibility of a no-fit, order the wood early in the morning and have it delivered, or pick it up yourself if you can handle it; and if it doesn't fit, you'll have time to go back to the lumberyard for some more cutting to get smaller lengths.

If you go into your house through a door leading directly into a big, wide room, you won't have a problem, but if you have to enter a door on the side of a narrow hall, you may have maneuvering problems. Premeasure the diagonal lines in doorways . . . see how far in your wooden extension ruler will go horizontally before it hits a wall.

THE HARDWARE STORE —
THERE ARE MALE
CHAUVINISTS THERE, TOO

At this point in my life, a hardware store is the magic place that a toy store is to my children. Maybe the part of me that is gadget-gathering contributes to this feeling, but the real joy is finding things, hardware or tools, that make my tasks easier.

Before going into how to operate in a hardware store, I want to emphasize the words *hardware store* as the name of the place to buy tools and materials, not "houseware store." Houseware stores are where you go to buy trash baskets, sponge mops and the like. Usually, the hardware they carry (nails, screws, hinges, etc.) comes in small quantities, prepackaged—and packaging costs! Also, at houseware stores forget variety and versatility. They don't exist there. (How could there be room for everything you might need with all those garbage cans, dish-drying racks and brooms taking up so much space?) So buy housewares from the houseware store, and be wary of hardware sold there. (This philosophy goes for paint, too. Paint stores can stock more variety, color and type, and often have the facility to mix colors for you.) I think I would also have to include a caveat about large supermarkets, because, again, their supplies are limited. In no sense do I mean to disqualify the convenience of their availability for a quickie purchase of some nails, screws, or an electric switch, but rather I would encourage you to locate the best supplied hardware store in your community and go there as a general rule.

Two features of this approach are important. First, I do believe that the price will be lower in a hardware store for items which can be bought unpackaged (like a pound of nails), and even for some packaged things. Second, as you go there more often, you will become more familiar with their supplies and the layout of the store—where things are. (And you should always spend a few minutes browsing, anyway, just to see all the wonderful things that are available and how many variations on a theme there are.) In addition, the frequency of your visits will eventually make you a familiar face to the salesmen and saleswomen.

As a recognized customer you will find it easier to ask questions and get a knowledgeable reply, and probably the item you want. Compare this to the often-heard response in a houseware store: "That's all I have, lady." Or the supermarket, where it's help-yourself-and-take-it-to-the-cashier. God help you if you don't see what you want and aren't too sure what it's called; I'm sure I don't have to tell you what a forget-it scene that is.

How do you know if you're in a real hardware store? (Yes, a good hardware store could sell garbage cans and brooms.) Look around. You should be able to see a large variety of sizes and styles of hammers, big carpenter's levels (2 feet long and longer), open counters sectioned and stocked with millions of things you can help yourself to: a handful of nails, one washer or many, electric plugs, switches, teeny jeweler's screwdrivers; and if you are especially lucky, as I am, they will also have sections with faucets or just faucet handles, etc. Hanging up on the walls will be all wonderful varieties of never-seen-before tools and gadgets and hardware. They will usually carry a healthy supply and variety of glues, plaster compounds, paint, tapes, and cleaning, stripping and staining materials for refinishing furniture . . . and many other things.

And now, how do you operate in the hardware store, presuming you have found one of these great stores? Well, if you are there to buy thumbtacks, or one of the often-used white glues like Elmer's or Sobo (mothers' glues—right?), or even some nails, you will not have your presence in the store questioned or challenged, and you will have little trouble filling your order. However, if you are there to buy a faucet handle, and you linger over the decision (and are observed by the salesman), your eventual choice will almost surely be questioned. "Are you sure that's what you want, lady?" Or "What kind of a sink do you have, lady?"

I remember once, when I found the most wonderful thing in the hardware store, right before Christmas. It was a round metal disk with holes in it; its use is as a drain in some kinds of sinks. I saw it as a suitable object to paint, sprinkle with glitter and use as a tree ornament and I bought twelve. Naturally, the salesman had to ask his question, "Why are you buying so many, lady?" to which I replied, "I'm going to hang them on my Christmas tree!" I didn't bother to tell him that they would look quite different and certainly not like drains, and he apparently didn't have the imagination to dream what I was about, so he just gave me one of those "WOMEN!!??" looks and rang up my purchase.

The problem of always being challenged here is similar to that in the lumberyard. Actually, I have often found the salesmen's attitudes to imply more than challenge. They are often annoyed—before you even open your mouth, they appear to be distressed with the whole proposition of having to deal with a woman. I always imagine that they are telling themselves that now they will lose precious selling time with a woman customer. And there's one more problem, which still happens frequently enough to really annoy me—that of being bypassed by the salesman for a male customer who has come in after me. I see two possible reasons for this: the first, simply that he doesn't want to wait on a woman for the reasons above; or, and this is the bad one, that I'm probably there with my husband, right?

I think that the best advice I can offer you is to be sure you know the name of what you want. Look in a catalog and also, if possible, know the vernacular name for the item, if there is one. I have tried in this book to give you as many terms for the same thing as I know (Sheetrock = wallboard = plasterboard, for example). It is more than just nice knowledge; it may be the difference between getting what you want and not getting it.

STORAGE SUGGESTIONS FOR TOOLS AND HARDWARE . . . AND WHERE TO BUILD

I have a deep closet in my dining room. In the back I stuck an old bookcase (that I found in the street and knew would come in handy).

On the top of the bookcase, about 4 feet high, I have a revolving tool holder, which holds the screwdrivers, chisels, awl, pliers, wrenches, etc. In the bins in the lower section I keep the little steel tape measure, nail set . . . small stuff like that. On the wall beside this I hang, on nails, my hammer, level, framing square and 3-foot steel ruler. On the other shelves in the bookcase I have four or five plastic boxes with little drawers, in which I keep different-sized nails and screws, separated by size and type (round-head screws in a different drawer from flathead screws), nuts and bolts, toggle bolts, etc. Large boxes of things like nails and screws, from which these drawers are filled, are kept in the cellar, along with coffee cans filled with infrequently used items such as pilaster clips (because I bought too many), or nails or screws

I bought by the pound, electrical supplies like wire or plugs, etc. I tape one of whatever item is in the can to the outside of the can so I can tell what's in the can. In addition to this, I found I had accumulated much prepackaged stuff that I forgot I had and bought new when I needed it. Eventually, I put up some pegboard in the cellar and hung up all these packaged items—hinges, expansion plugs, etc. My power tools are kept under the bottom step of the staircase, a step with a hinged top, but if I didn't have that I'd keep them on the bottom shelf of that bookcase in the closet. And I keep all my heavy-duty extension cords (for the power tools) in an old wastepaper basket in the closet. One last thing: I keep my power tools in Pan Am bags—one for the saw, with all the blades in a Baggie in the bag; and one for my drill, with all the drill bits in Baggies also in the Pan Am bag. This way I can just grab the whole bag and operate.

OK, that's fine for you, you're saying, but what if I don't have a cellar or a deep closet?

My first suggestion is to go junk shopping (or scavenging in the street). You need some kind of a cabinet with big, wide-area storage and also some deep drawers. Or you can build it. It is preferable to have everything together and as visible as possible. (I'm not happy with the cellar storage and would have it all upstairs if I had the proper setup . . . yes, I need to build one of those cabinets.) Visibility is perhaps the most important thing, to be able to see immediately the tool or piece of hardware you need. This is why I like the revolving plastic tool caddy; I can flip it around and grab the screwdriver I need in a flash. (And this is why I hate toolboxes, much digging and disorder and time wasted and sometimes anger spent . . . no, don't go that route.) In the cabinet you find or build, you can use the wide areas to keep the tool caddy and your power tools. You can hang the hammer and such on the doors. In the drawers you can keep the boxes of nails and screws, which are usually labeled on the top, so you can grab what you need. If you have enough drawer space you can also divide the drawer into sections for the loose items and hardware bought in bags. (Bags of hardware are a pain if you keep them that way after you buy them.) I think it is advisable that nails and screws and the like (pointed objects) be kept in some kind of container with a lid, a can, box or jar. Baby-food jars are a big thing these days, in the handyman books and magazines. They are OK if you use the big ones; and if you are able to put hardware stored in these jars on a shelf, you have the added feature of visibility, no labeling required. Also suggested in these magazines is that you nail or screw the lid to the under part of a shelf . . . neat, eh? Don't do it! Remember, all these tips are for men, men who usually enjoy the luxury of "Keep the kids out of here" while they build. They don't have to worry about small hands knocking over open jars of nails, about open jars left out while the phone is answered. When you, a woman with children, build, you may rarely be able to hand over the kids to your mate. (If you don't have a mate, and you have to build sometimes while the children are around, remember—you also have to answer the phone!) So use containers with lids while you build. More often than not, I will bring up from the cellar the box of screws I need, rather than pull out the drawer from the plastic box of drawers in the closet, because the drawer has no lid, and I've had plenty of accidental spills, many of which were my own fault. Besides the no-lid aspect of the plastic drawers, I have another gripe—the drawers get stuck all the time.

WHERE TO BUILD

A friend of mine, reading the early parts of this book, commented, "I'd like to try to build something, but I don't have a place to work. You have a cellar."

"I don't build in the cellar," I told her. "I build in the dining room." Actually, I build anywhere it's convenient. A part of my good fortune relating to this ability is that I am not hindered by wall-to-wall carpeting anywhere in my house. We're lucky to have a scatter rug here and there. (People just don't throw out rugs that are usable much, but I keep watching.)

My friend didn't have wall-to-wall carpeting in her living room, so I told her that she could just roll up her rug a bit and go to it. Sweep up the sawdust and wood chips with a good mushy broom, and maybe vacuum after that . . . no, don't vacuum first, too much sawdust could eventually give you clogs in the vacuum.

If you have wall-to-wall carpeting everywhere, build in the biggest room—and vacuum. (See page 304, "An Approach to Broken Appliances," if the vacuum goes bad. That shouldn't happen too soon, though, and maybe even never. I'm the overcautious type.)

HOMEWORK—

PROJECT #1:

AN UNDER-THE-BED

DRAWER

What follows next is a sample of planning and executing a project. It is something a friend of mine asked how to build; she wanted storage under her son's bed. The pages and pages that follow are far more elaborate than any you or I would ever need for a project, but there are many lessons to be learned that are blown up for you to see. Eventually, the steps will be simple and you will make a quickie sketch and run off to the lumberyard. (No, no, make a neat list for that.)

Read the planning and execution steps for the lesson. Try it if you need a thing like this and feel ready to do it.

DRAWER UNDER BED ON CASTERS

looking at

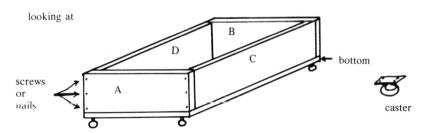

screws
or
nails

bottom

caster

looking down into

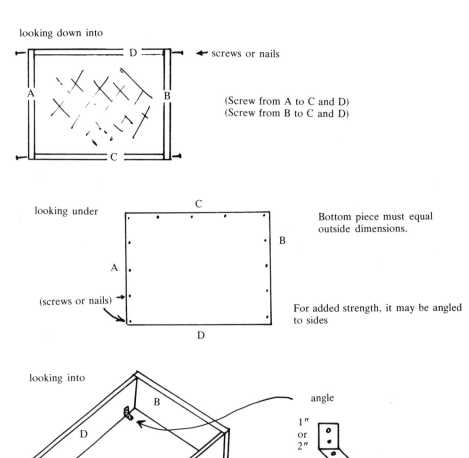

← screws or nails

(Screw from A to C and D)
(Screw from B to C and D)

looking under

Bottom piece must equal
outside dimensions.

For added strength, it may be angled
to sides

looking into

angle

1"
or
2"

1"

Glue is a good idea,
where *A* meets *D, C*
and where *B* meets *D, C*

STEP 1.   Buy 4 casters. Buy the kind that look like balls rather than wheels; they work better. Some screw in; some have claws and you hammer them into the base. Screw-ins are best for durability. With the claw kind, the wheel part is separable from the part that attaches to the base, so that you must hammer them in. Determine right away with one unit how high off the floor they will cause the box (drawer) to be.

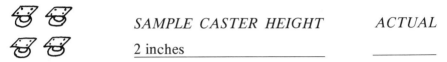

	SAMPLE CASTER HEIGHT	*ACTUAL*
	2 inches	

STEP 2.   Determine *outside* dimensions of the drawer.

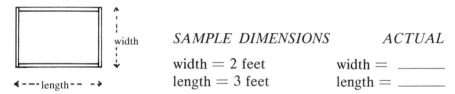

SAMPLE DIMENSIONS	*ACTUAL*
width = 2 feet	width = _____
length = 3 feet	length = _____

STEP 3.   Determine *lengths of wood* for A & B, C & D (use ¾" thick pine).

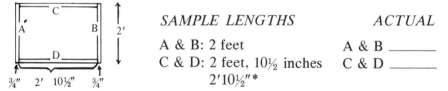

SAMPLE LENGTHS	*ACTUAL*
A & B: 2 feet	A & B _____
C & D: 2 feet, 10½ inches	C & D _____
2'10½"*	

STEP 4.   The bottom. Since you are attaching casters, it is necessary to use wood rather than Masonite. Wood will be sturdier, too. The bottom should be plywood, which comes large enough so that the bottom can be one piece. It comes in sheets 4' x 8', of thicknesses ¼", ½", ¾" and maybe even thicker. Get ½" for this project. (¼" is not too strong.)†

*If you have an actual case like the one above, where C & D come out odd inches and you decide to go for the whole 3 feet for C & D, you will have to go back to *Step 2* and adjust the outside dimension—length—to 3' 1½", and do it immediately. Also affected will be Step 4, which follows.

Another reminder: If this is being made to hold something of a specific size, check *inside* dimensions to be sure they are large enough.

†It is not recommended that you use wide pine boards (difficult to get in widths of over 12–14") for the bottom because you will need more than one, and they may warp, each in a different way. Thus it won't ever be a smooth surface.

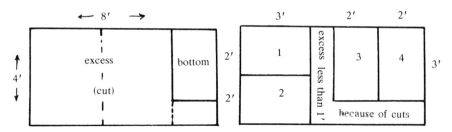

Have the bottom piece cut at the lumberyard, and maybe have the excess cut into more manageable pieces. As you can see from the example, much will be left. You can easily get 4 drawer bottoms out

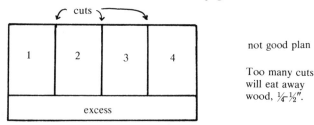

not good plan

Too many cuts
will eat away
wood, ¼-½".

of the sheet at the sample dimensions. The dimensions must be equal to the outside dimensions of the drawer. See Step 2 illustration.

	SAMPLE	*ACTUAL*
plywood bottom (½" thick)	2' x 3'	_____

STEP 5.   Determine *width of wood* for sides *A, B, C* and *D.* (Wood comes in "named" widths of even inches—1 x 2, 4, 6, 8, etc.—and those widths are actually ½" less. A reminder.)

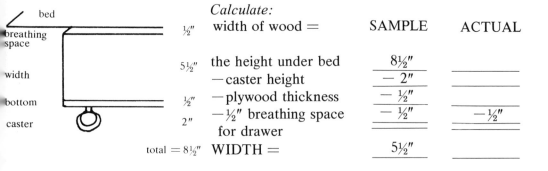

Calculate: width of wood =	SAMPLE	ACTUAL
the height under bed	8½"	_____
—caster height	— 2"	_____
—plywood thickness	— ½"	
—½" breathing space	— ½"	—½"
for drawer		
WIDTH =	5½"	_____

Thus, in the sample, wood for the sides will be one by six, which will actually be ¾″ x 5½″ . . . 2 pieces 2′ long, 2 pieces 2′ 10½″ long.

STEP 6.   If you want to attach knobs, one or two, in the front of the drawer, here's the picture. Knobs come with a bolt which can be removed. The important thing to know about the selection of the knob is the length of the bolt. It must be as long as the depth of the wood it will pass through, plus no more than a bit less than the size of the knob it screws into.

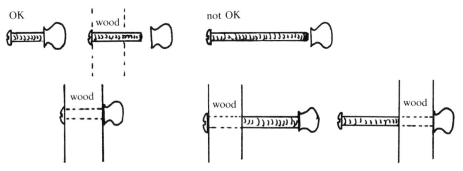

For the sample, the bolt must be a bit longer than ¾″.

STEP 7.   The planning stage is now complete. Make a shopping list.

Lumberyard

	SAMPLE	*ACTUAL:*		
		(#)	(Name)	(Length)
Sides *A, B*	(2) 1 x 6, pine, 2′ long			
Sides *C, D*	(2) 1 x 6, pine, 2′10½″			
Bottom	½″ plywood (D-D), cut out piece 2′ x 3′			

Hardware store

Nails or screws. 1½″ long. (At least 24–30 will be used, so buy a whole box, for future use.) Nails and glue will be OK. Screws, with or without glue, will be best.

Glue. Ask for their best wood-to-wood glue. An animal glue like Franklin's will work well. (Set the plastic container in a pot of hot water for a few minutes first.) Or Elmer's Glue-All is very good, too.

Angles. 1″ x 1″ or 1″ x 2″

Screws for angles. (Not nails!) No longer than the thickness of the side pieces or the bottom, whichever is *thinner,* or they will come out the other end.

Knob(s) with screw a bit longer than the thickness of the sides

Casters. 4 per drawer

Note: You could skip the knobs and cut out a hand hole in the front:

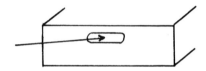

STEP 8.   Go shopping.

ASSEMBLY PHASE

Materials

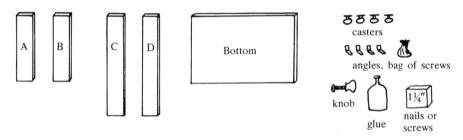

STEP 1.

Draw lines *x* by standing side *B* on its edge at one end of *A,* and then at the other end. Do the same thing with the edge of *A* on *B*.

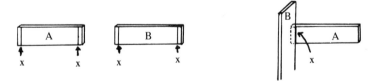

(The nails or screws attaching *A* and *B* to *C* and *D* go in between the line and the edge, centered.)

STEP 2. Mark with a pencil the position where the nails or screws should go in. They should be centered between line *x* and the edge, and about $\frac{1}{2}''$ at least from the corner.

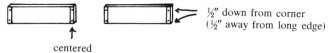

$\frac{1}{2}''$ down from corner
($\frac{1}{2}''$ away from long edge)

centered

STEP 3. Mark the position of the knob (or knobs) on *A*.

1 knob: Draw a diagonal line from corner *1* to corner *4,* and a diagonal from *2* to *3.* Where the lines cross will be the center, where the knob is to go.

2 knobs: Draw the same lines as for one knob. That center mark is *K.* Measure the distance from *K* to the edge and draw a line from *5* to *6*—line *5–6.* Now the board is divided in half and we find the center of each, drawing lines *1–6* and *2–5* for the left side and lines *5–4* and *3–6* for the right side. The knobs will go at K_1 and K_2.

STEP 4. Drill holes for attaching sides and for knob(s) at marked spots.

Use a drill bit for the knob hole(s) which is at least the same diameter as the bolt, so that it will slip through the hole easily. Because this is a bolt, it need screw into the knob only, not the wood.

If the sides are to be nailed together, use a drill bit smaller than the diameter of the nail.

If the sides are to be screwed together, select the drill bit carefully, using the techniques suggested earlier.

STEP 5. Use angle clamps for assembly.

If you do not have any, there's a technique that may be helpful.

Use available wall space as a brace. Glue edges C_1 and D_1, stand on edge, and place *A* on edge against them. *B* should be placed between the other ends of *C* and *D* and the wall.

Nail A_1 to edge C_1 and A_2 to D_1.

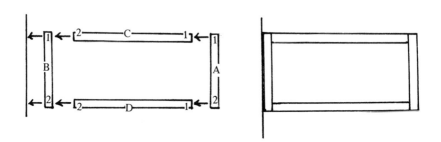

Reverse the setup carefully and attach B_1 to C_2 and B_2 to D_2. Don't forget to glue first.

STEP 6.   Lay the bottom on the box and put one nail in each corner; this will square it. Then put the rest of the nails in.

STEP 7.   Turn the box over and attach the inside angles, if you are using them. (See illustration on page 94.)

STEP 8.   Turn the box over again so that the bottom is up, and attach the casters in the corners. (It's easier to do this after the angles have been attached. The box would roll around while you were attaching the angles if the casters were already on.)

STEP 9.   Put the knob(s) on.

END OF PROJECT

HOMEWORK—

PROJECT #2:

BOOKCASE—MULTIPLE

CHOICE, CHOOSE THE

EASIEST

Because all of this knowledge has come to me as the result of need, there has always been a time factor involved in doing projects (needed yesterday, better do today!). Building from expediency does not allow time for the most complicated types of construction, very little time for elaborate or handsome design and no time for perfection. And inevitably this is how I work. It's OK for me; the job finished performs its function. I have a friend, a widow, who taught me much, so much, about tools and materials that she should really be writing this book. But she tells me never, never to say she had anything to do with my teaching. She can't bear to hang around and watch me do one of my bang-bang jobs. (That's what I call it—she calls it "cellar construction.") The fact is that I simply couldn't live in a state of rubble and ongoing renovation, and thus I have moved swiftly, using quick methods. There was old and ugly wallpaper in the downstairs dining room that had to go. I didn't know how to remove wallpaper, so I simply painted big, wide, black-and-white stripes—later for the wallpaper! (Strangely enough, this summer my friend finally painted over the linoleum-tile wall covering in her hall, after four or five years of living with their aged ugliness, waiting for time to remove it. She too applied the bang-bang philosophy—but I didn't tell her!)

What I'm trying to tell you is to find your own course and be happy in your work. If you want to be like me, pick the easiest-looking things to make, and you'll make much—and you'll be happy. (Maybe you'll be the only one—so what? Invite me, I'll be happy with you.)

The bookcase variations that follow will give you many ideas. I include the bricks and wood first, because it is absolutely the easiest and the fastest, if you know where to get bricks. Some of what is shown for bookcases can also be done in existing closets and cabinets. I always feel comfortable when I look at pictures of things I think I might be able to build. I hope some of these things get you excited enough to try.

BOOKCASES—MANY WAYS

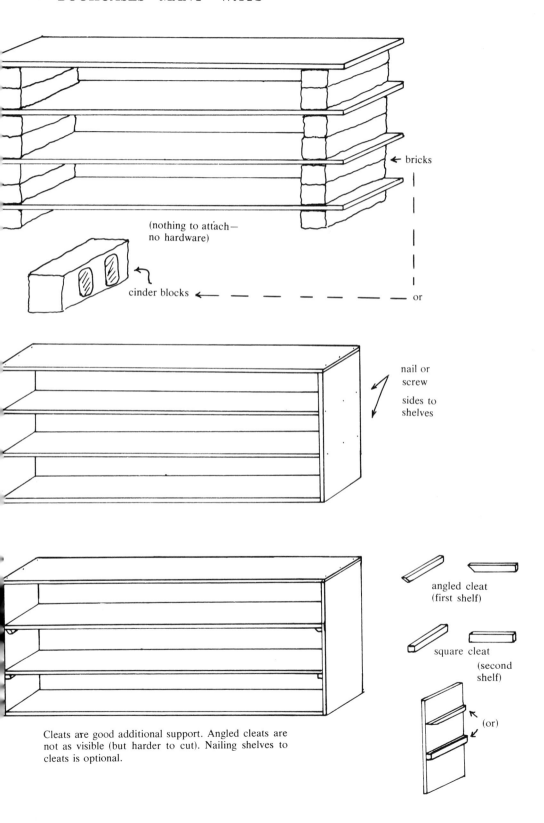

bricks

(nothing to attach—
no hardware)

cinder blocks ← — — — — — — — — — or

nail or
screw

sides to
shelves

angled cleat
(first shelf)

square cleat
(second
shelf)

(or)

Cleats are good additional support. Angled cleats are not as visible (but harder to cut). Nailing shelves to cleats is optional.

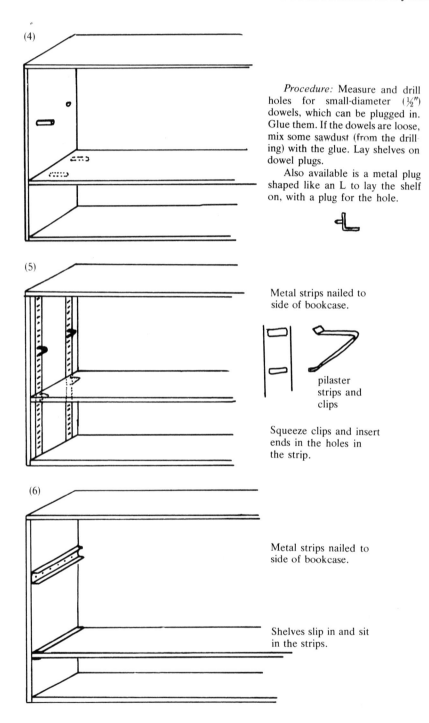

(4)

Procedure: Measure and drill holes for small-diameter ($\frac{1}{2}$") dowels, which can be plugged in. Glue them. If the dowels are loose, mix some sawdust (from the drilling) with the glue. Lay shelves on dowel plugs.

Also available is a metal plug shaped like an L to lay the shelf on, with a plug for the hole.

(5)

Metal strips nailed to side of bookcase.

pilaster strips and clips

Squeeze clips and insert ends in the holes in the strip.

(6)

Metal strips nailed to side of bookcase.

Shelves slip in and sit in the strips.

Nail (or screw) and glue sides to shelves

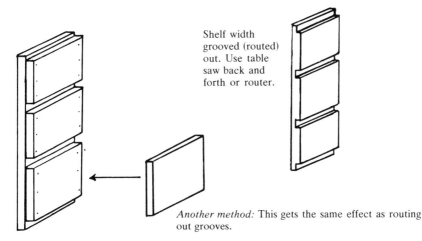

Shelf width grooved (routed) out. Use table saw back and forth or router.

Another method: This gets the same effect as routing out grooves.

Cut small pieces of wood and nail to side. Spaces between should equal thickness of shelf.

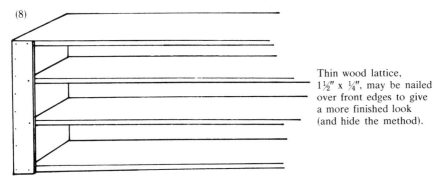

Thin wood lattice, $1\frac{1}{2}''$ x $\frac{1}{4}''$, may be nailed over front edges to give a more finished look (and hide the method).

Note: These two methods (7 and 8) are the best approaches to use for glass shelves.

(9)

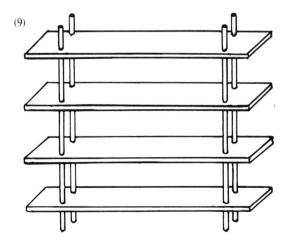

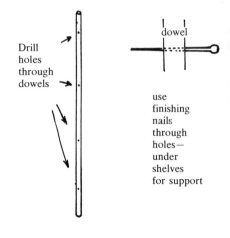

Drill
holes
through
dowels

dowel

use
finishing
nails
through
holes—
under
shelves
for support

Procedure (and you may need
a friend to help):
Put nails through the lowest holes,
put on bottom shelf; then put nails
through for the next-to-last shelf,
put on that shelf; etc.

Drill holes in shelves. Size equals
the diameter of the dowel
(1½″ diameter suggested).

(10)

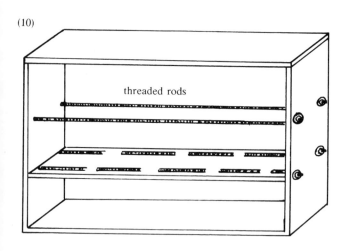

threaded rods

nut

rod

nut

metal washer   metal washer

Threaded rods come
in long lengths
and can be sawed
to proper length.

Caps are also available
which screw over end
of rod protruding
from nut.

Lock washer
looks like a
cracked washer,
holds better (locks).

Procedure: Drill holes in bookcase sides. Put rods through holes, put on washers and
nuts. Do not tighten too much. Lay the shelves on the rods. Tighten nuts.

(11)

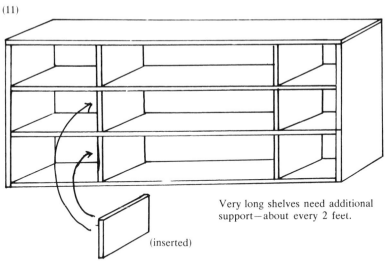

Very long shelves need additional support—about every 2 feet.

(inserted)

shelves as in bookcase #2, with additional supports toenailed in

or

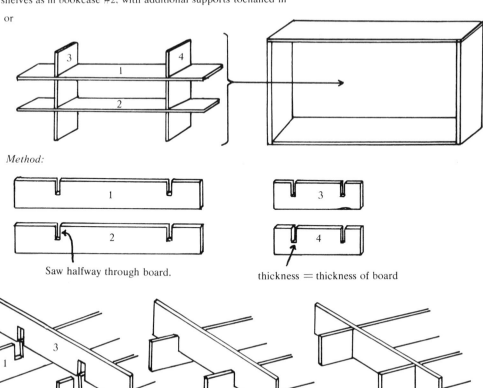

Method:

Saw halfway through board.

thickness = thickness of board

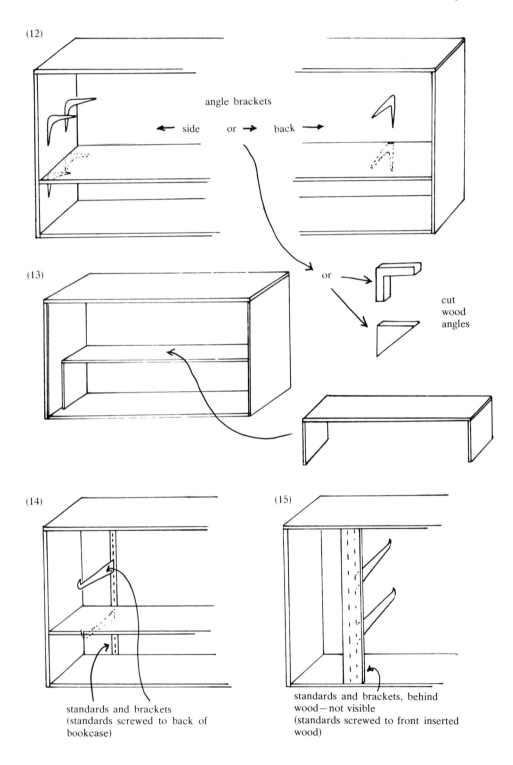

(12)

angle brackets

← side   or →   back →

or →

cut
wood
angles

(13)

(14)   (15)

standards and brackets
(standards screwed to back of
bookcase)

standards and brackets, behind
wood—not visible
(standards screwed to front inserted
wood)

(16) In an unused doorway—bookcases both sides:

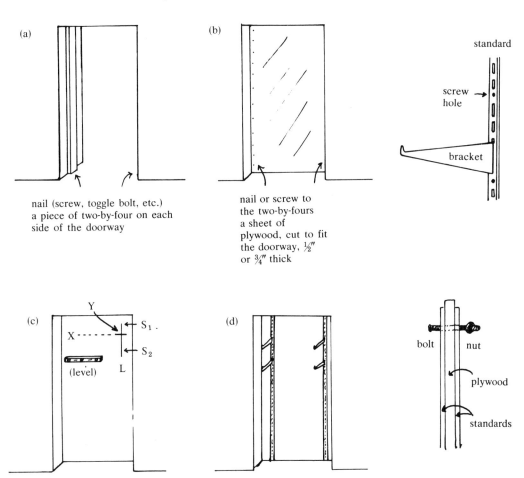

(a) nail (screw, toggle bolt, etc.)
a piece of two-by-four on each
side of the doorway

(b) nail or screw to
the two-by-fours
a sheet of
plywood, cut to fit
the doorway, ½″
or ¾″ thick

standard

screw → hole

bracket

(c)

(d)

bolt   nut

plywood

standards

1) Measure in from left 6″ and down from the top 6″ and mark X.

2) Measure in from right 6″ at 2 spots, S_1 and S_2, above and below where you think X would be on the right side. Draw a line between S_1 and S_2, line L.

3) Hold level under X and draw a line across to line L. The point where they cross Y will be the spot similar to X on the right side. (If the level isn't long enough, use a long ruler or straight piece of wood, with level held under it.)

4) Hold a standard with the screw hole over the X spot and nail it in lightly, leaving some of the nail sticking out, so it can be removed. Mark all the screw holes on the plywood.

5) Do the same on the right side, nailing into the Y spot.

6) Drill holes through the plywood for all the markings.

7) Slip bolts through standards on one side, then through plywood, then through standards on other side, and put on nuts and tighten (a friend needed).

OTHER WONDERFUL THINGS TO BUILD (ONLY WONDERFUL IF YOU NEED THEM)

It would serve no useful purpose to start out with elaborate building projects here. If this is truly an introduction for you, then you can't build a bureau (as well) if you don't first try building a simple cube. You probably shouldn't try a staircase before building a bookcase, for example. No, I won't say "Don't," because I certainly have been trying to make you believe you can do ANYTHING! But I am making a suggestion for the direction to go toward. However, if what you really need is a bureau, go to it!

Most of what follows are plans without measurements. My reason is simple. Each person's needs vary. You decide the measurements. How? Look at other things already built and pick up the rules for measurement (if needed) from them. For instance, if you want to build an end table to go beside a chair, look at another end table that you or someone else has. See how its height compares with the height of the chair seat. Or in other cases, custom-design it. If you want to build a cabinet to hold phonograph records, measure a record jacket. Make the cabinet depth (inside depth) equal to or an inch or so greater than that side, and do the same for the height. Measure how many records will fit together on a shelf width you'd like and make as many shelves as you need. If you don't want to chisel out space for hinges when hanging doors and lids, don't do it. Be happy in your work. Use some of my "cellar" techniques while you get comfortable with your new tool supply. Rely heavily on your instincts as well as the techniques you develop on your own. Guesstimate, develop a habit of really looking at how things are made. Try it! . . . that thing you think(?) you could make. So what? If it doesn't work out, stick it in the cellar. That's what cellars are for! What do you think everyone else has in his/her cellar? (The mistakes! The pieces of wood that cracked, the pieces too short, the bookcase that wobbled. . . . Join us. Think of the wood inventory you'll be accumulating.)

What follows is not the elaborate but the functional, but as your skills for building grow, so also will grow your capacity for improvisation. You will see the fancies you can add to your own handiwork; your exposure to materials will be expanded every time you go to the lumberyard and hardware store. Every time you open a home-decorating magazine, you'll get an idea. You'll find yourself browsing through handyperson magazines, and you'll discover a new type of book collection growing. And then one day, if you really keep at it, you will find yourself very privately wondering if maybe you couldn't build a little shack in the country and you know what? You could! (I must warn you, however, that as you mull over these thoughts, that shack will grow into the glory of all your dreams—all the storage space you can have, and this here, and that there, and of course you'll build in the beds, and the cabinets . . . and then you'll begin to think about all that wonderful hardware you've always wanted to use but had no place to put—door latches, knobs, hinges . . . then you'll be into the lighting . . . (I'd better stop. You get the picture, don't you?)

So let's get started on that house. First, build a cube.

CUBES

(1)

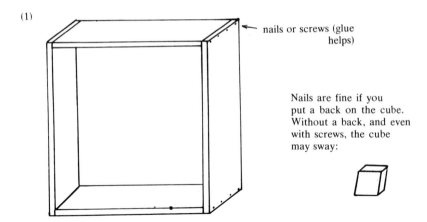

nails or screws (glue helps)

Nails are fine if you
put a back on the cube.
Without a back, and even
with screws, the cube
may sway:

Masonite is best for the back, especially when it won't show. The best way to measure for the back, if you have a piece of Masonite larger than the size required for the back, is to lay the cube on top of the corner of the Masonite and draw lines for the two sides to be cut. This will also guarantee the perpendicularity of the cube.

draw lines ⟶

Masonite

(2)

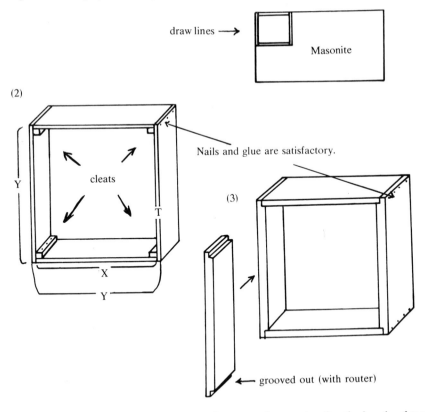

Nails and glue are satisfactory.

cleats

Y

T

(3)

X

Y

⟵ grooved out (with router)

In a cube, the outside dimensions are the same; after construction the lengths of top and bottom can vary from the sides, depending on the method of joining the corners. In the above cube (2), the top and bottom will be shorter than the sides. The difference will be 2 times the thickness of the sides: $X = Y - (2 \times T)$, T being the thickness.

RECTANGULAR BOXES (LIKE A WINDOW BOX)

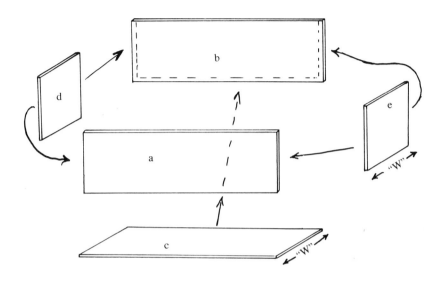

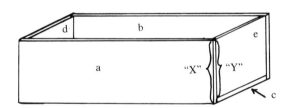

Sides *a* and *b* are on the outside.
Bottom *c* is between the bottom edges of *a* and *b*.

Sides *d* and *e* are between the side edges of *a* and *b*, down as far as *c*. Side dimension, "*Y*," of sides *d* and *e* is equal to side dimension of *a* and *b*, "*X*," minus the thickness of the bottom *c*.

As may be obvious from the diagram, the width, "*W*," is the same for *d*, *e* and *c*.

(Setting the bottom in the way pictured instead of between *all* the sides always appeals to me as easier.)

BOXES WITH LIDS AND HINGES

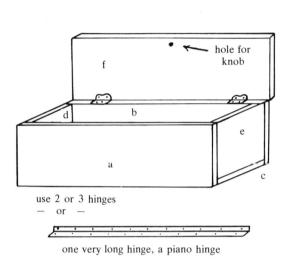

f

hole for
knob

d · b

e

a

c

use 2 or 3 hinges

— or —

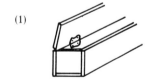

one very long hinge, a piano hinge

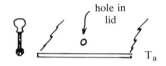

hole in
lid

o

T$_a$

If a knob on the top is desired, drill a hole
in the lid, far enough in from the edge of
the lid so the protruding end of the screw
of the knob doesn't hit the top edge of
side *a* when closing, thus the hole must
be in at least the thickness of *a*: T_a

Be careful how you put hinges on. Try them first without attaching them, to see the effect of how you are planning to use them.

In the above picture, one part of the hinge is attached to the *top edge* of side *b*. The other part of the hinge is attached to the flat undersurface of the lid *(f)*. The effect of placing the hinges this way is that there are flush edges:

The same effect is possible if you attach the hinge to the edge of the lid and the flat outer surface of side *b:*

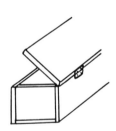

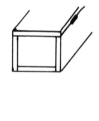

If you attach the hinge to both inner flat surfaces (1) or both outer edges (2), the effect will not be flush:

(1)

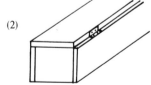

(2)

And if you attach the hinges to both the edge of the lid and the edge of side *b,* which are, as viewed, inner edges . . .

... the box
won't close.

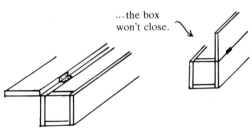

LADDERS—TO BUNK BEDS, TREE HOUSES, ETC.

Use 1″ x 3″ wood (actually ¾″ x 2½″)

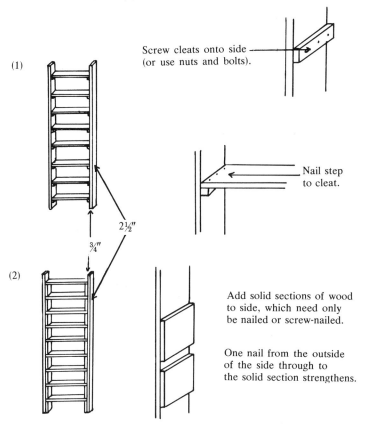

(1)

Screw cleats onto side (or use nuts and bolts).

Nail step to cleat.

2½″

¾″

(2)

Add solid sections of wood to side, which need only be nailed or screw-nailed.

One nail from the outside of the side through to the solid section strengthens.

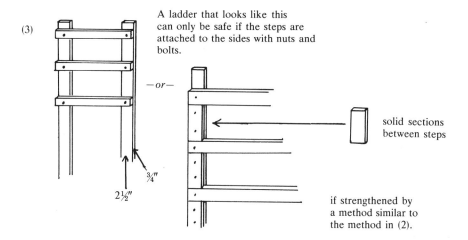

(3)

A ladder that looks like this can only be safe if the steps are attached to the sides with nuts and bolts.

—or—

solid sections between steps

¾″

2½″

if strengthened by a method similar to the method in (2).

BOOKCASES—TWO MORE WAYS

Cubes and Boards

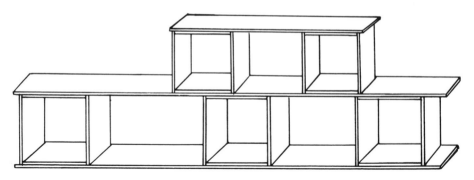

An effective touch is cubes painted black, boards stained
walnut or some other wood variation.

Ladders and Boards

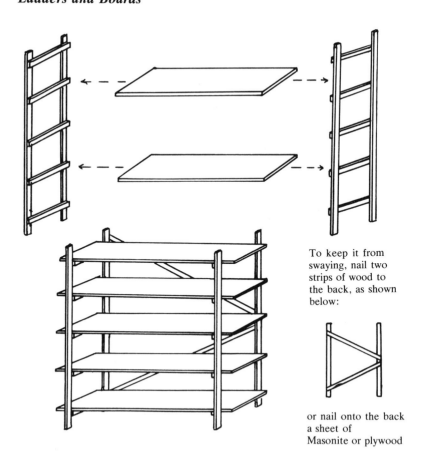

To keep it from
swaying, nail two
strips of wood to
the back, as shown
below:

or nail onto the back
a sheet of
Masonite or plywood

AND ANOTHER BOOKCASE!

Here's an idea. I used it under my steps. There were two nice two-by-four supports; rather than bury them behind a wall panel, I made a bookcase. This could also be done in the frame of an unused window; nail the two-by-fours to the sides of the frame.

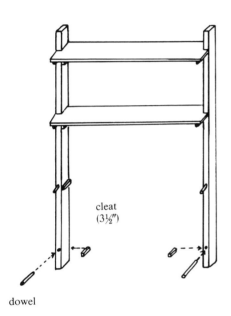

cleat
(3½")

dowel

Drill the front for inserting dowels. Squirt glue into hole first.

Use cleats under the part of the shelf within the two-by-four; nail cleats to the two-by-four.

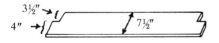

3½"
4"
7½"

Saw corners off shelves. (1 x 8's)

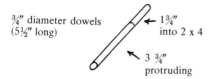

¾" diameter dowels
(5½" long)

1¾"
into 2 x 4

3 ¾"
protruding

TWICE AS MUCH

Make some
of these.

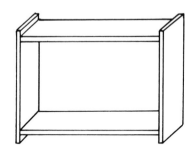

Now watch—

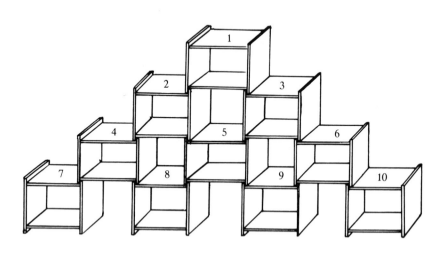

EASY STORAGE–DISHPANS AND CLEATS

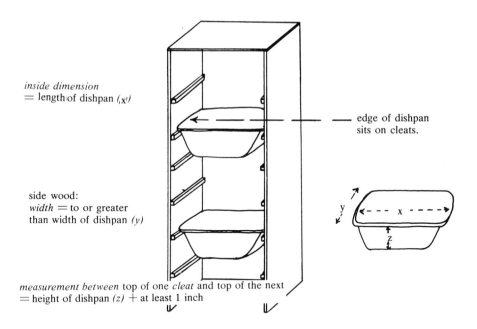

inside dimension
= length of dishpan *(x)*

edge of dishpan
sits on cleats.

side wood:
width = to or greater
than width of dishpan *(y)*

measurement between top of one *cleat* and top of the next
= height of dishpan *(z)* + at least 1 inch

CLOSET–ADDING A SHELF AND/OR A CLOTHES BAR

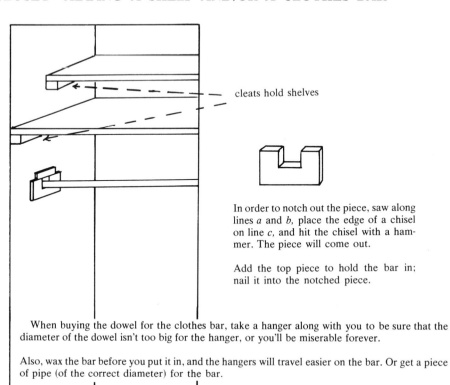

cleats hold shelves

In order to notch out the piece, saw along lines *a* and *b,* place the edge of a chisel on line *c,* and hit the chisel with a hammer. The piece will come out.

Add the top piece to hold the bar in; nail it into the notched piece.

When buying the dowel for the clothes bar, take a hanger along with you to be sure that the diameter of the dowel isn't too big for the hanger, or you'll be miserable forever.

Also, wax the bar before you put it in, and the hangers will travel easier on the bar. Or get a piece of pipe (of the correct diameter) for the bar.

ADDING DIVIDERS IN DRAWER

(looking down into drawer)

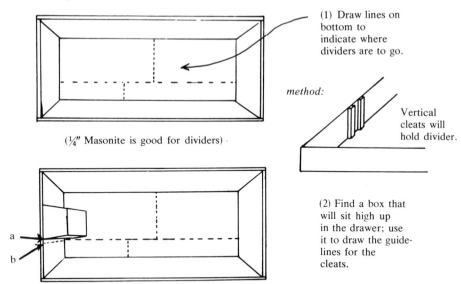

(1) Draw lines on bottom to indicate where dividers are to go.

(¼″ Masonite is good for dividers) ·

method:

Vertical cleats will hold divider.

(2) Find a box that will sit high up in the drawer; use it to draw the guide-lines for the cleats.

a

b

Set the box ⅛″ to one side of the line on the bottom of the drawer and draw guideline *a*. Then set the box ⅛″ to the other side of the bottom line and draw guideline *b*.

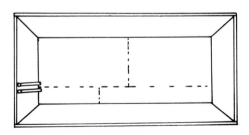

(3) Glue cleats to side of drawer. Cleats should be ¼″ apart to allow Masonite divider to slip in.

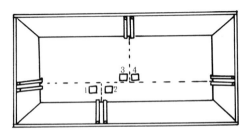

(4) Use the box to mark the other points, and glue in the cleats.

Put dividers in, position correctly, and glue in four more cleats: *1, 2, 3, 4.*

TABLES AND DESKS

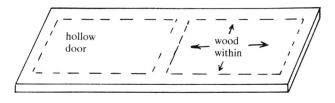

hollow door

wood within

available as a rectangle

Good because of the finished quality, but not too good for cutting down (see diagram).

or

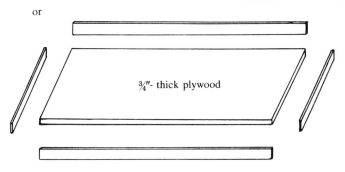

¾″- thick plywood

Good because of available size of 4′ x 8′, can be cut down to square, circular or rectangular shapes.

The rough edges of plywood have to be covered. Squares and rectangles may be covered with ¼″ x 1″ lattice, glued and nailed.

Also available for covering edges of plywood are:
(a) veneer—very thin, almost curly wood which can be glued on;
(b) wood tape with adhesive.
Both are alternates to lattice, and are what to use for circles.

Chipboard should not be used with legs shown, because it has no grain, only chips, and may not hold screws well.

wooden legs

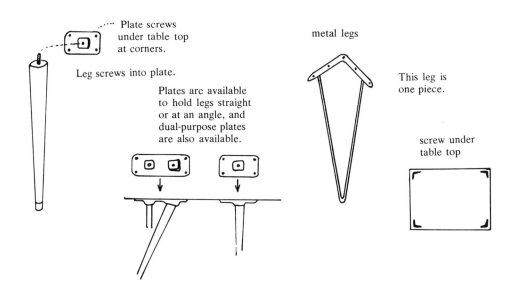

Plate screws under table top at corners.

Leg screws into plate.

Plates arc available to hold legs straight or at an angle, and dual-purpose plates are also available.

metal legs

This leg is one piece.

screw under table top

The Whole Table Built, Legs and All

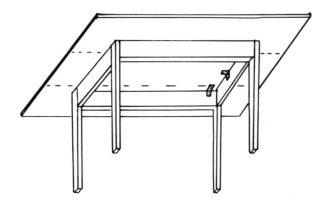

Top can be solid
or boards,
angled on from
underneath.

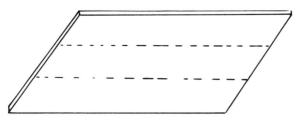

Corners doweled
and glued would
be good.

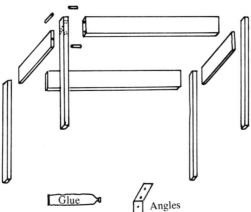

Glue   Angles

BED

Nowadays, one can buy a mattress and spring, with legs screwed into the spring. This is often adequate. In my bedroom, this is exactly what I have, nothing more. However, perhaps one day I may get fancier. This is the route I might take:

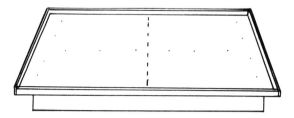

Plywood under the spring, I think ¾ inch thick, would make me feel secure. My bed is a king-size, thus it would need two sheets of plywood, cut so that when placed together they would measure about 1 or 2 inches more than the sides of the spring. To the edges of the plywood at the bottom, I would nail some 1 x 3 or 1 x 4, to give it a better look, and also to cover the rough plywood edges. I would then make a base of 1 x 10's for the plywood to sit on, recessed about 6 inches or so. I would premeasure where the base would sit and nail or screw the plywood to the place at a few strategic places (where the dots are in the illustration above).

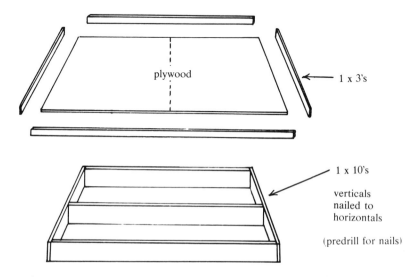

plywood

← 1 x 3's

1 x 10's

verticals
nailed to
horizontals

(predrill for nails)

One sheet of plywood would be all that was necessary for a single, and you could even do without the spring if you wanted.

Now, if you just let your head wander a bit further . . . you could extend the base and add, using it for support, a headboard-bookcase with two shelves (or one or more) and a lower panel to lean the pillow against. (Yes, I know, you're already to the point of "And I could even build in end tables. . . .") It's fun, isn't it, this new exploration?

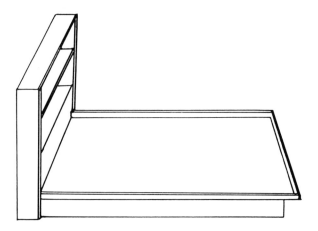

TRUNDLE BED

Finally I have found a summer house for me and the boys. It's a very old house and it will take years to furnish, because I'd like it to be somewhat the way it was when built, and that means almost-antiques (or good junk-shop finds). In any case, beds are the first priority, and I'd like a lot of them because I'm a people person and want lots of guests. Browsing through a book of pictures of antique furniture, I came across an old trundle bed that looked like this:

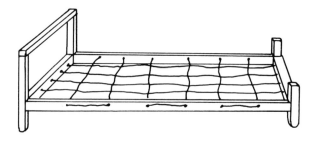

. . . and I got an idea. . . . Why not build trundles under all the beds that also have to be built? Why not start with the trundles? I'll make a trundle for myself, which will eventually go under my bed, and trundles for the boys (they can help) . . . and a simple design shot into my head. Why not have guests make their own beds (trundle)?—and the beds will be done in no time! (As for the mattresses, well . . . one each time I can afford one, that's all.) So far, three of my friends are delighted with the idea, so the plan may be a boon! Here is the blueprint for a weekend visit:

The finished product will be made from two-by-twos, lap-jointed together (glued and screwed). Holes will be drilled in the four sides before joining. Rope will be threaded through the holes after joining. In the old days, wet rope was used, and because it shrank as it dried, it made a snug spring; so maybe we'll wet the rope.

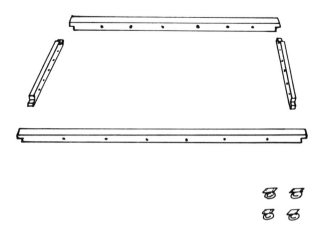

Then casters in the four corners. Presto . . . a trundle!

COUCH AND CHAIR

With all the foam-rubber shapes and sizes available these days, and also puffy fillings, a couch can be a simple project. If you look at some friend's Danish modern, for example, you will notice how easy it is to duplicate. These couches usually have metal springs wired into the base, but you know about rope now, or you can always go "junking" for an old spring. Or you can always opt for a hard seat and use a solid piece of plywood under the foam or puff. The legs are a screw-into-the-base type.

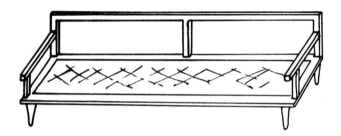

Someday when I have time again, here is the couch I would like to have—easy to build and satisfying my lazy needs and my storage needs (shown bare of bolsters or puff). Footrests, extra seats and/or endtables would be stored underneath—just boxes, the lids sitting on top. The foot pillow could be attached under the lid and the lid reversed when you used the box as a footrest, or the pillow could just sit in the box. And there would be casters under the box for mobility.

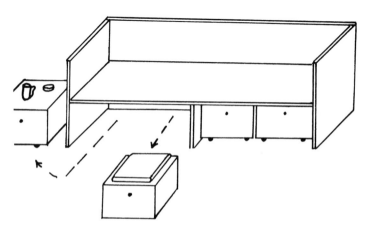

This project should be simple. I would use butcher block if I were very rich, but as I'm not I'd probably use plywood, 1 inch thick. And I would limit the couch to 8 feet, to be able to have a one-piece solid back. And I would cleat for the seat piece.

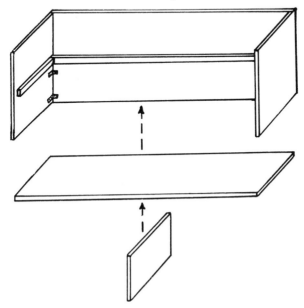

Back is glued and screwed into the sides. Cleats (1″ x 2″) are glued and screwed into the sides and back. Glue the top areas of the cleats and lay the seat piece on. Nail it down in a few places. Put center bracing piece under the seat and nail the seat down to it. The seat could instead be a frame with rope or spring. Some angle braces will make for more security, one under the cleats at the corners and one at each corner bottom. Angled bolsters will give comfort, but don't forget to make the seat deep enough to absorb the bottom of the bolster and still have room for your own seat.

Don't forget some edging (1″ x ¼″) for the plywood edges. Apply it with glue and some brads.

Boxes are boxes. I don't have to illustrate, do I?

As for a chair or two; adapt the couch plan, with or without the box-footrest-endtable.

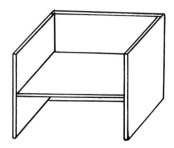

BOX COFFEE TABLE

While we're talking about boxes and storage, I'd like to show you one I built for my living room. A tempting buy-now-pay-later offer of a circular saw with a free metal table came in the mail one day. The saw was cheap and I had never heard of the brand, but it *was* cheap, so I sent for it. (Why haven't I talked about a circular saw yet? I still haven't used it. I used a borrowed one once. They're scary, so wait a few years and then get one. The best use for it, probably, is to cut thick plywood. However, it is a difficult saw to control. The little table that came with the one I have has some guides on it which help when the saw is attached to the underneath part of the table, blade coming up through a slot. But holding it loose in your hand takes getting used to.) The damn thing was big. and I had no place to keep it—thus my new box (hideaway) coffee table.

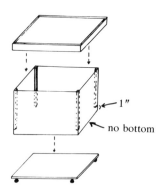

The project was done with ½″ plywood. I covered the piece for the top with leather and nailed ¼″ x 1″ around the edges. The four sides of the box were nailed to 1″ x 1″ inside the corner pieces, not as long as the side. The bottom piece was cut to fit inside the box sides. It sits on the bottom because the 1″ x 1″ inside corners sit on the four corners of the bottom. The table and saw sit on the bottom and can be lifted off the bottom more easily when the side has been lifted off first.

DOOR

We have three cats, and I wanted a living room that would be free of cat hair. However, I didn't want to cut off the air supply with solid doors. The answer was (almost) just a frame made from two-by-twos, with lap-joint connections and some yellow plastic clothesline strung through holes drilled into it.

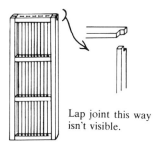

Lap joint this way isn't visible.

I said "almost." In spite of how tight I strung the line — and I made the space between each line no bigger than half a cat's head, about — when the project was finished, my most brazen cat walked up to the door . . . and walked through the space; the rope spread easily and her body was through! Damn! The door which had been so inexpensive to make became very expensive, because I went out and bought some hard, see-through vinyl plastic, cut it to fit the lower two sections and wove it in between the rope. The top area has none, and I've fooled the cats! They would surely jump up and go through if they knew . . . and we do get some air.

Some things don't always work out according to plan, but that's part of the game.

WINDOW SEAT

This is another of my "one of these days" projects, but I've mulled over the plan enough so that it should be an easy job.

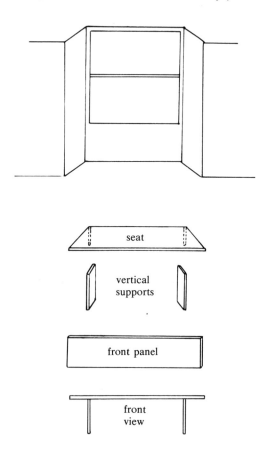

For the seat use a board, or plywood if you want a very wide seat. Place two pieces under the seat in the position indicated by the dotted lines, recessed, at least at the thickness of the front board. Nail the top down, and then nail the front on.

This method is better than nailing the verticals under the angled edges, because the front edges of the supports would then be angled, not flush to meet the front panel. (See this exaggerated illustration.)

If you have a radiator, you should not seal it in (no heat!). Instead you could put a thin board, the length of the top seat, on the floor, nailed into the supports, and one at the top, under the seat board; then nail slats across the two.

Or the front panel could be doors to storage, hinged to vertical supports.

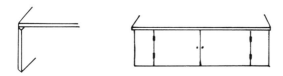

The angle? How do you figure out the ends of the wood? Measure the width of the wall beneath the window a. Measure next the length from the outer tips of the walls b. (This will be the length of the board you need to start with.) Lay your angle ruler on the floor, as shown, and measure distance c. Do the same thing on the other side to get distance d . . . the house could be crooked, so don't assume c and d are the same. Mark the board for c and d and saw off the excess. (And if you're lucky, what you'll be left with is a.)

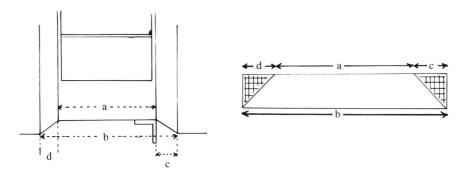

CUPBOARD

The difference between a cupboard and an ordinary box is that you want the cupboard to be structurally strong (cans and dishes are heavy), and you want it to hang on the wall. Thus the design is just a bit more complicated.

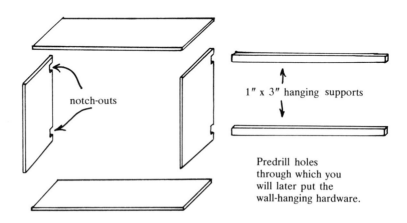

notch-outs

1″ x 3″ hanging supports

Predrill holes through which you will later put the wall-hanging hardware.

We start with the four sides of a box—no top or bottom. But first prepare the vertical sides for the hanging feature. Use ¾″ plywood. Notch out the sides to receive 1 x 3's set in. These will be used for hanging. Glue and screw box sides together. Glue and screw hanging supports to back.

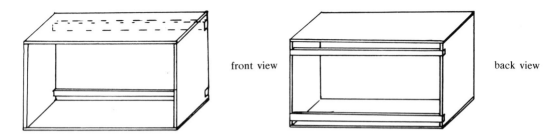

front view

back view

Next we add styles to the front edges, all 1″ x 2″, or 1″ x 2″ horizontally and 1″ x 3″ vertically. These add more strength to the box and provide a better base for hinging the doors.

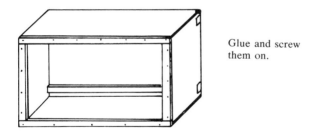

Glue and screw
them on.

Next the doors, which are an easier deal if you make them to sit outside instead of fitting them within the space, so cut them larger. Use
¾″ plywood for the doors, too. Predrill for knob bolt before hinging
door. If the cabinet will sit high, put knobs low.

　　Hang the cupboard on the wall. Use the strongest wall hardware,
through the one-by-threes into the wall.
　　For a bigger cupboard, add another vertical inside *(v)* and another
style *(s)*.

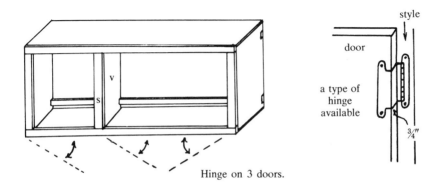

Hinge on 3 doors.

KITCHEN COUNTER

I had a wonderful book of great plans, which I used when I built my counter. I've been looking for it for about two years now, but without success. Thus, I just had to go down and take mine apart with my eyes (and hands, feeling around) to see how it was built. I'll give you the measurements, since they're probably standard.

It looks roughly like this:

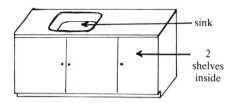

First a baseboard frame is built: 2 x 4's are used, the long ones 60½ inches, the short ones 17 inches, nailed together. The outside dimensions will be 60½" x 20" when nailed, because 2" x 4" is really 1½" x 3½", and the thicknesses of the long pieces at x and y are 1½" + 1½", which equals 3", + 17", which equals 20".

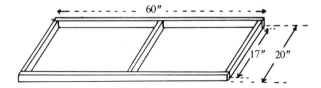

Next, a piece of ¾"-thick plywood, cut 22" x 60½", is nailed to the base. This is the floor of the counter. The extra 2" overhang in the front is for the comfort of tucking toes under. (Remind your husband of how thoughtful you were of his comfort some night when he's washing the dishes!)

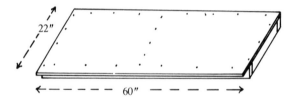

   Two sidepieces (¾″ plywood) must be cut measuring 22″ x 36″. From the top back corner of each, notch out—saw off—space for a 1 x 3 to fit (¾″ x 2½″). Lay the edge against the plywood and pencil the area. Then saw it off.

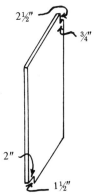

   From the bottom front, saw off 2″ x 1½″ (2″ is toe recess, 1½″ is the height of the 2 x 4). Make sure of the actual dimensions of the 2 x 4, because it might not be exactly 1½″ x 3½″, remember?

   (You may need a helper.) Place one side on the floor against the base and flooring piece. Nail the side into the base (2 x 4). It will wobble without help, maybe. Now do the same with the other side. Next, nail a 1 x 3, cut 62″, to the top backs of the sides; setting it in the notched-out spaces (62″ because the thickness of the side pieces are each ¾″, the floor base 60½″ . . . 60½ + ¾ + ¾).

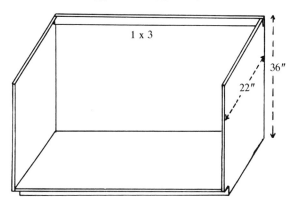

   Next, cut the styles, one 62″-long 1 x 2 and three 32½″-long 1 x 2's. Also cut the inside vertical piece to divide the sections, 1″ ply, 33½″ x 22″, notched out on top for the 1 x 3.

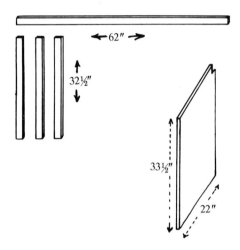

(a) Nail the long (62″) 1 x 2 to the tops of the sides.

(b) Insert the inside vertical divider. Nail to floor (toenail) and to back brace (1 x 3); then nail through top style to it.

Nail vertical styles to left side, divider and right side (*c, d* and *e*).

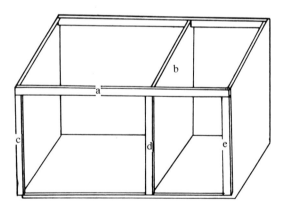

Without a bottom horizontal style, you should cut doors to fit between the styles so they are flush with them; you can add a bottom style, nailed to the counter floor, and hang outside doors similar to the cabinet type described earlier.

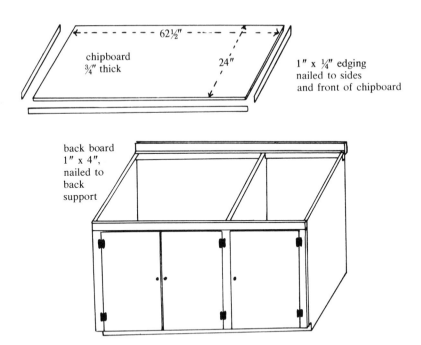

top

Top nailed down. You can nail some cleats inside the right section and add shelves.

Chipboard is a standard for the tops of counters and should be used when you put on Formica.

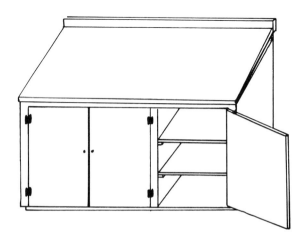

One final word about mine. Weeks before I made this counter, I had found three old table tops on the street (oh, all right, beside someone's garbage can . . . that's fair pickings). I stored them in my cellar, knowing they would come in handy one day. They did! They were the wood I used for the vertical sides! A word about findings, then, is: pick it up. You might even find nice cabinet doors for some cabinet you will build a year from now. (If you don't have a cellar, find a friend with one, a friend who likes you . . . and your new craft.)

Doors for Cabinets—Another Way

You can have an old, country look by making doors from 1 x 5's, this way:

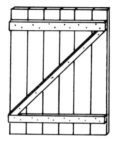

This Z brace goes on the inside, usually.

Make a bunch of boards held together by two crosspieces. Then nail in the diagonal to keep the door from getting tipsy.

BUNK BEDS AND PLAY STRUCTURES

There are all kinds of bunk beds . . .

. . . from simple . . .

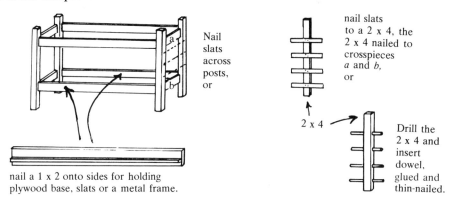

Nail slats across posts, or

nail a 1 x 2 onto sides for holding plywood base, slats or a metal frame.

nail slats to a 2 x 4, the 2 x 4 nailed to crosspieces *a* and *b*, or

2 x 4

Drill the 2 x 4 and insert dowel, glued and thin-nailed.

. . . to hanging . . .

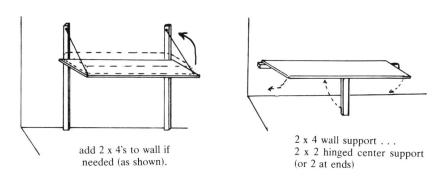

add 2 x 4's to wall if needed (as shown).

2 x 4 wall support . . . 2 x 2 hinged center support (or 2 at ends)

. . . to the play unit . . .

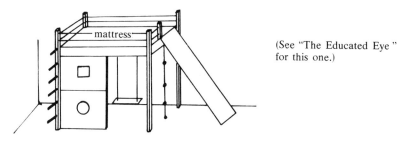

mattress

(See "The Educated Eye " for this one.)

dowels into post for ladder (any post convenient for climbing)

But here is the plan for my children's room, if I ever find the time! To fill a room with beds, when they're only used for sleeping, is a waste of space. Kids need a room to play in. (God help my kids! They're going to live in a jungle.) The back half—swings and rope—is already there.

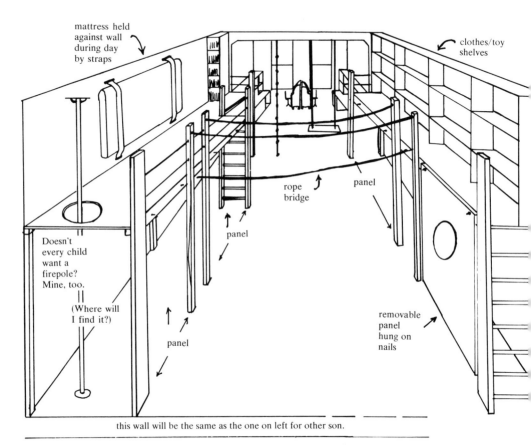

mattress held against wall during day by straps

clothes/toy shelves

rope bridge

panel

panel

Doesn't every child want a firepole? Mine, too.

(Where will I find it?)

panel

removable panel hung on nails

this wall will be the same as the one on left for other son.

THE STAIRCASE—AND
THE PRINCIPLES
THEREOF

Because this staircase is my one claim to fame, in this neighborhood at least, I'd like to share the whole learning experience with you.

In my quest to find an easy-to-build staircase, I went through at least a hundred home-decorating magazines, bothered all my patient friends with questions and poked around the lumberyard. Also, I looked at every pair of steps I walked on. Eventually I went to the library because I was still uncomfortable with my findings and had decided to divert myself by learning the concepts and terminologies of staircases. I pulled out every serious-looking building book there and sat down to learn. The name of one of the publishers was familiar, and I suddenly remembered all those books my father had had on plumbing and steamfitting, books which shared the one bookcase in our living room with a set of fifteen classics (unread) and my mother's copy of *Gone with the Wind*. The publisher's name was Theodore Audel, who seems to have put out volumes on all phases of construction, not on a handyperson's level but on a craftsperson's level. The books are well illustrated and not difficult to understand. (Some things not in here are surely covered in greater depth in the Audel books. I recommend them as browsing material, at least.)

Those old memories of home and the bookcase gave me a warm feeling, and I opened the Audel book first. It was the only book I had to look at. All the principles were there and easy to grasp.

The step, the part you put your foot on, is called the tread. The distance in height from one step to the next is called the riser. The two sidepieces that hold the steps together are called stringers. For comfortable stepping, Audel recommends a formula—no, probably he stated that it was a *rule:* Two times the riser dimension plus the tread dimension should equal 25 inches ($2r + t = 25''$). If you want a riser of 8½ inches, then you should have a tread of 8 inches ([8½ + 8½] + 8 = 25), according to the comfort formula.

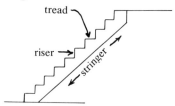

The brownstone houses beside mine had the same plan as my house. All have steps to the lower floor in exactly the same place as I planned to put mine.

I removed part of the floor and the floor braces in the closet above, and the walls and some of the studs of the closet below, as illustrated in the diagram following. (I ascertained that none of the studs were load-bearing. See the difference on page 66.)

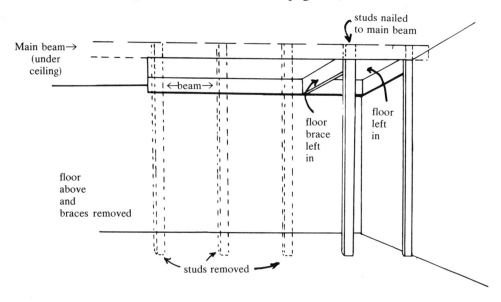

At some point I measured the distance from the top of the landing to the floor below. I measured the distance from the floor under the landing to the wall of the outer hall, because there had to be walking space between the wall and the bottom of the steps.

I had already decided that I wanted about an 8-inch riser, from testing (walking up and down) and measuring other staircases—not just for comfort, but for safety. The boys would be running up and down many times a day.

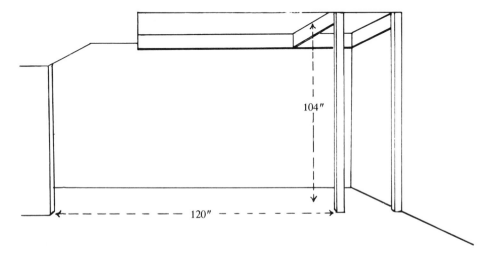

I did some quick arithmetic. How many 8-inch risers in 104 inches? $104 \div 8 = 13$ steps . . . no, 12 steps and the floor. (A riser of 8 inches meant a tread of 9 inches [8 + 8 + 9 = 25, the *rule*]). Twelve steps of 9-inch tread meant 108 inches. Disaster! That would only leave 16 inches' walking space to the hall.

I grabbed a piece of graph paper and drew the steps to double-check myself. Graph paper is an absolute must for planning a project like this. The best benefit of it is that it offers a way to determine how long the stringer should be. I don't know how builders do it—trigonometry?—but I measured the length with a piece of graph paper. See the next diagram for a graphic illustration of my setback.

Back to the decorating magazines . . . maybe one of those circular staircases that come prefabricated . . . ? No, the opening at the top isn't wide enough and a main beam is in the way of widening. . . .

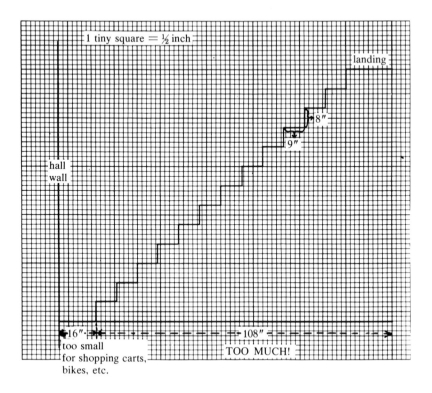

1 tiny square = ½ inch

landing

hall
wall

8"

9"

16"
too small
for shopping carts,
bikes, etc.

108"

TOO MUCH!

I considered a higher riser, but decided we'd all kill ourselves on a steep staircase. . . .

The final design came from a friend who had seen a similar staircase at a party she'd been to. She called it a "people staircase" because it had provided seating for half the people at the party. She drew me a sketch.

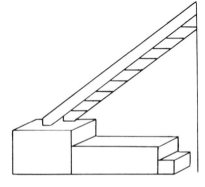

It was perfect! As I looked at the sketch, I realized it would provide more than people space; it would also give me badly needed storage space, a reading corner for the kids (if they ever learned to read) and—best of all—it would be a stage for the boys to give shows on. Quickly I got another piece of graph paper.

Three boxes—easy? No such luck. These boxes were horrors, mostly because they had to be strong. That meant an understructure of two-by-fours. Notching, sawing and screwing into two-by-fours is not something I'm very happy about doing. The task of building the boxes took all weekend.

Back to the steps. Hopefully, if you have to build a staircase, the steps can go to the floor, so let's consider for the rest of this discussion that the top of the highest box is the floor.

When I awoke on the weekend following the box-building project, I was still trying to decide how to build the steps. Only two plans were in my head:

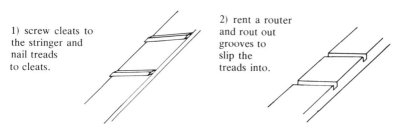

1) screw cleats to the stringer and nail treads to cleats.

2) rent a router and rout out grooves to slip the treads into.

In any case, I went to the lumberyard to buy the wood for the staircase. Stringer wood comes 2 by 8 inches. Treads were available in 1 by 9 inches (actually true 1″ x 9″ plus a curved front edge), called "1 by 9 tread." My steps were to be 24 inches wide, including the stringers, therefore I needed nine treads 21 inches long ($24 - 1\frac{1}{2} - 1\frac{1}{2} = 21$). The stringer thickness is actually $1\frac{1}{2}$ inches, not 2 inches. And I decided to have the steps cut at the lumberyard with their table saw to guarantee straight cuts . . . and to watch every minute to be sure they measure right. The length of the stringer wood had to be at least 120 inches but I had to cut angles off, so I bought them 122 inches to have some sawing space.

In order to determine the length of the stringers, one evening, after playing around with some trigonometry which left me unsure, I cut a piece of the graph paper $4\frac{3}{4}$ little squares wide (to represent $9\frac{1}{2}$

inches) and laid it over the graphed drawing of the steps, letting corners *A* and *B* be just barely visible. I Scotch-taped it to the drawing
and measured.

While I was at it, I got out a protractor and measured the angle
at point *Z*, crossed the lines *X* and *Y*. It was 42°. A right angle was
represented by the crossing of the lines *X* and *W*, thus I would cut
off at an angle of 48°, the shaded area. At the top I would leave an
angle of 48° and cut off 42°. How nice that all worked out! I'm sure
there's a principle of math at work here, but I don't know it.

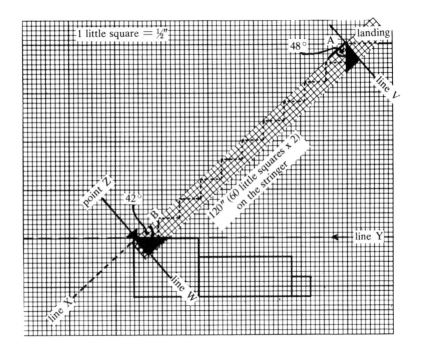

An interruption to illustrate using the protractor:

I placed the protractor this way to determine the angle at the top.

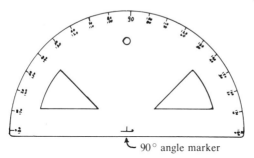

90° angle marker

The right angle (90°) I want is the one made by line X (stringer top), and line V, which meet at point A, because it contains the angles I need to know about, the angle to cut off and the angle to remain. Similarly, at the bottom of the stringer, the right angle of concern is made by line X and line W, meeting at point Z.

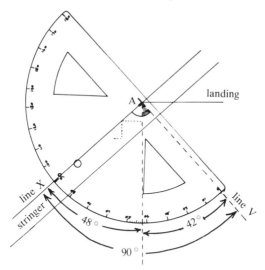

The angle marker is set thus:

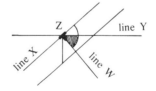

Now, to continue with the solution for the building method I finally used to attach the treads to the stringers:

As I was unloading the wood from my car, a friend came along. "What are you building now?" he asked.

"A staircase . . . one of these days. I'm probably going to use cleats, but I'm not happy about it," I answered.

"You know," he said, "I saw an interesting bookcase the other day, where the shelves were sitting on threaded rods that went through the sides and were tightened with nuts, thus holding the shelves to the sides." (See bookcase plan #10, page 106.) Bells rang in my head. Bang, bang . . . drill a few holes, glue, cut the angles and up we go!

"Thanks, you saved my life," I yelled, as I jumped into the car to go to the hardware store. "Eighteen quarter-inch-diameter threaded rods, please. How long do they come?"

"Three feet, lady." "Could they be cut shorter?" "Yes, with a hacksaw."

"OK, eighteen, please, and thirty-six nuts to fit . . . and, oh, thirty-six washers."

God, I was excited. Could it be that there would be a staircase in my house tonight?

I called my friend (and teacher) in the midst of this excitement, and she suggested that maybe I ought to borrow her brother's circular electric saw to cut the angles off the stringers. My saber saw might not be strong enough to plow through the thick stringer wood. I called him and he stayed throughout the whole venture.

The first thing I did was to cut a piece of cardboard in a rectangle, 8 inches by 9 inches. Then I measured off the top and bottom angles on the stringer (with my little protractor) and drew lines to indicate the cuts on both stringers. I picked up the circular saw, which was uncomfortably heavy. My start was clumsy and I was unsure about guiding it and I stopped. My friend offered to do the cuts—he was used to the saw—and I let him. Then we lifted one stringer into position and it fit perfectly! My friends just stared at me in disbelief. I guess I had trusted the graph-paper method all along, naively; and they, experienced builders, couldn't believe that such an unorthodox method could work.

Next, I measured down 8 inches along the top cut edge, marked it off, laid the cardboard with the 9-inch edge from the bottom of that 8-inch mark to the side of the stringer, and began to draw the guide-lines for drilling the holes. The learning process is slow and sometimes disastrous. I had a flash—a mental picture of the tread sitting on the rods. The treads were 1 inch thick. That would leave me with a 7-inch riser at the top and 9-inch riser at the bottom. Start over, sister. . . . This time I also remembered that the diameter of the rods was ¼ inch and I wanted to mark for the center; so this time I measured down along the angled cut edge 9⅛ inches and marked the rest of the line with the cardboard. The following illustrations show the procedure I used.

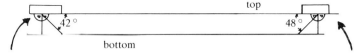

protractor laid on top of stringer, held straight against edge by bracing it with a piece of wood

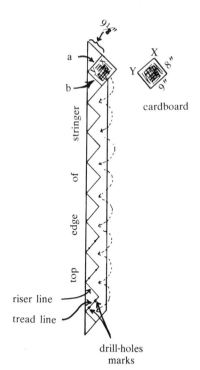

cardboard

Place corner *X* of cardboard at 9⅛" mark.

Place corner *Y* at edge of stringer.
Draw lines *a* and *b*.

Move cardboard down.
Place corner *X* at inside end of line *b*.
Place corner *Y* at edge of stringer. Draw lines.

Continue until all lines are drawn, then mark x's 1″ in from each end of the tread lines to indicate where the holes are to be drilled. Drill ¼"-diameter holes for the rods.

The final assembly: Here's how to do it, if you have to: Put all the rods through the stringers. Put the washers on the rods. Then screw on the nuts, only so far that about ¼″ of the rod protrudes. Push the rest of the rod through the stringer so that the washer and nut are against the stringer. Do this on only one side of the stringer. On the other side put on the washers and nuts but leave space between string-

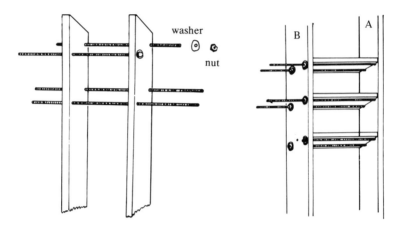

er and treads. Glue the edges of the first tread and lay it on the rods. Holding the nuts secure on side *A,* tighten the nuts on side *B,* not too tightly, yet until all treads are placed. Then tighten all, very tightly. Then saw off all but $\frac{1}{4}''$ of the rod protruding on side *B* . . . yes, a hacksaw. For final security, hammer some nails through the stringer into each tread, one on each side, to keep it from going anywhere if it ever becomes loose.

The final stage is to lift the step construction and place it into position — with help.

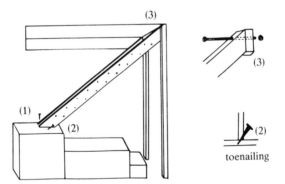

(1) Predrill holes and nail the tips of the stringer at the bottom to the platform.

(2) In order to prevent the steps from slipping in time, predrill holes and toenail from the outer side of the stringer, down, in the direction of the push, into the platform.

(3) Now that the bottom is secure, drill holes through the upper tips and through the crossbeam. Use long nuts and bolts through these holes to secure the top.

If the angles are correct, it will sit in place without being held.

Now it must be attached permanently; secure the bottom first, then the top.

And there you have it—my claim to fame.

THE EDUCATED EYE, OR SIMPLICITY IS IN THE EYE OF THE BEHOLDER

Years ago, I would look at pictures of furniture and built-ins in newspapers and magazines, and wish I could afford those I particularly liked. Then gradually, as I built more, learned new techniques and handled a wider variety of materials and hardware, I noticed myself reacting to similar pictures differently: Wow, what a lot of money! Bet I could build that!(?) Actually, what was really happening was that my eyes were looking at the furniture and my mind was disassembling it and reconstructing it, sometimes even improvising on the idea, like substituting something cheaper for the expensive butcher block in the picture.

I suspect that now I have reached a peak, for I really have difficulty buying anything, even if I can afford it. It seems such a waste of money. (Yes, sure, my time is worth money, and there's precious little time these days, but occasionally I can squeeze in a project.)

What I am going to do in this chapter is to fill in the gaps, provide the missing links and show you that even if just exactly what YOU are interested in building isn't diagramed in this book, it is really here; or rather it's in you, and will grow in you as you progress—seeing, touching and working with the real stuff.

Before we get into the meat of illustration, I have to mention one more facet of my building philosophy, the collection of thrown-away-but-not junk. I have a friend (the same one who taught me so much

152

about building) who shares with me the art of collecting. So much of what is thrown away is readaptable that I want you to begin to take a second look at that pile of "junk" down the block. Often I go off to work in the morning with an old (and marvelous) frame tucked under my arm, wrapped in part of my newspaper, reclaimed from somebody's garbage can on the way to the subway. (No, I don't open the lids of all the garbage cans I pass — only if some interesting junk is sitting on top do I browse, quickly.) I'm still a little new at this and not too cool about it yet. However, my friend is a true pro and can spot an antique half a block away. One time at the sanitation dump, when she was helping me dump boxes of plaster I had chipped from the walls to expose the brick, she found a magnificent walnut pulpit! This and many more of her treasures are sitting in my cellar, for she long ago ran out of room in her own cellar. (And I have on occasion reclaimed some of her less valuable treasures, for which she had no immediate use.) For the doors I made for the living room last year I needed some nice latches. I remembered the shutters in the cellar.

One night late, she came to the door and asked me to come with her to help, she had spotted some shutters. The woman upstairs watched my children and off we went in her station wagon. In front of a brownstone some blocks away was a mound of shutters — obviously thrown out as trash. Some were not too special. "Do we have to take all of them?" I asked. There were at least twenty pairs, and I was getting nervous.

"Yes, of course, if for nothing else than the hardware!" There is always the possibility of finding beautiful, old, ornamental brass latches and hinges. And the shutters are still in my cellar, minus a plain, unornamented brass latch I reclaimed, soaked in paint remover and attached to my living-room doors.

So keep your eyes open (and aimed at trash piles). One person's garbage can be another's jewel.

My first example illustrates a combination of reclaimed and new.

THE SODA FOUNTAIN

My younger son spotted a children-sized soda fountain in a toy catalog, shortly before his birthday last year. "Mom, would you get me this for my birthday?"

I looked at it. "Not on your life, it's fifty-five dollars!" . . . and I looked at it again . . . "but maybe I could make it for you."

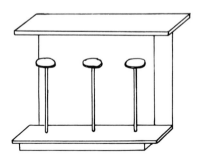

This is a picture of Sam's best birthday present ever! he says. It looks almost the same as the one in the catalog.

Later in the evening, the night of the promise to Sam, I sat down with the catalog and my educated eye and here's what happened:

(1)

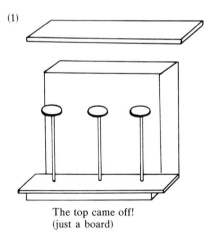

The top came off!
(just a board)

(2)

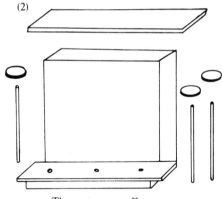

The seats came off.
(thick dowels and wood circles)

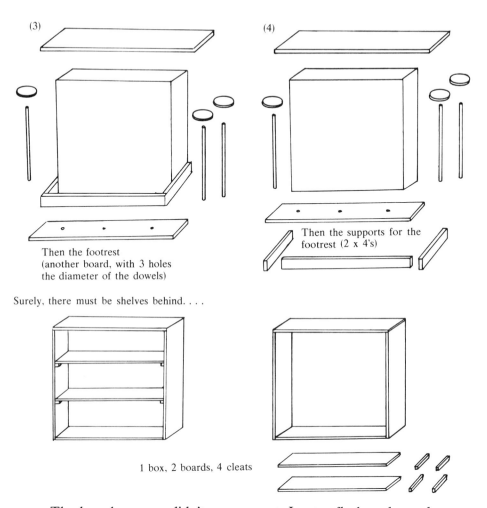

(3)

Then the footrest
(another board, with 3 holes
the diameter of the dowels)

Surely, there must be shelves behind. . . .

(4)

Then the supports for the
footrest (2 x 4's)

1 box, 2 boards, 4 cleats

The box, however, didn't come apart. I got a flash and ran down
to the cellar to look at some huge drawers my friend had salvaged
earlier in the month . . . and they were perfect! A quick phone call —
"Do you mind, I'll only use one?"

"Well, OK," she relented. (She doesn't part easily with her treasures. Who does?)

As I was making a sketch and figuring the dimensions in relation
to the drawer, I realized I was in trouble. How to brace the seats and
dowel supports? I looked at the catalog again, but try as I could, I
couldn't see through the footrest. OK, so what holds up a dowel and
supports it so that it will be straight? More than one board with holes

. . . or . . . I got an idea, worked it over in my head and decided to give it a try. It worked.

I added a board under the footrest between the sidepieces of the footrest support, flush to the front piece. From under the board I nailed in three strong nails, predrilled holes in the bottom of the dowels, smaller than the nails, and put the dowels through the holes in the footrest and onto the nails.

The seats were more complicated, the boys would be wiggling and they had to be secure. I used a small block of wood, drilled a hole for a dowel of joining size in both the block and the large dowel and joined, with glue, the block and the large dowel. Then I nailed the block to the circular wooden seat, adding glue in between.

(Many luncheon scenes in my house!)

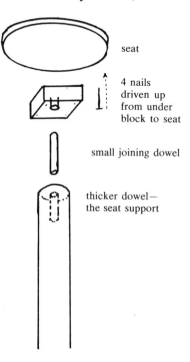

seat

4 nails
driven up
from under
block to seat

small joining dowel

thicker dowel—
the seat support

THE COATRACK

Here is an example of something which should at this point look simple, and it is. I would like to use this example to illustrate how you can adapt an idea for your own purposes, and, particularly, how you can determine the first dimension and so go from there. I will also include the improvisation that I would do on this plan.

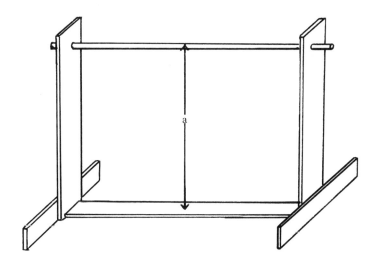

Available space is certainly one of the factors, but function is the key. A coatrack has to hold clothes hung on hangers, and for this illustration let us assume that this is a children's clothes rack. The first dimension, therefore, has to be the inner height *(a)*. It is important, now, not to measure just the longest child's coat, but also the coat hung on a hanger (from the top of the curved hook on the hanger to the bottom of the coat). Then add to that a growth factor of as many inches as you feel comfortable with. In this illustration I have allowed 28 inches *(a)*, and this is a clue you might not ordinarily get from a photo or a sketch in an advertisement. So, let me demonstrate how you can determine the measurements, or rather the relationships of the dimensions, from such an ad.

Use a rule with inches divided into at least sixteenths for this example, maybe thirty-seconds for a smaller picture. Let $\frac{1}{16}$ on the ruler equal 1 inch, for a start. The lesson to be learned is the method to use in measuring.

The true dimensions can be obtained only by measuring along the edges, and in this sketch these edges are not all horizontal. The true "related" dimension of the width of the sidepiece can only be determined by laying your ruler along line *1,* not across as in *x,* for *x* is a distortion of perspective.

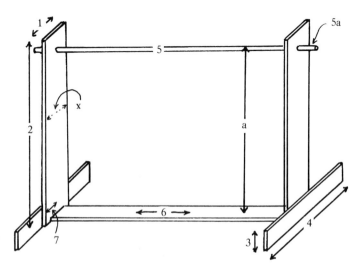

OK, lay your ruler along *1;* it measures $\frac{5}{16}''$. (Let's skip the sixteenths part of it from now on.) *1* = 5, the relative width of the sidepiece. Now lay the ruler along line *2: 2* = 31, the relative length of the sidepiece.

Next, the bracing pieces: measure *3; 3* = 3, the relative width of the brace. Measuring line *4,* we get *4* = 18½. Make it 18—for simplicity. So *4* = 18, the relative length of the brace.

Assuming that we'll be using 1 x ?' pine, which means ¾" thickness (or thereabouts), it looks as though we can actually use exactly what we came up with as relative dimensions as real ones, inches. One-by-five sidepieces and one-by-three brace pieces seem perfect. If they weren't, you could double, halve or apply some ratio to *all* measurements to get them to a reasonable size (the *same* ratio to *all!*). This means the following: if you wanted a wider sidepiece, apply a 1½ ratio to each relative dimension:

1: $5 \times 1\frac{1}{2} = 7\frac{1}{2}$.
2: $31 \times 1\frac{1}{2} = 46\frac{1}{2}$.
3: $3 \times 1\frac{1}{2} = 4\frac{1}{2}$.
4: $18 \times 1\frac{1}{2} = 27$.
And so forth.

However, I'm content to live with our original dimensions (since it's obviously a setup!). To continue.

Measure the entire length of the dowel *(5),* from tip to tip: $5 = 48$. How much is sticking out? Measure *5a:* $5a = 3$. Two pieces of the dowel are within the sidepieces, as are two pieces sticking out, so in order to get the inner dimension, subtract them from 48: $48 - 3 - 3 - \frac{3}{4} - \frac{3}{4} = 40\frac{1}{2}$. (The $\frac{3}{4}$'s are the thicknesses of the sidepieces.) Thus we now know the length of the crosspiece along the bottom *(6): 6 = * $40\frac{1}{2}$.

And if you measure *a,* it is 28. If it was shorter or longer you would need only to adjust the lengths of the sidepieces to conform to your needs. Also, if your available space is less than 48″ you can shorten the length of the dowel and the crosspiece across the bottom; or if you want a wider coatrack, you can add the lengths of *5* and *6*.

Finally, don't hesitate to improvise. I would, for instance, add a shelf along the top for sweaters, hooks along one side for hats and clips on the other side for gloves and mittens. I'm sure you are already improvising for your own needs.

A clue for the construction: drill holes for the dowel first. Attach

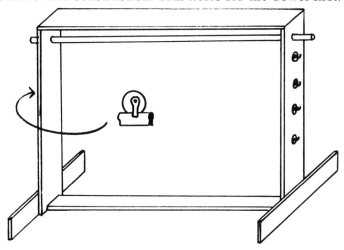

the top to the sides (use a corner clamp), and then nail in the crosspieces (from outside piece to crosspiece). Nail the braces to the sides.
Slip the dowel through, mark where the ends stick out, drill thin holes
through the dowel ends, put it back and slip nails through the holes to
hold it in place. (Or do it inside.)

NEWSPAPER AND MAGAZINE ADS

You don't have to buy building-project books to get ideas. Look
at the newspaper and magazine ads. Eventually you will begin to respond as I did with this ad: "I could surely build that cheaper." (Yes,
it would probably look cheaper, and rougher, but that's my cellar-
construction streak; you may be able to duplicate anything you see—
and as handsomely, with effort.) Naturally, I never place the added
value of my own labor on any of these projects. That's what keeps
the cost down (to just materials).

$99.50

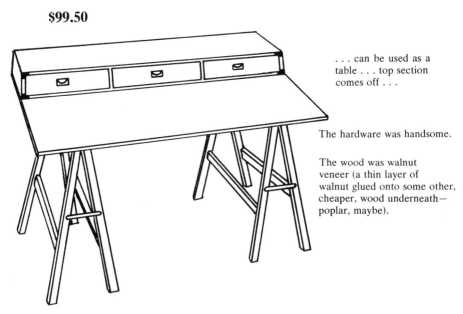

. . . can be used as a
table . . . top section
comes off . . .

The hardware was handsome.

The wood was walnut
veneer (a thin layer of
walnut glued onto some other,
cheaper, wood underneath—
poplar, maybe).

As nice as veneer looks, because it's a bit of the real thing, I'm
still satisfied with staining pine. Tomorrow for veneer. . . . So, could
you make it cheaper?

OK, use your educated eye and . . . . LET 'ER RIP!

top section: a rectangular box (with insets)

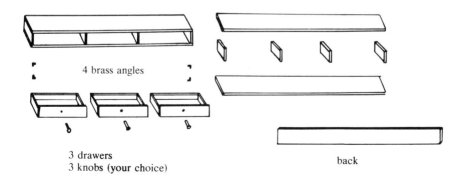

4 brass angles

3 drawers
3 knobs **(your** choice)

back

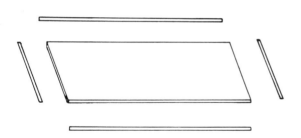

a piece of
plywood
and
veneer edging
or
$\frac{1}{4}''$ x $\frac{3}{4}''$
wood edging
if
$\frac{3}{4}''$ plywood
used

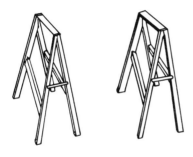

sawhorses!

(another good
table-leg variation)

THE TEST OF YOUR EDUCATED EYE

How do you make a drawer?

Go and look at some of the drawers in your house . . . see how they're constructed. Yes, this is a dirty trick—there are routed-out grooves for the bottoms to slip into. How do you do that?

The grooves are made by a router or by a circular table saw, the blade of which comes up from under the table through a hole in the top of the table. The wood is guided over the saw by a jig, which is a contraption, store-bought or self-designed, to keep the wood between barriers, so that it will go only one way, not shift left or right.

Both of these tools are advanced, not recommended for beginners. Me, I confess to being a beginner, too. I have had a router for over a year and have never used it, only lent it to friends who know how to use it. Yes, I'll learn one of these days, when a project calls for its use.

So . . . how do you build a drawer?

Improvise: build a box and wax the edges . . . buy drawer-guiding gadgets which attach to the side of drawer and cabinet (perhaps you already have these on some of your drawers) . . . use the technique suggested for bookcase #8 . . . . or get a router and learn to use it. (A contradiction of what I said above? This is, hopefully, not an authoritarian manual. Here anything goes.)

If you learn how to use the router, will you come and give me lessons?

PLUMBING

HAPPINESS IS HOT AND COLD RUNNING WATER, NO LEAKS... AND NO SEXY PLUMBER!

The subject of plumbing is not a happy one for me, most particularly when it comes to the theory of what goes on in the toilet tank. About three months ago I began to search the handyman books for a good description of the principles involved in that contraption of plumbing within the tank, because there was an ever-present passage of water. I tried all the things I knew about to check it and discovered no solution. So finally I called the plumber, in hopes of getting some more information, picture diagram in hand in order to best express myself and understand.

There are plumbers who have gone to plumbing school, and there are plumbers who have learned all they know from their fathers or uncles, but with both varieties I have been totally unsuccessful in communicating. My biggest hangup, I think, has been the principle involving water pressure, and now I'm beginning to wonder how many plumbers understand what water pressure is! And I've been to the horse's mouth—my father. (Isn't everyone's father the best in his field, whatever it is?) But my father, the plumber, couldn't explain water pressure to me, nor could my brothers, also plumbers. (They all forgot to say the word "pump" to me.)

Water pressure, simply, is water traveling with force. That force comes from a water pump at the waterworks (wherever that is). A pump is necessary to move water from reservoirs to our houses.

What did I do with my troublesome toilet tank? I went to the hardware store and bought new guts—plastic guts!—for about six dollars and I took out the old and put in the new. Peace on earth, and no muscle needed!

Muscle is another thing that makes me unhappy about plumbing—my lack of it, I mean. Pipes are heavy to carry and hard to manipulate when you are assembling them. Waste pipes are the very heavy ones and the ones that often are the problems. Smaller pipes are trouble because they often have to be custom cut and threaded to fit a particular unit; this means expensive equipment.

My plumbing career thus far, and as a result of the above, has been involved with the little and painless things that I can fix or replace, and the big things only in terms of exposure to vocabulary. Learning the names of everything is something I recommend, for an interesting reason: you get a better job done. If you call the plumber and say, "My toilet keeps leaking," he will come and fix it, and the leaking may start again two days later because he didn't do a complete checkup. But if you call the plumber and say, "The flush ball does not seem to be meeting the flush-valve seat properly," he'll say to himself, "Wow, this woman knows something about plumbing, I'd better do a good job." And if you're lucky, he will.

SHUT-OFF VALVES (STOP VALVES)

The first thing to acquaint yourself with is the place where the shut-off valves are in your kitchen and bathroom. (If your kitchen and bathroom are back to back, there may be one set of valves for both rooms.)

What are shut-off valves? They are handles connected to pipes that disappear behind the walls, and they are usually low along the wall, near the floor or under or behind the sink or toilet. There are two shut-off valves, one for the hot water and one for the cold water. In elegant plumbing situations, there might be separate sets for the sink, toilet and tub. If you have discovered that when someone flushes the toilet while you're taking a shower you lose the cold water and get scalded, this is because the water to both the tub and the toilet (and probably the sink) comes into the bathroom in the same pipe, and also that there is probably only one set of shut-off valves for the bathroom.

Now, stop reading and go to the bathroom and kitchen and locate the shut-off valves. . . . OK, now you can handle a flood, or at least one kind, the kind emanating from pipes between the shut-off valves and the sink, toilet or tub. There are similar shut-off valves in cellars, usually under the rooms receiving the water. Pipes go across the ceiling from the main source of entry into the house, and in various places connections are made and pipes go up into the ceiling, bringing water upstairs. Near the connections are the shut-off valves, and they will shut off *all* water from getting upstairs. The connections look like inverted *T*'s and in fact are called tee fittings.

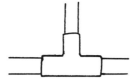

There is also a main shut-off valve near the place where the water comes into the house, which shuts off all water supply to the entire house in case of a total-disaster flood. There is only one shut-off valve at this point, because only cold water comes in. Shortly after this point, you will notice a connection that takes some water toward the direction of the water heater or boiler—whatever heats your water—and there should be a shut-off valve on the pipe right before the water reaches the heating mechanism. From some other point of the heater will be a pipe that carries the heated water, and this pipe will eventually meet and travel beside the cold-water pipe that did not go through. If you have access to the cellar in your house, go and have a look.

Now, make yourself a note for the next time you go to the cellar. Take with you some kinds of tags on string and red and blue marking pens, or red and blue paint, or red and blue wool. Hang tags, tie wool, or paint the shut-off valves—red for hot, blue for cold. You can tell which is which because the hot one will feel hot and the cold one cold. Also mark, if you can't determine it easily, which rooms they shut off. And maybe on the same day you can try all the valves, to be sure they are marked properly and also to be sure they all work well. If the water doesn't stop completely, call the plumber and have them fixed—before the flood! (If the flood comes in the middle of the night or on a weekend, and you can't get a plumber right away, you might have to shut off the main valve—no water for anything in the house!)

Shut-off Valves—Incoming Water

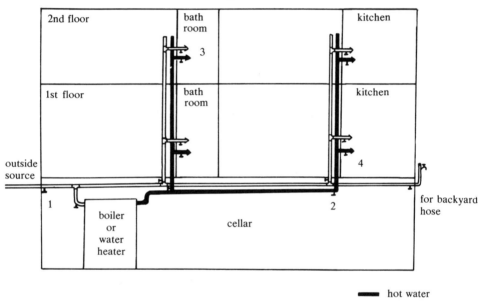

☐ hot water
═ cold water

⊥ are shut-off valves. They shut off all incoming water past the valve. For example:

1 shuts off *all* water into the house
2 shuts off hot water to all kitchens
3 shuts off cold water to the bathroom on the second floor
4 shuts off hot water to kitchen on first floor only

The pipes for incoming water are narrow, from 2 inches in diameter for large buildings to ¾ inch for smaller buildings. The pipes for waste, outgoing water (not shown here) are larger, about 4 inches in diameter.

TOOLS YOU WILL NEED TO PLUMB

(Definition of *plumb* for this book: (a) stop minor leaks—many leaks are minor; (b) unclog clogs in the drains and pipes—the hair, plastic astronauts, socks, candy wrappers, paintbrushes . . . you know the list well.)

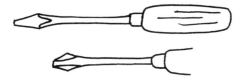

Screwdriver

Often the screwheads in the faucet handles are Phillips type. Although a Phillips screwdriver will give extra strength for the hard-to-unscrew screws, a regular screwdriver will serve you just as well in most cases.

Pliers

This is the tool that will give you the power your fingertips or hands don't have to grasp the "other end" of the sections to be dismantled. However, for want of a wrench, for many years the pliers have been my wrench. It was always sweating-cursing tough with pliers, but by no means impossible; the job always got done. ("Bless me, Father, for I have sinned. I cursed about"—let me see . . . sixty seconds in a minute, it took half an hour—"about a thousand times, Father. . . .")

Wrench

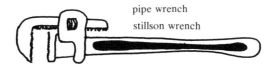

pipe wrench
stillson wrench

Life became easier for me one day after I investigated the plumbing tools my father left a couple of years ago. Shortly after he put in a bathroom in an apartment I had before the house, he got sick and never recovered. The untouched tools in my cellar were my private grief and my private reverence. But one day—and this has to be the Irish superstition in me—I knew I could hear him cursing at me from wherever. "For Chrissake, girl, use the damn tools! You need them!" In the box were a couple of wrenches, one about two feet long, which may come in handy later in my career, and one a perfect size for all the work I had been doing with pliers. (Thanks, Pop.) A 10-inch stillson wrench is a perfect size.

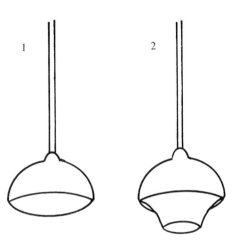

Plunger

A couple of weeks ago, I braved it and went to a plumbing-supply store, the place where the plumbers go, to buy a couple of faucets, a plunger and a snake (see below). It's surely the cheapest way to shop, and I must say it was kind of fun. Oh, yes, I was an oddity to all in the store, but, well, maybe I have a soft spot in my heart for plumbers, and I didn't react in my usual way to the typical cracks. "You want a job with me, lady? Anytime!" The manager was particularly nice, and as he handed me the purchases, tossed out, rather nonchalantly, bits of useful information related to whatever he had in his hand. The plunger he gave me looked like the one in Figure 1. Then he reached inside it and withdrew the part folded inside, so it looked like Figure 2. "Out for the toilet, in for sinks and tubs," he said, and went on to find the snake. No wonder I could never plunge the toilet successfully! I never had the kind with the extra fold. So, be sure to get this style.

In order to accomplish the best downward-into-the-pipe force, there should be water within the cup of the plunger before you push. Sink it in the toilet first, or if working on the sink or tub, fill it a little with water and sink the plunger into the water before pushing. Start plunging slowly and gradually develop a strong, steady thrust.

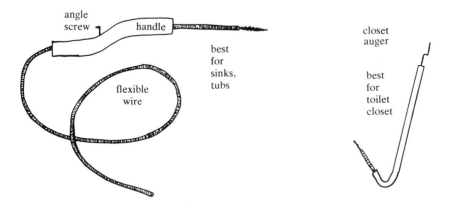

angle screw

handle

best for sinks, tubs

flexible wire

closet auger

best for toilet closet

Snake (auger)

This will go where the coat hanger could never reach, and do what the hanger couldn't do. It's fantastic! The wire is flexible. The little angle screw in the handle tightens the flexible wire within the handle so you can push it into the pipe by rotating the handle with your two hands. Loosen the screw, push some more wire through the handle, tighten and rotate-push some more. If it feels as though it is really stuck, pull it out, and if you're lucky the pointed tip of the snake may grab and bring the clog out with it.

LEAKS

How many times did you hear from your mother when you were young—or maybe you even tell your children now—"Cola takes the paint off cars, imagine what it does to your stomach!" (I'm addicted anyhow. Besides, my stomach isn't coated with paint!)

Now let's talk about water, that used-to-be pure, God-given-best thirst quencher. Have you ever seen a sink or tub where the dripping leak has gone unattended for a while? Slowly the enamel turns green (chlorine?), and eventually the enamel begins to be eaten away (eaten away!), and you can actually see the black steel under the enamel.

True! So if you'd like to prevent all that leaking, chemically treated water from ruining your fixtures, fix the drips, and to hell with the landlord. A washer costs only a nickel or so; subtract it from the rent. The going rate for a plumber, and they usually come in pairs, is about $9.50; subtract the value of your time, too.

What is a washer? It is a little round piece of rubber that acts as a seal when placed between sections of fitted-together plumbing fixtures. Sometimes it's screwed in, sometimes it's just lying there between two tightly fitted and attached sections, as you will see as we go along.

A Leak in the Faucet

TURN OFF THE WATER FLOW—THE SHUT-OFF VALVES! or don't attempt to do anything. And put the stopper in the sink so you won't lose screws.

God only knows how many different styles of faucets there are; I certainly don't. However, I will illustrate how two kinds come apart. The concept should carry for the rest.

To remove the entire faucet, loosen the fitting (a fitting is a nut attaching two pieces of pipe). Let the loosened fitting slide down the supply pipe. Then loosen the tightening nut holding the faucet rigid to the underpart of the sink. As you do this, pull the faucet up, and when you have unscrewed the nut from the under-pipe of the faucet, it will come off, as will the thin metal washer that should be there, too.

Leak from faucet: (Is it a hot or cold leak?) Replace appropriate washer at bottom of spindle. Or . . . it could be that the seat needs smoothing or replacement. Look into the hole after you remove the spindle. See that squarish hole? That hole is the center of the seat. Both the seat remover and the seat smoother are inexpensive tools.

Leak from around base of faucet: (Is it screwed in tight?) Check, and replace if necessary, the thin washer within.

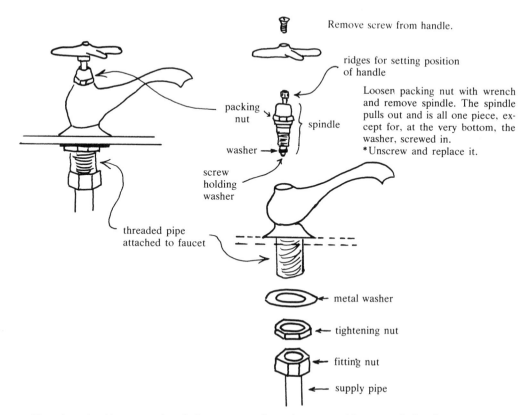

Remove screw from handle.

ridges for setting position
of handle

packing
nut

spindle

washer

screw
holding
washer

Loosen packing nut with wrench
and remove spindle. The spindle
pulls out and is all one piece, except for, at the very bottom, the
washer, screwed in.
*Unscrew and replace it.

threaded pipe
attached to faucet

metal washer

tightening nut

fitting nut

supply pipe

*In order to be able to grasp the spindle to unscrew the washer screw, either screw the handle
back on to hold it, or use pliers as shown, grasping the top of the spindle. (The ridges at that top
allow you to set the handle in any position, so now you can correct the COLD.)

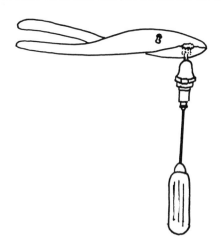

A Hot-and-Cold Mixing-Type Faucet

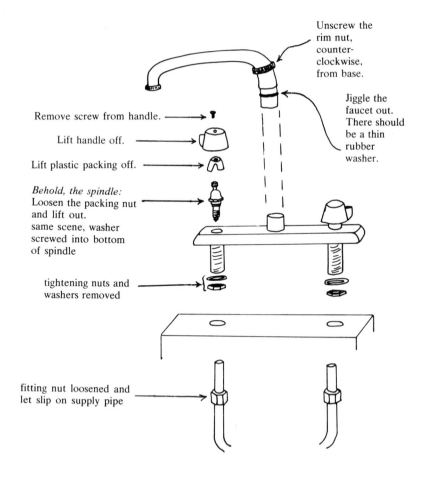

Unscrew the rim nut, counter-clockwise, from base.

Remove screw from handle. ⟶

Lift handle off. ⟶

Lift plastic packing off. ⟶

Jiggle the faucet out. There should be a thin rubber washer.

Behold, the spindle:
Loosen the packing nut and lift out.
same scene, washer screwed into bottom of spindle

tightening nuts and washers removed ⟶

fitting nut loosened and let slip on supply pipe ⟶

Leaks at Fitting Nuts

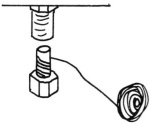

Loosen fitting nut.

Wrap packing thread (available at plumbing-supply stores and hardware stores) around pipe, the part of the pipe that the nut will slip along to get to the threaded section it will attach to.

Wrap it in the same direction that the nut will be screwed on; if the nut goes on clockwise, wrap the thread clockwise, too.

If you still have a leak, it could be that you put too much thread on, and the nut cannot tighten enough, or you put on too little, and haven't accomplished the effect possible. The desired effect is that the thread sqwoosh into the area between inside platform of the nut, which should hit the lower edge of the threaded pipe to which it's attaching, thus providing a washerlike function, a seal.)

Note: Although I happily use a pipe wrench, pictured earlier, because that's what I have, liberated from my father's toolbox, and it feels nice and strong, I have been pooh-poohed lately for my "stupidity." ("A pipe wrench is for holding pipes!" someone said. "You should use a monkey wrench, or an open-ended wrench, where the grabby

monkey wrench

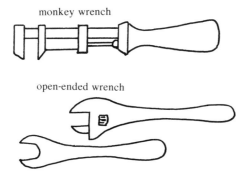

open-ended wrench

edges are flat, not ridged, like the pipe wrench. You'll mar the chrome with those ridges.") So someday I'll get a monkey wrench, maybe, or a full set of open-ended wrenches so that I have a size to fit all the different nuts in this plumbing scene. In the meantime, I'm perfectly happy with my all-purpose pipe wrench.

Tip: You can protect the chrome by wrapping some masking tape around it (especially if you're going to attack it with ridges!).

Tip: A basin wrench, with its extra-long handle and flip-flop grabbing end, is good to make an investment in for those troublesome jobs under the sink and toilet.

CLOGGED PIPES

I have never been the master of waste pipes and what goes down the drain. The changing presence of babysitters is inevitable in my working-mother life. ("Coffee grounds are good for the drain, they cut the fat." "Coffee grounds are bad for the drain." . . . Etc., etc.) And, there are two small boys who couldn't read the rules if I pasted them above the toilet or sink or tub. ("Mommy, my astronaut went down the tub with the water!") Alas, clogged pipes have to be dealt with occasionally.

Let's start with plunging, which should be the first method of attack.

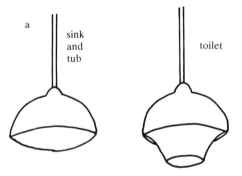

Fill the fixture—sink, tub or toilet—with enough water so that it's as high as the wood emerging from the rubber plunger *(a)*. (This may not be necessary if you've got a healthy clog!) Sink the plunger in the water so that it fills with water inside the rubber. (Water is better to push with than air.) Start slowly and plunge forcefully (sqwoosh up and down) with steady strokes. This may be enough to loosen the clogging matter and clear the pipe. (While plunging, say a prayer to whoever your god is.) But if the plunging doesn't work or if it's the tub, and you can't get the plunger in a good position to do any good), here are the next steps.

If it's the sink, try the trap first. What's the trap? Let's talk about traps and their purpose a bit.

Waste creates a gas which is poisonous, called appropriately sewer gas. You can identify it by its smell: it smells like a sewer.

I learned about sewer gas accidentally, and the boys and I had a fine adventure as a result of it. This old brownstone of mine is sadly in need of new pipes, particularly waste pipes, maybe only waste pipes, but that costs money. I have places here and there in my house where there are holes in waste pipes that often have to be fixed. And I leave the holes in the ceiling there, so that the pipes are accessible to the plumbers. They come and put some new kind of pasty-dries-hard patch on them every so often. (I'm never home when they come, to watch and learn how to do this rather simple thing that I pay $9.50 times 2— and I can't imagine the purpose of a "helper" for a job like this, except that it's a recession. However, I've asked them what this almost-magic substance is, and it's epoxy putty.)

Back to the sewer-gas adventure. I had had one patch put on a big waste pipe in the ceiling over our upstairs bathroom, about two or three months before the adventure. The leak developed again, but I was short of cash and decided to put off calling the plumber until pay-day. It was still only a dribble; I could put up with that a few days more. A friend dutifully told me I was foolish. "Don't you know sewer gas is poisonous?" I paid no heed.

One night a few days later, I was sitting in bed, reading, and I noticed an awful odor. I went over to the crack of open window and put my nose to it, expecting it to reveal the source of the smell, "to-night's latest pollution." But the air was clear. I walked back to the boys' room to check the back window, passing the bathroom. Nothing at the back window, but again passing the bathroom, I noticed the smell was powerfully strong in there. Bells rang—sewer gas! My God, we'll all die of poison gas! I threw open the windows and hopped back into bed with my book, intending to call the plumber in the morning, payday or not. The smell remained strong. I began to wonder what the properties of this gas were, if it did any good to air the place. I got up and searched the home-repair manuals I had. Most of them didn't even say it was poisonous, and none told what to do if . . . any-thing! "Boys, wake up," I said as I shook them awake and out of bed, "we're going to have an adventure. We're going to camp out in the living room tonight." I had already set up the sleeping bags for them, and dragged blankets and pillow for myself down and was all set up. I felt like an ass, but who can you call at 1 A.M. and ask about sewer gas? The boys woke up enough to enjoy the change in the routine, and that's always an adventure, and they never think Mommy is crazy, like some people do.

The next day, the plumber, while laughing at my past night's survival plan, said in the same breath, "Oh, yeah, it's poison all right." I guess that meant that open windows were an OK solution.

So in the waste pipes is sewer gas. How is it kept from coming back to you in your house? The traps!

The trap is designed so that it retains water, as shown in the diagram. This blocks the sewer gas from coming back into the room.

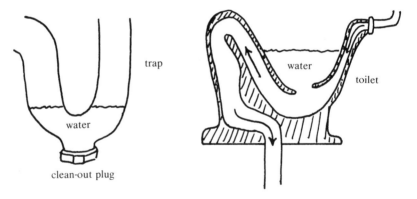

Perhaps you have never realized it, but the toilet bowl is designed as one big trap. I always took it for granted that water sat in the bowl, but I never thought there was purpose to it, did you?

As for the tub, I'll take a guess (I'm not about to rip up another ceiling) that there is a trap under the drain. There has to be, right?

For years I thought the purpose of the trap under the sink was to "trap" all the lost combs and knives and paintbrushes and astronauts. Not so, but it does help keep some things from going farther.

Now for Step 2, if plunging doesn't work. If the clog is in a sink with a visible trap, first put a pail under the trap to catch all that water when you open it. Next, use a wrench and remove the nut at the bottom of the trap. Be careful! Use rubber gloves to mess around in there if you're a big Drāno user, because some residue may be at the bottom of the trap. (*Note:* Washing soda, once every couple of weeks, run down with hottish-warm water, is a great pipe cleanser, and far safer for your pipes in terms of corrosion . . . and pollution?) You may be able to clear the clog just by poking around and digging out the #Z*#* stuff stuck right in the trap.

If your trap doesn't have a nut (clean-out plug) at the bottom of the trap, loosen the retaining nuts until the trap comes free, and clean it out. (A piece of heavy chain is a good unclogger of this type of trap.)

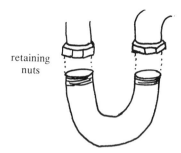

Now, the last resort step: If your fingers don't work in the first kind of trap . . . or if the above trap, cleaned, wasn't the answer . . . or if it's the toilet or the tub . . . use the snake.

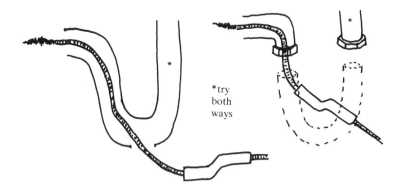

Snake around, through whatever you're going, slowly but ever for ward. You should feel the clog when you get there. Gently force it and jiggle and try to loosen it, or pull the snake out if it hits an impasse, and it may bring the clog out with it at the point of the snake.

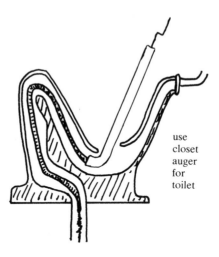

use
closet
auger
for
toilet

THE TOILET-TANK GUTS, HOW IT WORKS,
HOW TO FIX IT WHEN IT DOESN'T

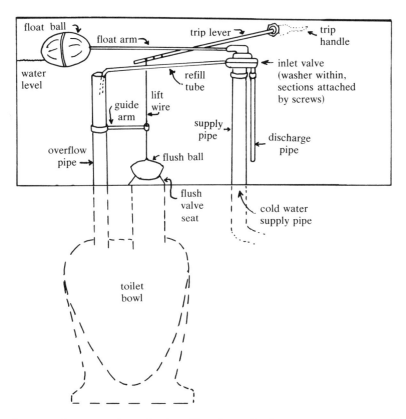

As you depress the *trip handle,* the *trip lever* comes up, pulling with it the *flush ball,* thus opening the *flush valve.* Water from the tank surges into the toilet bowl, and combined with the water in the bowl, is enough to cause a force allowing the water to go down the drain.

The *float* falls as the water leaves the tank, thus opening the *inlet valve.* With this valve open, a new supply of cold water is allowed to enter. Some goes through the *refill tube* into the *overflow pipe* to the bowl, and refills the bowl to create the trap. The other portion of water passes through the *discharge pipe* to refill the tank.

As the tank refills, the *float,* sitting on top of the water, comes back up and eventually closes the inlet valve, thus stopping the flow of water to the tank and bowl.

Problem: An Ever-Present Passage-of-Water Sound

a) Try pulling up the float arm higher than the water level. If the sound stops, that means that the intake valve wasn't closed enough. Bend the float arm a bit. This will allow the float to cause a tighter closing action as the water comes up to the same level, because the angle has been adjusted.

b) That was a quickie test in (a). If the sound didn't stop, now you have to determine what the sound is. Is it water flowing from the discharge pipe and refill tube, or is it leaking through the flush valve seat? Next, another quickie test: Push down on the flush ball. Sound stops. Empty the tank (flush) and hold the float up so that no more water comes into the tank. Try dropping the ball over the valve and try to determine if it's falling directly over the hole, or hitting a bit to the side. (Yes, I know you can't see through the tank—curse, curse.) If this is happening the guide arm needs adjusting. There is a little screw (it's gone? That's why!) that holds the guide arm in correct position by tightening the part around the overflow pipe. Loosen it, tap the guide arm around a bit, until the flush ball falls correctly over the flush valve seat, and tighten the screw.

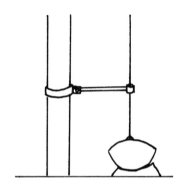

If the ball seems to be sitting correctly, buy a new one and hang it on the lift wire. Maybe it is worn. The part of the lift wire hooked over the trip lever may have to be adjusted if the shape of the new flush ball is different from the old. (Pick up a new lift wire, just in case you have a problem . . . bending, unbending, crack, break.)

If nothing works to stop the flow of water through the flush valve, CALL THE PLUMBER!

c) Is the refill tube connected properly? Is it gone?

d) Let's go back to the discharge pipe and refill tube. Suppose that is where the water was leaking from, and the float arm pull-up didn't stop it. Now you must investigate the washers within the inlet valve. STOP! TURN OFF THE WATER—COLD-WATER SHUT-OFF VALVE! because we're going to open the inlet, and that's the only thing that stops the flow of water. So unless you want a geyser. . . . Unscrew the screws necessary to open the valve. Inside between the two sections are washers, which may have to be replaced. Take them to your hardware store and buy new ones.

The type of inlet valve pictured earlier is the kind in a plastic-guts setup. I put one of these in the upstairs bathroom—it's easy working with plastic—and the cost differential, plastic versus metal, is just about negligible. Downstairs I have the metal setup, and since it is probably more like what you have, let's look at that kind of inlet valve.

The washer in this type is located under the valve stem and is screwed to the bottom in the same manner as a washer at the bottom of the spindle in a faucet. In order to be able to unscrew the valve stem, first remove the thumbscrews and unscrew the float arm, then slip out the upper parts. Unscrew the valve stem. Unscrew the screw holding the washer and replace it.

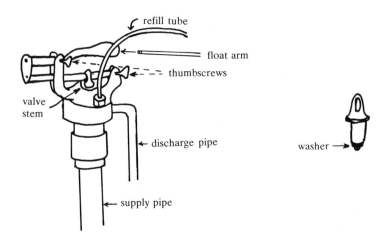

If this doesn't work, CALL THE PLUMBER! Or try putting new guts in. Sometimes the whole setup is too old to fix satisfactorily, and new guts can give you peace. You'll curse a lot, but it will be worth it.

Just for fun and future comfort, why don't you browse around in a hardware store now and price the parts? The whole replacement value is cheaper than one plumber's hourly rate, and you'd have to pay for the helper and the parts, too! (Price faucets while you're at it.)

THE FLUSH VALVE

If you do not have a flush tank, then you have a flush valve, which you may or may not be able to see. (The mechanism may be behind the wall.)

This mechanism is quite different than the flush tank, not just in design principle, but—and more importantly, because we are trying to learn—because we cannot watch the operation. As such, I can only explain it as I think it works, not as I've seen it.

First, there are two water chambers, the *upper chamber* and the *lower chamber*. Think of the upper chamber as one with a movable floor. Think of the lower chamber as one with a movable roof. Also, the illustration is a cutaway; the chambers are like cylinders, the lower one like a doughnut.

The upper chamber has a rod coming out of its floor and it extends down and sits perpendicularly against the rod of the *flush handle.* The rod and floor of the upper chamber are the *auxiliary valve.* The rod of the flush handle is called the *plunger.*

When you push the flush handle, the plunger tilts the auxiliary valve. This changes the pressure in the upper chamber, which is, somehow, overcome by the *diaphragm.* (The diaphragm is rubber, sort of bowl-hole-in-the-middle shaped, and is the roof of the lower chamber.) As the pressure reduction occurs, the entire assembly moves up —the floor of the upper chamber, the diaphragm, etc. With the roof off, the water in the lower chamber, coming from the *supply pipe,* spills over the walls and down to the *outlet pipe,* into the toilet, causing the flush.

At the same time, some water is traveling up through the *bypass tube* into the upper chamber. Thus, the pressure is eventually restored, the floor comes down again and the flush stops. (Note that there is a washer under the floor of the upper chamber, called the *auxiliary valve washer.*)

What can cause problems? Almost anything—worn-out washer or diaphragm, clogged bypass tube, broken mechanism in handle—as you can well imagine. Turn off the water supply, the shut-off valve controlling water to the supply pipe, unscrew the cover and take a look. You can lift out the upper chamber and auxiliary valve, but you need a spanner wrench to remove the disk holding the diaphragm in place.

. . . Or you can call the plumber the first time and watch. (This seems a bit trickier to me than the flush tank. You too?)

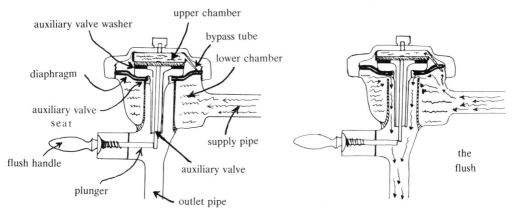

SINK STOPPERS

Pull up plug, drain is closed: But this drain stopper is in the way if you want to plunge or snake.

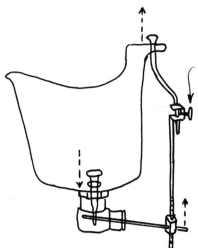

(Mine looks like this. Others may be less complicated.)

Unscrew the thumbscrew holding the mechanism together. Lift out the plug on the top of the sink. This will free the lower piece.

Pull out the rod going into the bottom of the stopper. (It's not attached in any way, just sitting there, held in by the outside mechanism.)

Pull out the stopper and unclog.

Unscrew the drain disk. If your snake doesn't fit through the hole, work from under, up through the trap.

OUTDOOR FAUCETS

If you have outdoor faucets and live in an area where winter weather will go below freezing, you must remember to turn off the water to these faucets. Otherwise the water in outside pipes and near outside pipes will freeze. When water freezes, it expands . . . and that means the pipes will burst!

How to do this? First go outside and turn on the water, letting it

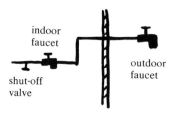

flow out of the faucet. Next go down to the cellar, or from wherever these pipes go outside, and turn off the shut-off valve, stopping the flow of water through these pipes to the outside. Next, open the indoor faucet (between shut-off valve and outdoor faucet); this will allow pipe to drain. Hang a tag on the shut-off valve with a note to yourself written on it: "Set for winter." These valves are located well enough within the cellar so that the pipes at this point are not in danger of becoming too cold. Lastly, go outside and make sure you've accomplished your task. There should be no more water flowing from the faucet(s). You don't have to turn off the faucets again. You are safe now. When summer approaches, just reverse the procedure . . . open the shut-off valves, turn off the faucets and remove the winter tag.

PIPE PATCHING

People always say to use a piece of inner tube from old tires, but I never have any old inner tubes. I have tubeless tires. I guess you could pick up some old ones for supplies at a junkyard. You can also buy a sheet of rubber at the hardware store. A piece of rubber sheet of some sort can be wrapped around a hole in the pipe, but it has to be held on securely any way you can think of if it happens before you get one or more of the following choices (or some waterproof tape will hold you a while):

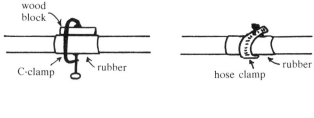

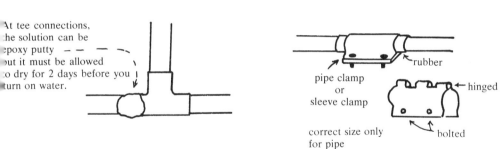

PIPE TAPS, SADDLE TEE

My ex-husband brought me installation instructions from a gadget he had just used to tap water from a pipe in order to install a washing machine, and said, "Here, you better put this gadget in the book, it works fine."

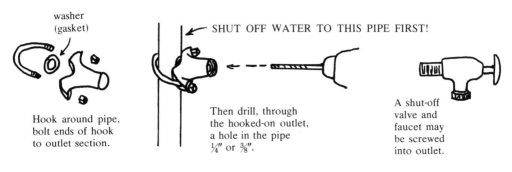

washer
(gasket)

← SHUT OFF WATER TO THIS PIPE FIRST!

Hook around pipe,
bolt ends of hook
to outlet section.

Then drill, through
the hooked-on outlet,
a hole in the pipe
$\frac{1}{4}''$ or $\frac{3}{8}''$.

A shut-off
valve and
faucet may
be screwed
into outlet.

HEATING SYSTEMS

I don't know everything, as you may have gleaned by now. Heating systems had always occupied a shady area in my mind. This book gave me a good excuse to do some research about heating beyond my own frame of reference, a gas heater, and I have obtained some fine general information which I will share with you.

Still, I don't mess around too much with my own heater, except for the very simplest things that one can do. What? Well, I call the plumber . . . for almost everything. Yes, I know, I should be able to relight the pilot light when it goes out; that's a rather simple thing . . . but you have to reach in so far! It scares me still, so I call the plumber, or rather, the gas company, who, at least here in New York, services gas heaters. "Services" is perhaps the wrong word; "diagnoses" is more accurate, for they do not fix it, they only tell you what is wrong and that you'll have to call a plumber to fix it. However, they will relight pilot lights.

The only other simple thing I do, twice a year, is to adjust the thermostat, before and after winter, but that's an easy one. And it's far away from the furnace. Nothing will blow up beside me. I know, the furnace won't blow up, the plumber always assures me. So, I still worry, that's my prerogative.

For me, however, worrying pays off, in that I don't just worry. I also take care of preventative maintenance, to ease a bit of worry out of my mind. Each year, right before it's time to have heat available, I call the plumber and ask for a thorough checkover of the furnace so that I'm in good starting shape. It doesn't take too long . . . does that mean he doesn't do a thorough check? Stop it, worrywart! Still, I do worry through the long winter, and this is directly related to the two bad experiences I've had out of the three times I've ever had to call the plumber because of no heat. (Two out of three is a bad record, except that the two bad times were the first two, and I have found a good plumbing company to deal with since those disasters.)

The first time (shortly after I had bought the house) the problem had to do with the accessories of the heater. The heater itself was fairly new, but the connections to it had not been replaced. A local handyman ("not too expensive") was recommended to me. He spent the whole day finding the problem and changing exterior parts, and the next day it still wouldn't work . . . he had put the new circulator on backwards! (Instead of bringing water into the furnace, it was pulling it out!) I stayed away from the cellar while the next plumber fixed. ("I don't want to know anything, just fix" was my policy.)

In my second winter in the house, the problem turned out to be simple enough for me to have fixed. However, it took three hours of two plumbers' time, taking apart the furnace, to discover finally that the electric switch had gone bad. Every time the furnace was turned on, it went right off automatically, thanks to the fine safety system built into the equipment. (Doesn't the plumber have a checklist which includes every feature of on—off, beyond just the plumbing features?)

Yes, I still believe that worrying is good, because what I really mean by my kind of worrying is *concern;* and in my search for more information about heating systems, I have certainly become more comfortable living above a furnace. Perhaps I can transmit some of this ease to you.

THE PURPOSE OF HEATING

Believe it or not—and I found this most interesting—the purpose of heating is not to warm your body! Your body creates its own heat. However, warmth moves to cold, heat moves to nonheat. Hot air moves to cold air, and so on. What am I talking about? Well, if the walls are cold, your body heat will be drawn out of you toward the walls and you will be cold. Thus, the purpose of heating is not to heat your body but to heat your body's surroundings so that your natural heat is preserved and retained in your body. I'd guess that conversely, when the surrounding heat is hotter than your own bodily temperature, you feel hot because the hot-to-cold direction is *to* your body, the colder.

It follows from what has been said that one can be comfortable if the cold areas are heated. The perimeters of a room, the walls, for example, would be the coldest surfaces. As you will note if you look around your house, the vehicles delivering heat, whether they be radiators, registers or electrical devices, are all placed on the floor along the wall or imbedded in ceilings. (We'll get to the refinements later.) They aren't placed against the walls because it's inconvenient to have a radiator, or whatever, sitting in the middle of a room; but instead they have been placed in the correct position to do the job they are meant to do—not heat air, but cold surfaces (in most heating systems). Air is a medium through which this heat travels.

Heat can travel and accomplish its task in different ways. *Radiated* heat is heat which moves through air (space) but heats only the surfaces it comes in contact with—walls, bodies, etc.—and in turn, surfaces radiate heat. The air through which this type of heat moves is not heated. *Convected* heat is heat which travels through air, water, etc., heating the medium of transfer. *Conducted* heat is heat which travels through surfaces, materials, objects . . . through walls.

Thus, most heating mechanisms are designed to accomplish the task of heating by a combination of these types of heat flow. For example—and I will surmise that this is correct—let's take a hot-water radiator system, hot water flowing through pipes and radiators. OK, the water is heated in the cellar water heater and travels up through the pipes. The type of heat which is traveling in the water is convected heat. As the heat in the radiator comes through the metal walls of the radiator, that heat is conducted heat. Once outside the radiator the heat is radiated heat, traveling in the air of the room, and also, probably, convected heat, heating the air it's traveling through.

(Bear in mind that the general picture is more important than the words.) What does this information all mean to us? Well, for one thing,

we are now in a better position to evaluate our various heating procedures and also, more importantly, to understand what causes heat
loss (and higher heat bills). For example, you may now realize that a
radiator under a window will probably be useless if the window is always open. The heat from it will be pulled out into the cold outside
air. So when you open the window, turn off the radiator. Any benefit
from it is too miniscule to pay for. Drafts cause heat loss; ever-present
drafts cause ever-present heat loss.

HEAT-CREATING DEVICES

Heat is created and then delivered. Let us look first at the process
of creating heat.

If the heat being created is hot-air heat, the unit in the cellar is
called a furnace. If the heat being created is hot-water heat or steam
heat the unit in the cellar making this heat is called a boiler. (A boiler

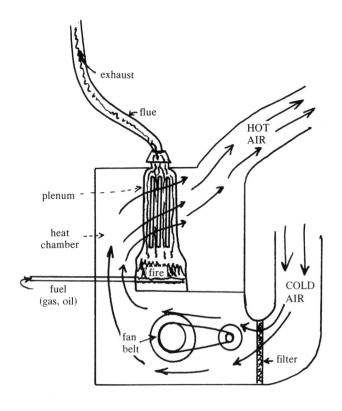

boils water.) (Now that's simple, finally, to me at least, for I have always used these two words, "boiler" and "furnace," interchangeably and ignorantly.)

Water is drawn into a boiler and is either heated to just very hot water or boiled to steam. In furnaces air is drawn in, heated and sent up heated.

I am not going to tell you how to fix boilers and furnaces, as I said earlier, primarily because I'm not qualified. However, perhaps you are interested in a general picture of how the devices work to make heat.

A HOT-AIR FURNACE   Cold air, drawn into the furnace and passing through a filter, is blown into the heat chamber. It passes around the plenum, the chamber heating device, and passes out of the furnace through ducts to the various places heat must be delivered to. In the plenum, the fuel, gas or oil, ignites, the fire heating the chamber, through which the air passes, thus heating the air. The fan belt blower is operated by a motor. The exhaust from within the plenum is expelled through the flue to the outside of the house through a chimney. (This exhaust may also be called "pollution.")

If the fuel is electricity, the air passes around glowing-hot (like the toaster's) electrical wires.

HOT-WATER OR STEAM BOILERS   The water is circulated through the boiler and back up into the radiators.

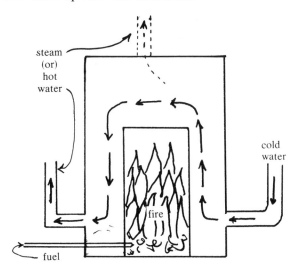

It is heated as it passes around the inner chamber—in which fire is raging—ignited by the entry of fuel, gas or oil.

If the end product is hot water, it must be pumped up and around. If steam is the end product, it rises without the use of a pump (heat expands) and returns by gravity to the boiler as water.

FUELS

The fuels used in boilers and furnaces can vary. Fuel is the substance which is burned to create heat. Coal, gas and oil are fuels. Electricity can also be a fuel for heating systems and it can also be the type of heat delivered—electricity delivered directly to wires or panels in rooms . . . but I'm getting ahead of myself.

Thus, when someone says he has a gas-heated house, he means that gas is the fuel which burns in the furnace or boiler. (The moving parts, such as motors and fans, are run by electricity.)

In terms of fuel-bill costs, and you probably know this, coal is cheaper than oil, which is cheaper than gas, which is cheaper than electricity. Aside from the cost consideration, one should also consider the upkeep and maintenance required when selecting one of these fuels. (I am always saying how I'd like to be rich enough to have electric heat so I'd be done with furnaces and boilers, but I realize after I say it that besides heat in a house, one needs hot water flowing to the sinks, and that means a boiler of some sort!)

Having mentioned the variance of maintenance in these different fuels, I'll be more specific about the differences.

Coal is no longer a popular fuel, but it is still used. The coal is delivered to a place on the floor near the furnace. It is up to the homeowner to deliver it into the furnace. (My mother tells long stories of how unpopular this particular household task was to her and her four brothers and sisters, and how constant was the infighting about whose turn it was. I guess that might be true of most houses that were coal-heated.) Another thing one has to do with a coal furnace is to empty out the ashes, which are part of the residue of combustion. The gas by-product goes up the flue and the dust particles, all of which don't go up the flue, float through the cellar and up through the house, so I am told.

This residue problem is one of the biggest gripes one hears about oil heat, too. Remember the old science lesson: Matter can neither be created nor destroyed, but its form may be changed. *Oil,* when burned, turns into gas *and* what one might call soot, a substance of dust-particle consistency having an oily base. Some of this residue collects along the walls of the stack or flue, the chamber through which the gas residue passes up out of the house. And some of this soot, not all of which is completely dispelled from the house, floats through the air in the cellar and even up to the lower floors in the house. One friend of mine with oil heat compares her expenses to mine (gas heat) this way: "Your type of fuel, gas, is more expensive, but it produces clean heat—gas to gas, no soot residue. Although my fuel, oil, is cheaper, I have to add a cleaning- (curtains, etc.) and painting-cost component to my costs . . . and my cellar is a lot less usable than yours for storage, because everything left there gets covered with a fine layer of oily soot." This same friend, however, believes that service maintenance is better with oil heat. She has a service contract with the oil company. It costs in the vicinity of $25–$30 a year and includes an inspection of the furnace twice a year and a cleaning of the stack once a year. It also covers the replacement of some parts and the labor related to them. In addition to that, she says, in emergencies they are there usually within the hour. I don't know how available this type of service is to you, but I suggest that a service contract like this would be a fine investment. An oil-delivery schedule is maintained by her oil company; they automatically deliver more oil to her house when their records show it's due. That's nice (except, of course, when there's an oil-delivery truck drivers' strike, and that's one of those times the oil-heat people wish they had gas heat).

Yes, I guess I'm really glad I have *gas* heat, after all that, but I do feel there is a negative factor related to emergency maintenance, and, for that matter, to annual preventative maintenance. The servicing of gas heaters is supposed to be done by the gas company, at least where I live; and, as I said earlier, they really don't fix, just analyze the problem and tell you to call the plumber. They will, of course, restore an unsafe emergency condition to a safe condition. This usually means that they will turn off the furnace until it's repaired and make any adjustments necessary to remove potential fire, etc., hazards until the plumber comes. The drawback related to emergency no-heat-why?

calls to the gas company for service is that you often have to wait a very long time for them to show up; the colder it is, the longer the wait—that wait often turns into days, not hours. A commonly heard suggestion here in my city is to tell the gas company you have a gas leak, rather than the truth—no heat—and they will come right away. (The implication of a gas leak is the possibility of explosion and/or injury or death, thus these calls get priority.) No, I absolutely do not advise anybody to use this lie as a technique for getting quick service. Someone's life could be endangered by such selfishness. The thing to do is turn the electric switch, usually a toggle switch like the ones on your wall, to *off,* and wait for the gas people to come. Or if it's crucial that you have heat, or simply too inconvenient to be without it, call the plumber and pay for the repair. Naturally, in the very coldest weather, there will also be some delay even with the plumber. Besides, you can only call a plumber in the daytime. The gas company has 24-hour service. Yes, call them first, in any case . . . you could be lucky.

I must hasten to add that it may not just be the electric switch you have to turn off while you wait; but if, in fact, you have a water leak related to the heating unit, you must also shut off the supply of water to the heater, so familiarize yourself with the location of the shut-off valve for that pipe as well as with the electric-switch position.

The gas company also offers annual inspection of gas-heat units. Their policy is that if you call before August 15, the annual maintenance checkup is free. After that, because it's closer to winter problems, there is a nominal fee, three dollars or so, for the checkup. (And if you want to know how ignorant I am . . . I just found that out a few minutes ago, when I called them to find out if they had such an annual service. I've always been calling the plumber at the end of every summer—and paying!—to have a checkover. Pure stupidity on my part, and yet why didn't someone tell me, why isn't there a checklist of information to novice homeowners? Perhaps there is, but I've never seen one.)

One last thing about gas-heat delivery. That's the best part, for it's always there, sitting in the pipe, drawn in by the furnace or boiler as needed . . . no striking truck drivers can muck up our lives as a by-product of their strike.

This fact is also true of *electricity,* that it's sitting there in the wires for you when you need it, either as a fuel or as heat. The electric company functions similarly to the gas company in matters of maintenance and emergency, which means that if the electricity is the furnace or boiler "fuel," you may still wind up calling the plumber in the end.

A tip about plumbers, since it is inevitable that at some time or other you will need one if your house has heating units (heat and/or hot water): select the plumbing outfit carefully.

When still a tenant, I once had to find a plumber to install my washer and dryer after I'd moved. I asked around about plumbers and finally called the name that was mentioned most frequently. I asked homeowners only, not tenants, for they deal more in the raw plumbing (plumbing from the cellar up). I felt this was a good rule #1 to use. During the installation of the dryer, it was necessary for the plumbers to remove a pane of glass and set into the area the dryer-venting outlet. I noticed that after they finished the job and were about to leave, there was no sign of broken glass, either inside the house or in the yard. Nor, I hasten to add, was there any mess to clean up. I couldn't believe this; plumbers are notorious for the after-mess, and so I thanked them profusely for having cleaned up. They explained that the boss, Big Mike, who was the father, father-in-law or maybe even godfather of most of the plumbers working for the company, told them all to treat every house they worked in as if it was their own home . . . or else! And they did! That was the biggest plus point for calling them again the next time I needed plumbing repair. And each time they came, they did a good job. Thus I long ago decided to stick with them.

It is necessary to observe a plumbing company's abilities, but you need more than one opportunity. Don't decide after one successful time, try another, and then pick the one you think is best. Give each a decent chance. After you've decided on one, you'll become a "customer." And that means faster service and the better plumbers in the group, not the trainees. One last piece of advice: An absolute requirement for getting good service is paying the bills on time. If you have to be reminded to pay bills, it may be reasonable to expect that you may have to remind the plumber to come "soon"!

TYPES OF HEAT DELIVERED

Hot air travels up through ducts and out into the room through a grilled opening, usually placed strategically in the sides of walls. The

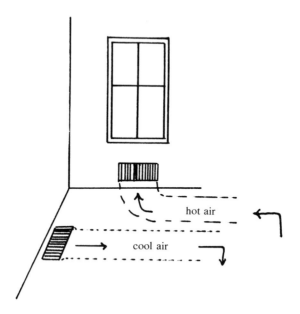

cooled air returns to the furnace through grills usually in the floors, and then through a different set of ducts. (Hot air rises, so the best place to capture the coolest air is at floor level.)

Hot water and steam travel up through pipes into radiators. In hot-water systems there is a separate pipe at the bottom of the radiator through which the water returns to the boiler for reheating. In steam systems steam cooled to water in the radiator travels back down through the same pipe it came up in.

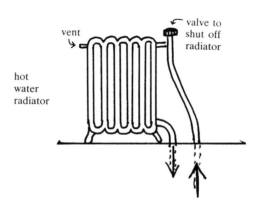

On hot-water radiators there is a vent. By opening the vent every year, you allow the air that accumulates in the radiator to escape, so that the radiator may fill entirely with water and do its best job. The vent can be opened either by a special key which unscrews a kind of bolt keeping the radiator sealed, or by unscrewing the knob on the end of the vent. (Some vents have those knobs.) If your key is lost, it can be replaced at the hardware store. This procedure should be done after the thermostat has been adjusted for winter (if you change it) and on the first day you have heat. Start at the bottom floor and work up, so my plumber has always advised me. Rattles and bangs in steam radiators usually means water is trapped. Tilt the radiator by putting a wedge under the feet of the radiator so that the water drains back down the pipe.

Hot-water and electric radiant heat Hot-water radiant heat is delivered through copper pipes buried in concrete floors. Electric radiant heat is delivered through resistance wires buried in the ceiling plaster (buried while the plaster was wet).

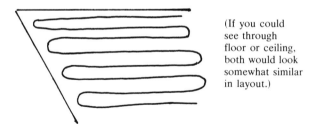

(If you could see through floor or ceiling, both would look somewhat similar in layout.)

I have only one comment about these types of heating. What happens when something's wrong in those ceilings and floors? No, thanks, I'll stick to nice, visible radiators! Radiant heat, baseboard type, may also be either hot-water or electrical. Yes, this makes me happier. The hot water comes through pipes within the baseboard, the electric heat through wires.

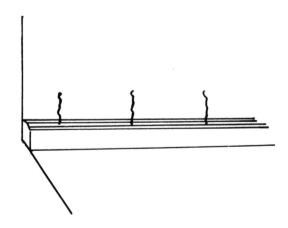

THERMOSTAT

A thermostat is a rather simple device which performs a function very similar to an electric on–off switch. Inside is a spring which is sensitive to temperature changes. It moves, either to close two electrical contact points, thus turning on the heating unit, when the temperature surrounding it is lower than the temperature set on the dial . . . or, in reverse, it moves to open the two points (they no longer touch), thus turning off the heater, because the desired temperature has been reached. This, therefore, is an on—off switch like the one you turn a light on and off with, except that this one reacts to temperature, not your finger. However, you may have noticed at times when you have made thermostat adjustments (have adjusted the temperature-set dial) that you hear a little click. If you were raising the temperature to get more heat, that little click was the switch going to "on" position. Yes, you can give this a try to see what I mean, but just once to try and once to set it back to the permanent setting. It is not advisable to change the settings frequently. Find the setting that makes the house most comfortable, and leave it there all winter. (All devices wear with use, even thermostats . . . and heaters!)

It is also recommended, whether you have a night/day setting type (one on which you can set a night temperature and a day setting, with a clock and time-setting dial indicating what time the night temperature is to take effect and what time the day temperature is to take effect) or whether you set the night temperature yourself every evening, because you don't have this option, that the temperature differential not exceed 6 degrees. The reason for this is that what you may save in fuel during the night may be lost in the amount of fuel consumed in the morning to build the heat back up to the daytime requirements.

SAFETY AND MAINTENANCE

A point that has just occurred to me, and one which solves a problem I've always had about the on–off switch being so far away, down in the cellar: If you sense or know of any condition, emergency or otherwise, that makes you want to turn the heater off, first push the temperature setting(s) on the thermostat all the way down to the lowest temperature. This should take care of turning off the heater quickly, for the thermostat is usually steps away. Then you can go down to the cellar, if that's where the heater is, and throw the electric toggle switch near (or on) the heater to "off" for permanence, until the maintenance person arrives.

Good heating systems have many safety features built in so that the heater will shut off in any number of conditions, each of which is a potentially dangerous one. An example of this is that if the pilot light goes off, a control indicator will cause the heater to turn off immediately. There are many other controls. To continue this example further, a pilot light could blow out as the result of a good cold draft . . . so when your heater does stop, sometimes you aren't in really bad trouble. You are in bad trouble if your heater does not have good safety controls built in. So, now that you've had the be-comfortable general-information course, I recommend that you read the owner's manual for your heater. See exactly what you have. Compare it to others. (Write to the manufacturer for a copy if you don't have one.) Also, if you've been lax about maintenance, perhaps now is a good time to get a thorough check of your heating plant.

A final word of caution for those of you in the same boat as I, possessing general information only: There are many books around that illustrate all kinds of maintenance that a homeowner can do on her own. Much is better left to the annual maintenance check you should have done. Some is scary, some is confusing and the steps are easily forgotten unless written down; so go easy on these recommendations, do what you can learn to do and feel comfortable about. Leave the rest to the plumber or gas or oil company.

I will give you two examples, both of which I am queasy about. (1) In boilers, pressure builds. If the pressure builds too high, some is released through a pressure-release valve, a pipe outlet that lets out water, usually aimed at a hole to the flue. Anyway, it is recommended in books that you periodically check this valve to make sure it isn't stuck, so that when it needs to work, it will (or the boiler could blow up!). This is a frightening thing to do, because as you depress the lever to give a quick test, a hiss of water shoots out. Watch out where you are standing if you try this . . . don't stand in front of the opening. That hissing hot water will hit you! (2) In hot-water heating systems, there is an expansion tank, which should be kept only partially filled with water, not filled. It becomes filled with water as some of the air cushion within the heater dissolves in the water. The air is a necessary cushion against which the heated water must expand, and so the air must not be totally depleted. Thus it is usually recommended that the expansion tank be drained once a year. However, before you do this, it is necessary to change the positions of two shut-off valves attached to pipes connected to the heater, in the proper sequence. Although I've hung tags on the two valves, written down the whole procedure, in sequence, and hung it on the wall near the heater, I'm still too uneasy to do it myself. I simply always say to the maintenance person doing the annual check, "Don't forget the expansion tank." (Everyone has some hang-ups. This is one of mine.)

It isn't really my intention to discourage you from learning anything. That I hope is already obvious by now. However, I feel that the best way to learn about heating systems, and what you can do to help yourself, is by observation. Have the plumber come and show you how to do it. Write down what you are seeing in whatever way it will make sense to you when you are alone. Nail all procedures on the wall near the heater so they are always available. This is imperative; don't trust your memory, not for the first couple of years or so, for you sometimes do these things only once a year.

This you can do: *When summer comes,* push the thermostat temperature dial all the way down and stop there. If you have a pilot light, leave it on, to keep the mechanical parts of your heater in better condition. (If hot water for your bathroom and kitchen facilities is made in your heater instead of a separate water heater, then, of course, you can't turn off the pilot. Don't do it ever.)

When winter comes, try to schedule the annual maintenance to coincide with the time you want to reset the winter temperature settings on the thermostat, and let it all be done by the maintenance person. Have her/him stay until there is heat throughout the house and you're off to a warm winter.

ELECTRICITY

PRISON ISN'T THE ONLY PLACE YOU CAN BE ELECTROCUTED

My prime reaction to electricity, and tasks involving it, is fright. It's a very basic fear—the fear of death! And this fear is real and well documented. In this very early stage of discussion about electricity, I want to encourage you to have this same fear, nurture it, cherish it, for with fear comes caution; hopefully the more fear you have, the more caution you will exercise, if, in fact, you are able to try your hand at things electrical at all. If you can't, if you feel you don't dare, skip it. You won't be alone. I would guess that over 50 percent of the people who dabble in it are scared.

Wait, don't flip to the next chapter yet. There are some things you should know about electricity, even if you never play with it, so that you may avoid danger and avert catastrophe, and to make you more comfortable in your home, if you live alone or your husband's away. Let's talk a little about wiring and current and fuses and circuit breakers and watts and volts—things you may feel too vague about.

I'm not going to be very technical, partly because I don't know all the technical terms and partly because I don't think it's necessary. If you grasp an idea, it doesn't make any difference how, or by what name. Later, if you get eager to add to your vocabulary, there are plenty of books around.

And I'm not going to talk about rewiring a house, or even about tampering with the wires in the walls. For that you should call a licensed electrician, and in these matters I defer to them. I must say here, however, that I do believe that the concepts involved in wiring seem simple and logical, and I would like to believe that I could become a licensed electrician someday; but the barrier is almost impenetrable, at least as I know it to be here in the city. First you must go to electrical school, then you must apprentice with a licensed electrician before getting a license. And that's not all—only a limited number of licenses are given (the elite are at it again)! And what male electrician would hire a female apprentice?

SWITCHES, FUSES, CIRCUIT BREAKERS AND AMPS, WATTS, VOLTS

As in plumbing problems, in which it is important to know how to shut off the water, so in electrical problems the most important thing to know is how to stop the flow of electricity. Switches, fuses and circuit breakers are devices which either connect or disconnect two ends of wire, allowing electricity to pass or stopping the flow. In each case, the wire stops on one side of the device and a new piece of wire starts on the other side of the device. The disposition of the device determines if current can pass from one side of the device to the other. If the switch is open, nothing is connecting the two pieces of wire, therefore no current can pass; if a fuse is not screwed in, or is blown, nothing is connecting the two wires; and similarly, when a circuit breaker flops off, it breaks the circuit—the flow of electricity.

A word about what a blown fuse is: A fuse has a piece of wire running through it, and along this wire passes the electricity from and to the wires connected to the fuse box. This special piece of wire will melt if the amount of current passing through it is more than it was meant to carry. Thus, in a 15-amp fuse, the wire will be warming at 15 amps and will melt at about 17 amps, and then the fuse is blown.

In the course of reading about electricity, I discovered that electricity has to push its way through wire (I don't know why, nor do I think I care). It is the pushing which causes heat, and different sizes of wire can hold different amounts of heat.

Now, I'll give you a bit of the vocabulary: *amps, watts, volts* and *ohms*. (This last is least important for you to remember for running your household.) Electricity pushes its way through the wire; the measure of this push is called voltage—"volts." The wire is resistant to this push (or it wouldn't have to push—right?); the measure of the resistance is called ohmage—"ohms." Now, if the measure of voltage is 120, and the measure of ohmage (resistance) is 12, only one-twelfth of the voltage passes through, or 10, and this measure of 10 is called amperage—"amps." This is complicated to me, I think, because I don't understand why wires are resistant, but I accept the fact. If you accept it, too, you now know Ohm's law.

What good does it do you to know this formula: Amps = volts ÷ ohms? Well, it helps you to think about a more important formula, one you should memorize, even though the concept may leave you. (In one ear and out the other, once you know how to apply it—that's my rule; don't waste space up there.) So, the next important formula is: Amps = watts ÷ volts. What are watts? Watts are the measure of the work that has to be done to get all the current through, and this is calculated by multiplying volts by amps. Watts = amps × volts. In the example of 120 volts and 10 amps, the watts equal 1200. The importance of this formula is in its transposition, so that you may calculate amps: Amps = watts ÷ volts. (Volts in your household will usually = 115; substitute 115 in the formula.)

This is the thing we always need to know: How many amps? The reason we need to know is because usually all our switches, fuses and circuit breakers are rated in amps, and the amount of current that a wire will safely carry is measured (rated) in amps. In order not to overload the wires (which will burn when overloaded), blow fuses, etc., it is necessary to know how many amps are being asked for from a particular electrical device or a combination of them.

Fuse boxes and circuit breakers usually indicate amp capacity, thus showing the maximum capacity of the wiring to deliver the electricity. The rule, therefore, is never, in fuse boxes, to put in a bigger fuse than the rating calls for or you're asking for a fire. Because, as shown before, that special wire in the fuse won't melt until its rating is satisfied; the wires carrying the electricity from the fuse box are rated lower and will get hot and possibly burn before the fuse blows.

If the fuse box calls for a 15-amp fuse, don't put in a 20-, 25- or 30-amp fuse, no matter what anyone (including the electrician) tells you!

Circuit breakers are set by the electrician and should be set to meet the rating of the house wiring. Thus they are more desirable for safety. The circuit breaker is a device in which a switch is thrown, automatically disconnecting the wires, when the current asked for exceeds the capacity it's rated for.

Now is a good time to stop reading and investigate your amperage, particularly if you have fuse boxes. If the fuses in your boxes are higher than the rating stated on the door of the box, or thereabouts, get a supply of the proper-sized fuses (and get rid of any rated too high for your use—remove temptation!). To change a fuse, carefully unscrew the improper one and screw in the new one.

You are in a potentially dangerous position when removing a fuse. Do not stand in water, or in bare feet, or have a wet body. Do not touch any water pipes or gas pipes, for you may inadvertently provide the wrong route for grounding—yourself!—and get electrocuted. There are inexpensive insulated fuse removers in the hardware store.

You may find that you blow fuses more often with the lower-rated fuse, and if so, it means that you've been living dangerously, overloading the wires. I hope you are convinced, however, from all that has been said, never to live dangerously again. (Don't remove the fuse for the furnace, boiler, whatever, until you turn it off; there's an on–off switch somewhere on the unit, or should be.)

The next thing you should do is to make a diagram of what fuses or circuit breakers apply to what rooms or sections of rooms, so that you don't have to hassle it when the real time comes. Make sure a lamp or radio is plugged into every outlet and is turned on. Then test. Sometimes two fuses apply to one room. Leave the diagram near to or pasted on the fuse box or circuit breaker.

A word of caution about the nonscrew-in fuses. Do not try to remove them until you turn off the main power switch for the house, because a part of them remain live. After the main fuse is off, remove this type of fuse by prying it out with a fuse puller.

Keep a flashlight near the fusebox, or on the way to it, and test it often so that it doesn't fail you when you need it.

Time-delay fuses: Some appliances require an initial, starting-phase, extra surge of electricity—refrigerators, air conditioners, etc. The surge takes less than a minute, but often the amperage required for this surge can be double the amperage for normal running of the appliance. Time-delay fuses, Fusetron or Buzz fuses, are designed to accept an overload of electricity (more than they're rated for) for a small amount of time, seconds only, before they blow. However, they will blow out just like an ordinary fuse if the overload continues.

Appliance wattage and amperage: You will notice, if you look on the little metal plate in back or on the bottom of appliances (where the serial number is), that your radio may require 60 watts (or $1/2$ amp . . . 60/120 volts), and your mixer may require 150 watts (1+ amps), and your toaster requires 1200 watts (10 amps). This is because appliances with coiled heating mechanisms require more electricity than those with motors. And I'm sure the size of the motor is also a determining factor, because a washing machine requires more watts (about 400) than a mixer. Take a look at some of these plates and you will get a better picture.

Before we stray too far from the word "watt," let me explain one more thing, so that your electric bill may be more meaningful. The term "watt-hours" means the measurement of the number of watts used times the number of hours used. A 40-watt bulb burning for 5 hours uses 200 watt-hours of electricity. Our electric bill refers to kilowatt-hours. *Kilo* is the Greek word for "thousand." 1000 watts = 1 kilowatt. 1000 watt-hours = 1 kilowatt-hour. The electric meter registers the number of kilowatt-hours of electricity used. Thus, for example, if all you have on during a 10-hour period is a lamp with a 60-watt bulb and a radio (approximately 40 watts), you will use: (60 watts $\times$ 10 hours) + (40 watts $\times$ 10 hours) = 1000 watt-hours, or 1 kilowatt-hour.

At this point you should feel less a stranger in your own home . . . and now we can talk about some of the things you can make or fix in the electrical area.

ELECTRICITY —

IN AND OUT

The wires coming into your house to deliver electricity are two kinds (packaged together), hot and neutral. Consider "hot" the incoming electricity and "neutral" the outgoing. Electricity comes in, does work (like lighting bulbs, making electrical appliances work, etc) and keeps on going—out. It doesn't stop at that bulb, but passes through. Let's take a look at the start:

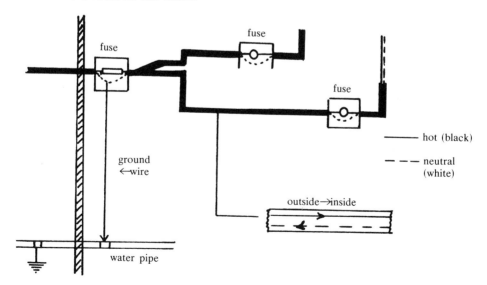

fuse

fuse

fuse

———— hot (black)

– – – neutral (white)

ground
←wire

outside→inside

water pipe

213

The cable the wires come in on is the package; inside the package are the two wires—or more than two, in which case the extra wires are hot.* Let's consider it the simple way: two wires, hot and neutral.

First, these wires are connected to the main fuse box in such a way that only the hot incoming wire passes through the fuse.

In addition, the neutral wire is grounded. This means it is connected to a wire which is connected to a water pipe which is grounded (i.e., in the ground). This is usually adequate in the city; but on farms, for instance, where often much extra electricity is required, grounding is also required at the pole, where a connection is made to a ground rod, which goes into the earth.

The clearest thing I can tell you about grounding, after much reading, is that its purpose is to reduce the danger of bad shock. Apparently, electricity must make an almost circular route through the house in order to be safe. Almost circular, because instead of going out of the house on the neutral wire within the package bringing in the hot stuff, it goes down into the ground near the point of entry. Further, I guess that the electric company has some built-in grounding outside, just in case the electrician didn't do a good job. I conclude that the electricity must be returned to the earth. (Didn't Ben Franklin get his from the sky?) However, I think we get electricity from water (or water power?) and now even from atomic power. Anyway, we get it and that's not the problem—the problem is using it . . . and respecting it.

Before we leave this mysterious question of grounding, I have another problem and a guesstimated answer. We've been told that materials such as metals, water and even your own body are "good conductors" of electricity, and that such materials as wood and rubber are "not good conductors." What does this really mean? I'm thinking about the suggestion to stand on a piece of wood when you are using an electric drill, for example, so that if the mechanism breaks down and electricity comes to the frame (encasement) of the drill, you won't get a shock. Does this mean, perhaps, that these bad conductors absorb the electricity and it goes no farther? As I understand it, you will get a shock when the electricity passes through your body to earth and on to the neutral wire, earth being the conductor. This means to me that the circle must be complete, around to the electrical service

---

*Two wires equal 120 volts; three wires equal 220 volts.

entrance, in order for you to get a shock. Yes, there seems to be a circle, at least within the house (and under it, if you're careless). My final question is, does this electricity traveling back along the neutral wire and properly grounded go back outside, or does it only go to earth? (You think your electrician can answer this question? Go ahead, ask him!)

Back to the diagram: The electricity comes into the house, first meeting the main fuse. Fuses control only hot wires, those delivering electricity into the house, so only the hot wires are connected to the metal ends of the fuse. Neutral wires bypass the fuses. (A horror story: My ex-husband, when young and still living with his mother, discovered while attempting to do some electrical repairs that taking the fuses out did no good; the hot wire was still hot. Reason: An electrician had wired the house wrong. The neutral wires, not the hot, were connected to the fuse encasement, either in the main fuse box and/or in the individual box for that floor. See testing device following pages.) As you can see from the diagram, after the main fuse box, the electricity is split to go to two individual fuse boxes. (There can be more but we'll use two for our example.) The wire coming into the house may deliver 60 amps to the house, and have the capacity to carry that much amperage. The wiring to the individual boxes (called branch circuits) will bring less than 60 amps, maybe 30 or 40 each, and will have the capacity to carry only that much. In my house I have two fuses in each box and two sets of wires coming from the boxes. The fuses called for are 15 amps each, and that means that the capacity of those wires coming out is only 15 amps. As each package of wires travels up into the rooms above, the wires are interrupted by switches and outlets which draw from the power for use on electric devices.

As we go upstairs, you will see what happens, and thus how to fix things.

Note: I think it best that you read this entire chapter before you attempt any repairs, so that you have the complete picture. That will prepare you for any complications.

BLACK TO BLACK, WHITE TO WHITE

Let's do an easy house—two floors, three rooms per floor, two individual fuse boxes, each with one 15-amp fuse. One box delivers to the first floor, the other to the second floor.

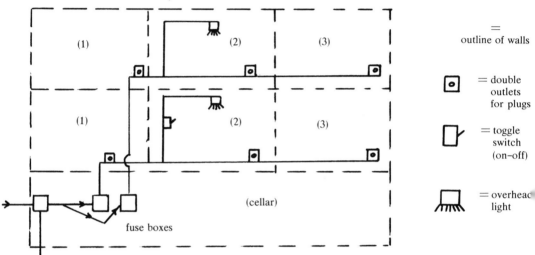

In each room there is one double outlet to receive plugs.

In the central rooms there are overhead lights; the first floor light is turned on and off by the toggle switch on the wall. The overhead light on the second floor, a light without a toggle switch, has probably a pull-chain control.

Let us look at each of these electrical devices.

THE OUTLET

The outlet is covered with a plate. The plate has two large holes for the outlets and a hole for the connecting screw.

The outlet, usually plastic, has two sets of receptacles for plugs. In the center between them is a threaded hole to receive the screw from the cover plate. On each side of the outlet are two terminal

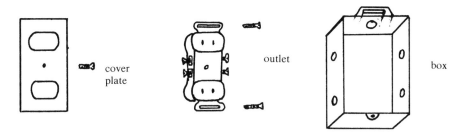

cover
plate

outlet

box

screws, which will only unscrew so far and will not come out. On one side the terminal screws are a brass-colored metal, on the other side they are a silver-colored metal. Lastly, there are metal pieces, top and bottom, with holes and screws. These are used to attach the outlet to the box in the wall.

The box in the wall, usually attached to a stud to keep it firmly placed, has holes in it, through which the hot and neutral wires enter. The wire package enters through one of the holes in the box. Within the box the black (hot) and white (neutral) wires are separated, the ends of insulation stripped off. The black wire is wrapped around one

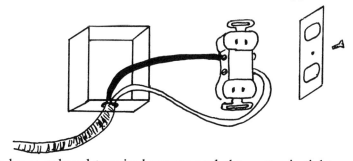

of the brass-colored terminal screws and the screw is tightened. The white wire is wrapped around one of the silver-colored terminal screws and the screw is tightened. In this case I have illustrated an end-of-the-line outlet, where only one set of connections has to be made. Hot-black is wired to the top brassy screw, neutral-white is wired to the bottom silvery screw on the other side. This is the type of outlet that would be in the fictional house in the right-side end rooms—the rooms #3. Both sockets in the outlet will function with the wiring as shown.

The reason for the double set of terminal screws is that they may be used to continue service to another outlet. Let's disregard the plates and boxes for the next illustrations, but, yes, they are always necessary in reality.

The three outlets on the first floor are probably wired this way:

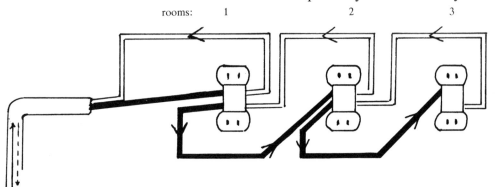

black into top, brassy screw *(room 1),* white into top, silvery screw *(room 1).* Then black (hot) out of bottom, brassy screw *room 1,* to top, brassy screw *room 2,* and white (neutral) out of bottom, silvery screw *room 1,* to top, silvery screw *room 2;* and so forth to the end of the line, which needs only the two wires.

It is necessary to mention that there are two kinds of these double outlets. There is the ordinary kind, in which one hot wire to one of the terminals will activate both sockets, as shown on the previous diagrams. The terminal screws, brassy, are screwed into the same piece of metal on the side:

There is also a kind called duplex, which demands that hot be brought to both screws in order to activate both halves. In this case the terminal screws are in separated pieces of metal outside.
Only one neutral out-wire is needed in these duplex outlets, however, and that means the terminal screws are within the same piece of metal. Wiring *room 3* outlet, in order to have electricity from both sockets, and using a duplex outlet, the outlet would look like this:

To facilitate this, you could use a slightly longer, exposed (stripped) end of wire, and wrap it around both screws, like so:

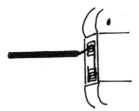

The usual purpose of this type of outlet is to allow one socket to be controlled by a toggle switch—on–off.

The wiring for two duplex outlets, in which one has both outlets always active *(a)* and the other *(b)* has one half always active and the other half controlled by a toggle switch, would look like this:

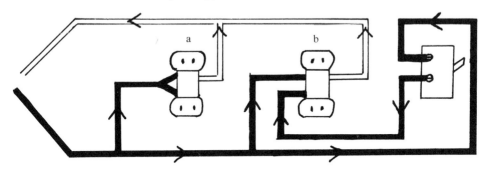

Now that you understand how these outlets are wired, you are prepared to replace one. First, *take out the fuse!* (My recommendation is to turn off the main fuse, if possible, when you are working with wires in the walls. You'll feel safer. I do.) Take out the fuse . . . or switch the circuit breaker to "Off." No, you're not ready to touch the wires yet.

Next, come back to the outlet. Test the outlet to see if it's still live. (Remember my ex-husband's horror story.) There is a fine gadget you should pick up during one of those make-your-face-familiar trips to the hardware store, a gadget called a neon tester.

From one end of the encasement protrude two wires (mine are colored red and black). At the end of each wire is a prong. On the other end of the encasement is a tiny bulb housed in a plastic cover. Put each end of the wires, the prongs, into one of the sockets, one in each hole:

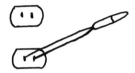

If the bulb doesn't light, try the other socket. If the bulb still doesn't light, you're safe—there is no electricity coming to the outlet. If the bulb does light, either way, CALL THE ELECTRICIAN! (Something's cockeyed with the wiring.)

Now, if you are safe, you may take off the cover plate and investigate the wiring. It might be a good idea to pull the outlet out a bit, gently, and make a note of the wiring before you unhook it. Also, take a look at the side to determine if you have ordinary or duplex type. If you do discover that it is a duplex outlet, make sure the toggle is "on" and retest that socket with the tester. (Just a precaution. It should be controlled by the same fuse, but check anyway. Besides, all of this is good experience, helping to build your familiarity with electricity.)

All right, you are ready. Unscrew each of the terminals to which wire is attached and remove the outlet. Replace it with a new one, wired in the same manner as the old.

The technique to use is to make a hook with the end of the wire and hook it around the screw. The hook should go in the same direction as the screw turns to tighten. (A hook going in the opposite direction will tend to come away from the screw as it tightens.) The wire secured under the screw either delivers electricity to the outlet, if it's the hot (black) wire, or it lets it out, if it's the neutral (white) wire.

THE TOGGLE SWITCH

This is a device which interrupts the hot, incoming electricity only. (Nothing interrupts the neutral; it does not [should not] pass through switches or fuses!) Thus, you should notice first when you look at one of these devices that the terminal screws, and the metal plate through which they each pass, are a brassy color . . . brassy for *hot*. Also, in addition to the toggle itself, which flips to "on" or "off," there are metal pieces at the top and bottom through which screws pass to connect the device to the box in the wall. These little metal pieces, on all these devices in boxes, are called ears. (Don't ask why. As I look at one of these devices sitting on my desk, there is only a faint hint of the shape of an ear.) Right below the top hole in the ear on top is another hole, and there is a hole above the bottom hole in the lower ear. These two holes receive the screws from the cover plate.

Switches, as well as outlets, etc., can go bad and need replacing. (The plumber was here one day for two hours trying to determine why my heater in the cellar wasn't working. Finally, he had an idea and tested the switch on the side. Sure enough, the switch was no good.) In order to replace one of these switches, you go first to the fuse box and remove the fuse (or flip the circuit breaker to "off"). Leave the switch *on* and whatever it's connected to *on;* when you return, the light, or whatever the switch is attached to, should be off. (If not, CALL THE ELECTRICIAN!) Switches, besides being used to interrupt service to an overhead light, can also be used to deliver service to an outlet nearby. (There are also devices which are a combination of one outlet and one toggle, which we'll talk about later.) What happens within the encasement is simple. When the toggle switch is in the "off" position, the metal strip is not touching the inside part of either terminal, thus there is no passage of electricity. When the toggle is in the "on" position, the metal strip touches both terminals and electricity passes through the switch on to the device requiring it.

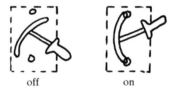

off   on

The box looks like this inside, with the white wire bypassing the terminals, either as one solid piece or cut and reconnected, the connection insulated.

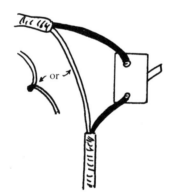

THE CEILING LIGHT

Last to look at in our fictional house are the ceiling fixtures in the middle rooms on both floors, rooms #2.

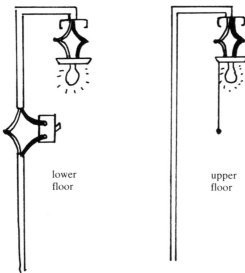

lower
floor

upper
floor

As you can see from the diagrams, on the lower floor service is interrupted by a toggle switch, controlling the on–off. On the upper floor service is not interrupted. Thus, it is necessary to obtain on–off control by a device within the fixture. The chain performs this function. Pulling it either causes a metal strip to connect two metal pieces within the fixture or it disconnects them. One piece of metal is part of the hot terminal inside, the other extends inside the bulb socket. When they are connected, electricity is delivered into the socket to light the bulb.

Perhaps you have such a condition as the top floor and you'd like to make a change so that the ceiling fixture is controlled by a wall switch rather than a chain. It can be done, but I think it should not be done by a novice. Watch someone do it first. What has to be done is to find the wire within the walls that is delivering the electricity.

The cable housing, called BX, must be sawed in half at the spot where you want the switch. (TAKE OUT THE FUSE FIRST!!) This will expose the black and white wires. The black wire must be cut so that each end can be connected to the terminals of the switch. The white wire may remain uncut, or it can be cut and reconnected, as shown in an earlier diagram. It's really not this simple, for the BX (armored) cable has to be sawed at an angle on one side and then twisted so that it breaks. If it's tight in the wall, this could be tough, to say nothing about the size of the hole you will need to make in the wall. Yes, watch someone do this. In fact, if you do want this done, call an electrician and watch him do it. It will be well worth the cost, if the exposure educates you enough to do the next one yourself, and now you have a great deal of preknowledge to watch with.

Some of this preknowledge is for talking to the electrician with, some is for using yourself. All of it hopefully will make you feel more comfortable in your electrified home.

About that ceiling fixture—how is that thing held up there?

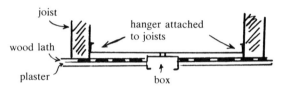

A piece of long metal, called a hanger, can be either of a shape that has sides that can be screwed to the joists or of a shape that simply lies on top of the lath. The latter is the kind you can cut a hole for and put in yourself . . . but don't hang a heavy chandelier from one that's just sitting on the lath! In the center of the hanger is attached the box, which hangs down and should be about flush with the plaster. There are different kinds of boxes, through which the wires enter, so let us look at a couple. In diagram *a,* the wires enter the top of the box. (They could also enter at the side; there are all kinds of boxes.) The ends of the wires are bare of their insulated covering, which is clothlike and black or white. The end of the black wire of the light fixture is twisted with the end of the black incoming wire. A solderless cover, also called an insulated cap, is wound around the twisted wires, screwed on. This prevents the black wires from touching the white wires, should they

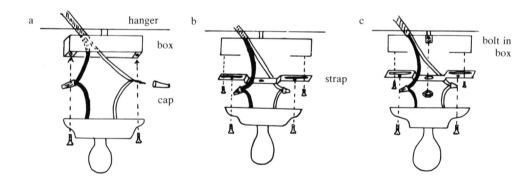

be exposed. Should they touch, it would cause a short circuit. (A short circuit is what happens when the electricity takes the shortest route back, bypassing the light fixture and going directly from black to white. It zaps the wires and blows a fuse. I think some of the hot electricity has to be siphoned off through a device before going to neutral; that's why shorts are bad.) The light fixture is fastened to the box by screws from the outside of the fixture to the holes in the box in *a*. Diagrams *b* and *c* show the use of a strap, a thin, strong piece of metal often used

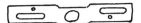

to lower the fixture attaching so that it will fit snug against the ceiling when the box is too high. Screws attach the strap to the box and other screws attach the fixture to the strap. The screws from the fixture screw into threaded holes in the strap. In addition, diagram *c* shows how a strap may also be attached to a bolt protruding from the top of the box. The center hole in the strap is slipped over the bolt and a nut underneath secures it.

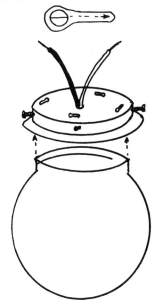

A Look at Some Other Ceiling Fixtures

This type and others like it are designed to hold globes over the bulb. The wires emerge from the top and underneath attach to the bulb socket. The slit holes in the top are used for the screws that attach

the fixture either to the box or to the strap, which in turn is attached
to the box. The screws on the side are used to tighten against and hold
the upper part of the globe, which goes inside the rim of the fixture.

A fixture like this one can be used in various ways . . . down from the
ceiling (as shown in the illustration) . . . up (the one in the picture
upside-down) . . . from a lamp base, etc.

Taking it apart, one can see how it is wired. Pull off the top. (The hole in the top is the entry for the wires.) Next, hold the top of the chain piece and pull away the bottom. (The bottom cover usually has a fitted piece of cardboard within. Leave it there.) Now we have the functioning part of the fixture. You will see that there are two terminal screws, one brassy, one silvery . . . black to brassy, white to silvery. (When you use this type of fixture in a lamp, you will notice that the lamp wires will both look alike, strands of thin copper wrapped in insulation. See later instructions for lamp-making.)

Actually, you just couldn't hang this fixture as is; it would be too insecure. Additional gadgets are required. That little hole in the top of the cover is also threaded inside to receive a hollow threaded bolt.

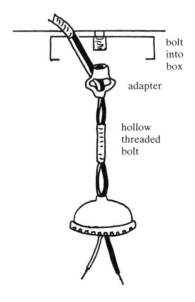

bolt into box

adapter

hollow threaded bolt

By also using an adapter, you can attach this bolt to the bolt from the box. The wires must then pass through the opening in the adapter, through the threaded hole in the bottom, through the hollow threaded bolt, and on into the hole in the fixture cover. Then screw the adapter to the bolt and the lower part of the bolt to the cover . . . or you could do all this first. Finally, hook the wires around the terminal screws, put the fixture back together and you're all set. (There are many variations on the theme, so do some browsing at your hardware store. You've got the basics now.)

Finally, I want to prepare you for two types of complications you may encounter up there in the ceiling when you are changing a fixture.

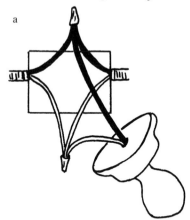

Diagram *a* indicates that service is continued through the box, on elsewhere. The light fixture may be controlled either by a pull chain or by a toggle to the left or right of the box, which controls this and the succeeding fixtures. (There are all kinds of possibilities.)

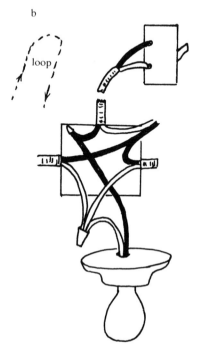

Diagram *b* indicates a more complicated setup . . . black to white??! Yes, under this condition it is permitted by the "Code."* This involves using a white wire where a black one should be, only to create a switch loop, using a piece of cable package with white and black in it to get to the switch. Think about it as if the switch were added later, and far away from the point where you could get at the incoming hot wire.

Before we go on to the easier (not so dangerous) stuff of lamps and extensions and the like, two final goodies to know about remain. (Oh, yes, there are many, many more goodies than this book will hold, but you're equipped to attempt reading the more specialized books now.)

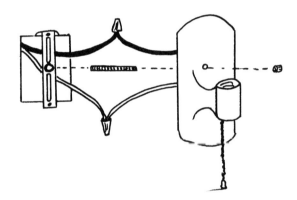

WALL LIGHT FIXTURE

(This is going to seem like pie after the preceding pages.) In the wall attached to a stud is a box. Screwed to the box is a strap; a locknut has been placed in the center hole of the strap. Into this locknut is screwed one end of a hollow, threaded rod called a nipple. The other end of the nipple comes through the hole in the fixture and a cap nut is screwed onto it to hold it in place. The wiring is done behind the fixture before this end of the nipple is attached.

---

*The "Code," the set of rules and regulations governing safe wiring methods, is the National Electric Code (NEC). Also, there are often local codes which meet NEC requirements.

Underwriters' Laboratories is a nonprofit testing lab, which tests all electrical devices, fixtures, etc. It is recommended that you only use devices with their seal of approval (UL) (or with the word "Underwriters' Laboratories" engraved on the devices, wires, cables, etc.).

TOGGLE-SWITCH–OUTLET COMBINATION

Here I sit at my desk looking at one of these devices, the outside only, and wonder exactly how it's wired. I've never looked. I'll take a guess and illustrate it. Tomorrow, when it's light, I'll take the fuse out and check it.

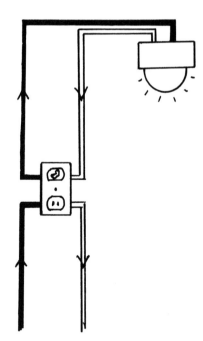

Let's see, the hot comes in and activates upper and lower half (toggle and outlet). The toggle half controls a ceiling fixture. If the toggle switch is "off," the light is off. However, the outlet works whether the toggle is "off" or "on," therefore the toggle does not control the outlet; the outlet is always hot. OK, when the toggle is "on," the juice goes to the light and it goes on; the juice comes back along neutral to the device and then out again from the device. Since the distance from the outlet to the light is far, probably a piece of cable (with black and white) has been extended through the walls up to the ceiling. This then creates a switch loop, the kind we mentioned earlier.

FIXING AND MAKING

TOOLS YOU WILL NEED

This is the easiest part, for the only tool you might not have is a wire cutter/stripper. The typical wire cutter looks like this; often, however, I have cut wire with scissors.

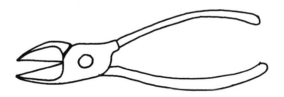

WIRE: SPLITTING, STRIPPING, TWISTING

The trouble comes with the stripping of the ends of the wire, and I have frequently chomped off more than just the rubber or plastic encasement around the wires. I've cut some of the little threads of wire within, and I'm never sure if I've cut off too much. Let's take a look at wire—the kind you would see coming from a lamp, not the heavy-duty type attached to your toaster.

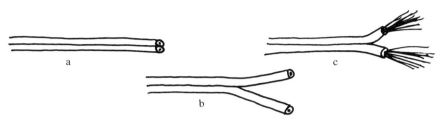

If you look at the cut end of wire *a*, you will see that inside the encasement there are really two wires—actually, two bunches of very thin, threadlike, copper wires, separated by the encasement. In order to prepare the wire for connection to some device, you must first split the encasement down the center a bit. Use the tip of the wire cutter to make a cut and then grab the two edges and pull them apart, so it's like diagram *b*. That encasement, by the way, is the insulation, so don't cut off too much. This wire, I must tell you, is encased in insulation material which is all one color—brown, white, black, yellow . . . lots of color choice. And as I said before, inside each section are threads of copper wires. Thus, at this low level of wiring for outside the walls, no differentiation is possible, no more black and white wire scene. Think about how nice this is while you read on. After you've been exposed to the things we are going to talk about next, I'll conclude my thoughts on the subject of no-more-black-and-white-outside.

Now for stripping. I have watched electricians, and they just seem to grab at the wire end with their wire cutter and pull out, and the section of insulation comes off—*poof!* Maybe they automatically twist around as they cut so that there is a cut all around the insulation. I don't know, but it never works for me.

Snip, snip, pull up at the same time and the insulation comes off! You may be more successful than I. I used to use my cuticle scissors, carefully cut the insulation all around and then pull it off. Those days are gone forever, because I have finally found the magic tool, a combination wire cutter and stripper. This is where to make an investment, if you need a wire cutter.

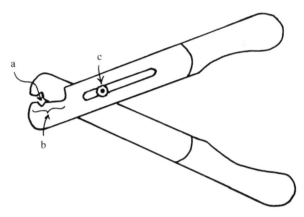

The entire edge indicated by the *b* arrow is a cutting edge, and mine is sharp and swift. (My wire cutters of the style mentioned earlier are worn.) However, the beauty of this tool is indicated by the *a* arrow, nicks in the cutting edge which fit nicely around a piece of insulated wire. A slight cutting action will cut the entire insulation around and through—and *poof!* (This is a real *POOF!*) The setscrew *c* makes it possible to hinder the cutter from closing fully; thus, if you play with it a bit, you can set it so that it allows just a cut of the insulation, not the wires within. I find it inconvenient to set the screw tightly, however, because then it has to be loosened for cutting. What I do instead is to cut and pull away at the same time, and as the cutting of just the insulation is completed, the cut-off piece will pull away and off the wire inside. (I am a right-handed person, and I cut into the insulation and pull to the right with the stripper at the same time.)

Wire, by the way, can be bought in whatever lengths you want it. If you've found that good hardware store, you will have noticed big spools of wire, and you can order 50 feet or so just to keep on hand. You might need to make an extension cord. Or you may begin to make your own lamps. (Lamp wire is 18-gauge wire.)

WIRING A LIGHT FIXTURE

I've been making my own lamps since someone showed me how easy it is, so let me show you how to do it. You can recycle at the same time (cans and bottles) or use any other inventions you come up with as housing for the lamp base. Or you can just rewire old lamps you find in junk shops.

terminal   terminal

hole for screw
for attaching
to a piece of wood, or whatever

Here is a typical ceramic fixture, terminals-exposed type. (Good for this illustration, but I would use the kind with a ceramic cover that screws on so that the terminals are covered after the wiring is done . . . see later illustrations of some varieties available.)

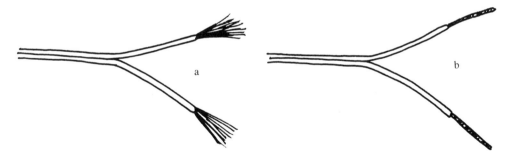

a   b

Take a length of wire *(a)*. Split one end and strip off the insulation on both pieces, about 3/4 inch's worth. Then twist each set of end wires around with your fingers, so that the wires are packed together and make a more solid unit to work with *(b)*.

Next, take one end and make a hook in it. Hook it around one of the terminal screws, between the head of the screw and the little plate underneath it. Unscrew the screw, if you have to, to make room for the wire. Place the hook around the screw so that it goes in the same direction as the screw will turn when you tighten it to the plate. (If

you hook it in the wrong way, the wire will tend to come away from the screw as you screw it in.) Tighten the screw so that the wire is held between the screwhead and the plate. (The plate and screw of the terminals are different-colored metals, but the wire is the same, either end, so it doesn't make any difference which terminal you start with.) Next, do the same thing with the other end of wire, hooking it and attaching it to the other terminal.

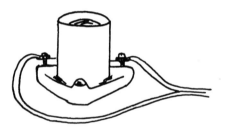

Go now to the other end of the wire. Here you have the choice of using one of the screw-terminal type of plugs or the newer kind, no wire splitting or stripping necessary.

WIRING PLUGS

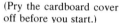
(Pry the cardboard cover off before you start.)

This type is the screw-terminal type plug. Split the end of the wire, strip the ends and twist them. No—first, push the end through the hole at one end of the plug and pull it through, then split, strip and twist. (Yes, that's a better way, why haven't I thought of that before? My stripped ends always get bent and gnarled on the way through.) After you've twisted the wire ends, hook them, push the wire back through the hole a bit, wrap the ends around the terminal screw and tighten. Slide the cardboard cover back over the prongs and snap it into place. (Never use this type of plug without the cardboard cover.) *Voila!* You have a lamp. Put a bulb in the socket. Plug the other end into the wall. Don't be afraid, only two things can happen—you will have light or a short circuit. No, I don't think you'll be electrocuted. If you have a short circuit, it will sound like a tiny explosion, and the fuse will blow. Go down and remove the fuse. Leave it out. Come back and pull out the plug and look at both ends. Either the wires in the plug were touching or the wires in the bulb socket end were touching. The electricity, instead of traveling from the end of one wire, through the screw and plate and into the bulb socket, met the wire around the other screw first and took the shortest route—to the wire, not the plate . . . thus a short circuit.

If all that splitting, stripping, wrapping around and screwing bugs you, as it does me, here's an easier way to do the plug. Use the new snap-together type.

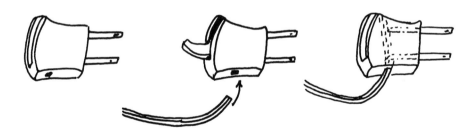

(a) Pull open the lever on the top.

(b) Push the unsplit, unspliced wire all the way through the hole in the side hole. (You can see if it's all the way in by looking through the opening at the lever.)

(c) Push the lever back in place. Inside there are pointed tips of metal, connected to the prongs, which penetrate the wires as the lever presses them together. (One tip penetrates one wire, the other penetrates the second.)

OTHER VARIETIES OF SNAP-TOGETHERS

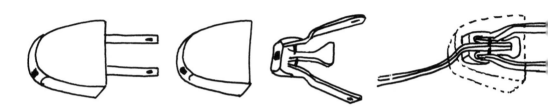

This type, which I like less than the one above, works in this way: Press the prongs together and pull the inside section out from the cover. Spread the prongs apart. Push the unsplit wire through the cover first, then through the hole in the inside section. Press the prongs together and push the inside back into the cover. In this type you can see the tips penetrate the wires.

This type of plug, the pronged-end, is also called the male plug. The receiving-end plug, with holes to receive the prongs, is also called the female plug. I have heard these terms for years, but honestly, only last year, when I bought a receiving-end plug, did it dawn on me which was which. I'll stick to "plug" and "socket."

Here are two types of snap-together sockets:

This type is similar to the first pronged-end plug illustrated above and functions the same way. Push the wire through the hole in the side and push the lever back down. (Yes, this is my first preference in the socket types of snap-togethers.)

This type I feel less secure about. The cover on top slides off. Lay the wire down into the inner section. You can see the tips. Press the wire into them and slide the top back over the lower section to cover.

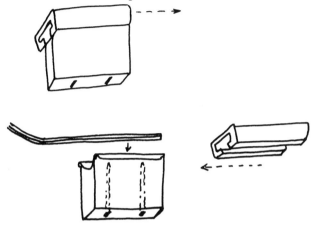

(I'm not happy about the sliding aspect, since it's the part you grab to hold.)

OTHER TYPES OF BULB FIXTURES

Some other bulb socket-fixtures, covered with a ceramic material, look like this:

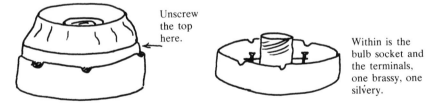

Unscrew the top here.

Within is the bulb socket and the terminals, one brassy, one silvery.

In all of these bulb fixtures, the terminals are one brassy and one silvery, I suppose so that you could also use them at a place where they are connected to the wall electricity. When you use regular lamp wire, no choice is required.

This next example contains a chain for controlling on–off, which the one before did not.

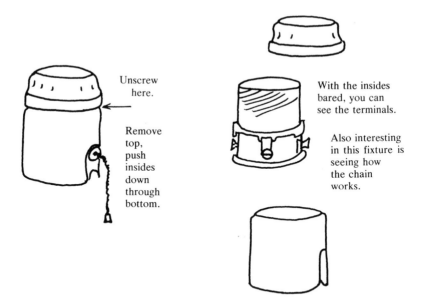

Unscrew here.

Remove top, push insides down through bottom.

With the insides bared, you can see the terminals.

Also interesting in this fixture is seeing how the chain works.

This last example is similar to the one above and has the additional feature of an outlet. Unscrew the top, push the insides down through the bottom. Here you can also see the terminals. The one facing you is into a piece of metal of dual purpose, a part for the light socket and a part that fits into the outlet area to activate the outlet. (This is a good type to buy and have a better look at.)

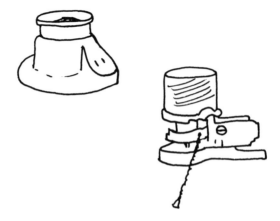

HOMEMADE EXTENSION CORDS

With the knowledge you now have about snap-together plugs, you can make your own extensions, any length you need (but not longer than six feet), instead of having all that overhang from stock-sized, store bought ones.

A word of advice: Make only your own light-duty extensions; buy ready-made heavy-duty ones, the kind with three-prong plugs and receptacles (or three-prong outlet and two-prong plug with ground wire).

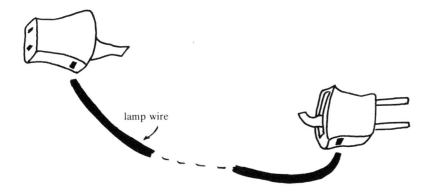

lamp wire

EXTENDED OUTLETS (DON'T!)

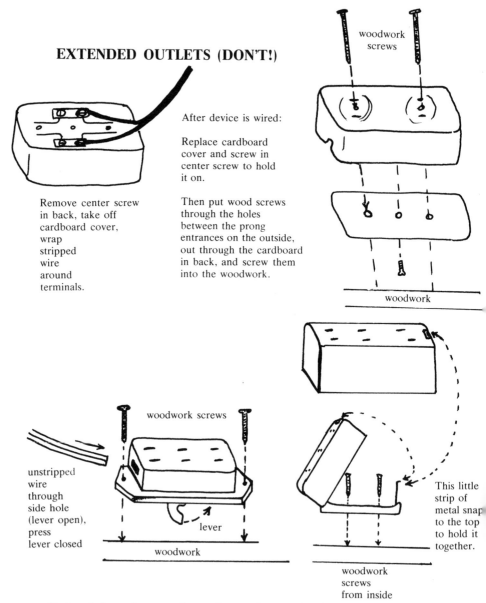

After device is wired:

Replace cardboard cover and screw in center screw to hold it on.

Remove center screw in back, take off cardboard cover, wrap stripped wire around terminals.

Then put wood screws through the holes between the prong entrances on the outside, out through the cardboard in back, and screw them into the woodwork.

woodwork screws

woodwork

woodwork screws

unstripped wire through side hole (lever open), press lever closed

lever

woodwork

This little strip of metal snaps to the top to hold it together.

woodwork screws from inside

Extended outlets, such as these pictured, which can be mounted to the woodwork, are not acceptable, my electrician warns, because they get painted over, sometimes so many times that they become almost invisible. Paint and time corrode the insulation and this can become a very serious hazard. So stick to loose-ended, visible extension cords. (Sorry.)

TOGGLE-SWITCH CONNECTIONS TO LAMP CORDS AND/OR EXTENSIONS

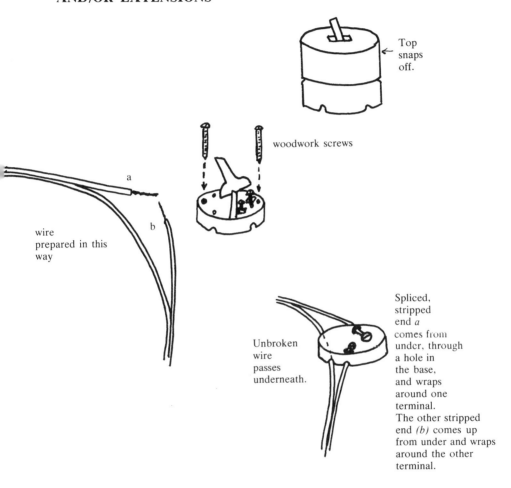

Top snaps off.

woodwork screws

a

b

wire prepared in this way

Unbroken wire passes underneath.

Spliced, stripped end *a* comes from under, through a hole in the base, and wraps around one terminal. The other stripped end *(b)* comes up from under and wraps around the other terminal.

This first kind can be mounted on the woodwork. Another DON'T!

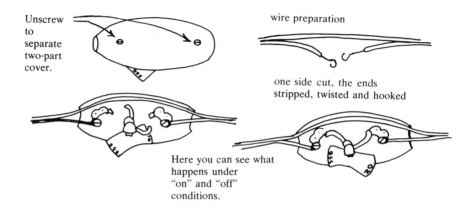

Unscrew to separate two-part cover.

wire preparation

one side cut, the ends stripped, twisted and hooked

Here you can see what happens under "on" and "off" conditions.

Toggle That Hangs on a Cord

(Remember, for toggles, only one of the two wires is broken and attached to the terminals.)

Snap-together Toggle Switches That Hang on Cord

This type needs minor wire preparation. Just separate the two wires and cut one side—no stripping, etc., of the ends.

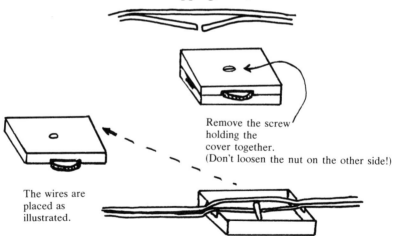

Remove the screw holding the cover together. (Don't loosen the nut on the other side!)

The wires are placed as illustrated.

Then the cover is replaced and the parts are screwed together. Prongs pierce the broken ends when the cover is replaced. As the circular toggle turns, a connection is made between the metal ends of the prongs. As the toggle turns again, there is no connection, thus no passage of electricity.

GROUNDING ELECTRICAL APPLIANCES

You will notice that most of your motor-driven electric appliances have three-prong plugs. The third prong, round, is the ground. There is a *very* important reason for this type of plug on those appliances.

Under some conditions, if the motor becomes defective, electrical contact could be made with the frame of the appliance—the outside metal cover of your drill, the outside metal cover of your washing machine or dryer, etc. This means that you could get a very serious, possibly deadly, shock. However, all these appliances have a built-in grounding facility, so that this electrical contact is diverted from the frame through a special grounding wire attached to the frame. This eliminates the possibility of shock for you, if an electrical connection is made between the grounding wire and the outlet.

The cable which contains the two power wires for the appliance also contains the grounding wire, and this wire is connected to the round prong.

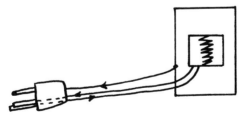

If you have three-pronged outlets in your house, you are in good shape to use this kind of plug. If you do not, and have the ordinary two-prong receptacles, you must take other steps so that the grounding can be accommodated. *The step is not to take the round prong out of the plug!!!* Your machine will not be grounded, and if your

motor becomes defective, you could be electrocuted. Yes! this is one
of those times. *The step to take is to use a three-prong adapter.* Put
your three prongs into one end. The other end has only two prongs,
which will fit into your outlet, *and* it has a *grounding wire.* You *must*
connect this little U-shaped piece of metal to the screw holding the

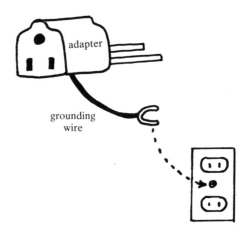

cover plate of the outlet on. (Unscrew the screw a bit and place the U
behind. Then tighten the screw.) The grounding continues through
this screw back on down to the cellar . . . if your house is properly
grounded. (This can be tested. Use your tester. Place one prong of the
tester against the screw. Put the other prong into one of the slots. If
the tester light doesn't light, move the prong in the slot to the other
slot. Now it should light. [It works only one way, in the positive slot,
since the screw, grounded, is negative, and you can't see from outside
which is which.] If you don't get a light either way, you're not grounded
. . . CALL THE ELECTRICIAN!)

The old stand-on-a-piece-of-wood advice is designed to protect you
if this happens and you're not grounded, and this might be adequate
(?) when you're drilling or sawing . . . but what about every time you
do the wash? Yes, the installer of these appliances is supposed to check
out the grounding. Are you sure about it?? Don't take any chances
with anything. Use safe methods and stay alive.

One other nice tidbit of information. Some appliances. like TV's,
have plugs where one prong is wider than the other. (Outlets have one
slot wider than the other, you may notice.) This wide prong is to assure

grounding. The wide prong fits in the negative side only. I've wondered about that for years; you too?

FLUORESCENT LIGHTS

There is electrical genius here that I cannot explain, but I will tell you the functions of the parts as I understand them, so that you may troubleshoot problems.

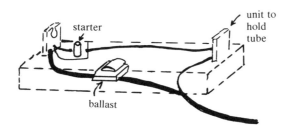

This first illustration is designed to give you your bearings. I removed the tube and the cover from mine for this illustration. (The remainder of the metal case is the dotted area.) The wire is black from where it comes in onto the ballast and as far as the left tube holder. Coming out from under the starter to the right tube holder and on out toward the plug the wire is white. Therefore the electricity flow is counterclockwise in this illustration.

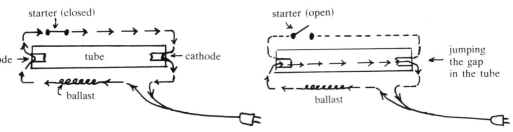

When you depress the starter button on the outside, here's what happens. Electricity flows in, past the ballast through the cathode at the left end of the tube, through the starter, over to the cathode on the right end of the tube and out. But more electricity is still coming in. Imagine a circle. The starter is a switch designed so that it will open and remain open right after some electricity passes through it.

Because the starter opens after that first trip, that route is no longer available. However, the ballast is so designed that when that happens, it provides a momentary surge of extra power. This allows the electricity to jump the gap between cathodes and pass through the tube. The electricity jumping the gap is the light. (Mercury in the tube vaporizes when this happens and helps the flow within the tube.)

Now you know why you have to press that button down until the light goes on—to get the electricity past the starter once, so that it opens and you have light.

The tube (as you know) is replaceable. The ballast, screwed into the case, is also replaceable, and so is the starter.

Before you replace all parts, or the wrong one, try to figure out what is not happening that should and which of these parts is related to the missing function.

REPAIRS AND
RENOVATION

WHY YOU'VE THOUGHT YOU JUST DIDN'T KNOW HOW TO DO IT (THE WRONG REASONS!)

A friend of mine, a single woman, gave me a long list of things that she wanted to know how to do, suggestions of things she hoped would be included in this book—not just for her sake, but for the many women who don't know how. This friend is one of the brightest, most talented and versatile women I have ever known, and I had great difficulty believing the contents of the list, insofar as it represented things she felt she couldn't do. Rather than just go ahead and add to the book all of the things she suggested that had not been already included, I immediately asked her why she felt she couldn't do some of these things without further inspiration, or why they *seemed* difficult tasks—especially those she had attempted and failed.

There was one particular item I questioned her about several times. It was how to put up drapery rods, a problem she was currently dealing with. "Usually," I said, "you just screw the end fixtures into the woodwork."

"Well, I don't know how to do that kind of thing," she answered the first time, in a totally befuddled voice. (This is not the person I know, I told myself.)

Within a week I brought up the same subject—same item—again. "But did you ever try it?" I asked hopefully.

"Oh, yes [and I sighed a quiet relief], and it was impossible, with my hands way over my head, trying to screw in those screws—they were all going in crooked, and I was quickly exhausted. I know there must be an easier way, a right way to do things like this," she responded.

"Yes," I said, "there is. Get a taller ladder!"

"Oh, my God, I never thought of that!" she said, almost embarrassed.

Immediately I knew the embarrassment was mine, not hers. I was sorry I had been so smug. I mentally reevaluated her list. I realized that at one time or another I had had a problem with everything on the list, and many of the things had been put off for years because I felt I couldn't do them.

I have underlined "felt" three times in anticipation of the point I hope to make, which is what you *feel* you can or can't do does not necessarily relate to your *ability*. Rather, the feeling of "can't do" relates to lack of knowledge about technique and/or the availability of helpful materials. (In my friend's list was "how to fix cracks in wooden legs of chairs, tables, etc.," and I think her feelings of helplessness came from not knowing that there are glues that mend and hold wood. This example brought to my mind the need to discuss many of these unknown materials.)

The feelings of "can't do" are based on insecurity, and the insecurity is really lack of information. I will give you, in these next pages, all the information I can think of. Most of it has been compiled through trial and error and endless questioning of experienced friends—and some research in books. Mostly, I think, questions and answers have been my most successful game; the questions have often come after trial *with* error! Sometimes the answers did not provide adequate information, because I did not ask the right question—more trial with error. But there is an answer to every question, somewhere, and more often than not you can operate with the answer rather than abandon the question.

Since I may do no more than scratch the surface in terms of necessary information, because of my own limited experience, what I'm really hoping to offer you is a philosophy about repairing: perseverance while gathering information. Although I almost hate to tout the old "If at first you don't succeed, try, try again" bit, I am encouraging you to follow a broadened version: If at first you don't succeed, ask a few more questions . . . and try, try, *try* again!

PAINTING

This is perhaps an area most women are proficient in. Men haven't drawn a line here: "You're a woman, you can't do that." Many men, as a matter of fact, are usually happy to leave this task to women. (Is it because they suspect that women are more careful, more patient, better suited to this job?) In any case, I don't feel that it's necessary here to go into great detail about the principles of painting. I will, however, tell you about the techniques and attitudes I employ when painting, for what they're worth.

First of all, I almost never use oil-base paint. The reason is twofold. (1) It makes me sick. Gall bladder/pancreas ailments cause me to react very badly to exposure to oil-base paint, as well as stains, varnishes, etc. So I avoid using them. (2) I'm lazy, and pressed for time (ever and always), and the cleanup procedure—floors, brushes, my hands and face (whatever got splattered)—requires time and turpentine (another no-no for my stomach). If and when I have to use oil-base paint, I do so in short time spurts, or outdoors, and I throw the brush away. Very uneconomical, I know, but my time has a value, I always try to remember when rationalizing this type of action. (There have been times when this attitude has done me in. For example, doors between the rooms in my house had been painted with oil-base enamel paint. I, being not too knowledgeable at the time, did not know that you cannot successfully paint flat paint over enamel. After it dries, many sections of the enamel show through. One door here has been painted at least five times with flat paint; among the paintings I tried someone's sander, and even liquid sander, a substance one paints on— all to no avail. So I have a purple door with bits of dirty white showing here and there. One day I'll get around to fixing it. What happens when you paint flat over enamel is that, because the undersurface is slippery, the flat paint doesn't adhere and kind of unevenly rolls away. A real mess.)

Another thing I *never* do is use spray paint. I simply cannot believe that some of it, flying around in the air, supposedly directed at the object being painted, doesn't float back toward you and get into your lungs. It's gotta be! And with everything else we're inhaling these days, I don't want to add to the misery. Purple lungs . . . no, thanks!

I watched an ad on TV the other night. A house painter was up on a ladder spray-painting a house, the paint guaranteed to last a life- time (or was it ten years?). No matter. How much was bouncing back into that poor painter? My children are also absolutely forbidden to use it, or even to stand near anyone using it.

I came home from work one day and my son proudly showed me his newly painted gold(!) bike. "That's very nice, dear, did you do that all by yourself?" I asked.

"Yes, my friend had a can of gold spray paint and let me use it."

I raved and screamed about never using spray paint—"How close were you standing?"—and slept fitfully that night, getting up frequently to check and see if he was still alive. Certainly he had stood too close and breathed in half of it, I believed. Well, apparently he hadn't. He's still alive, and I think that means only that he's lucky, and I'm lucky, too. And the ban stays on!

So I am left with the miracle of water-base paint, which, in this modern day, is available in both flat (no-shine) and enamel (glossy). I didn't know about water-base enamel when I was doing that purple door, but since I have discovered it, I know that the door can be sal- vaged. The nice things about water-base paint are: (1) no stomach reaction; (2) you can clean the brushes (and the pails and pans and sticks) by rinsing them out with water in the sink; (3) you can clean splats easily with a water-soaked rag; (4) you don't have to go to work with dark paint under your fingernails and cuticles, and all of the body splatters easily wash off, too; (5) it can be thinned simply with water—the base—thus at no extra cost. (Oil-base paint has to be thinned with $$ turpentine.)

Yes, I'm big on rollers. The job is faster. I'm careful not to have too much paint on the roller brush, or it'll splat all over—and some may even be ingested! My technique has improved during many years of painting walls. The trick is to work quickly but carefully, doing squared sections, going back toward the last wet square, not starting at the edge of the last one. The reason is that the paint consistency at the edge is thinner than the new starting paint in the next square, and it will not blend well. I guess I start in the middle of the square, go back to the prior one, then back to the middle and over in the other direction to complete the new square.

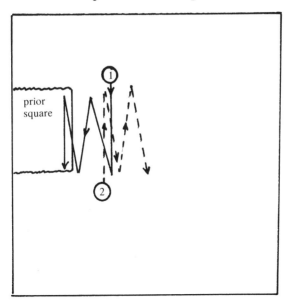

The illustration is intended to show direction left and right. In actuality, the strokes are much more vertical, and they travel through a bit of the edge of the last stroke.

PRIMER VERSUS SIZE (WHICH TO USE WHEN)

I have long confused these two things and have even used the terms interchangeably. Perhaps you, too, have some questions.

Size is really a glue; its purpose is particularly to seal plaster. It comes in powdered form and is mixed with water for use. Before painting or wallpapering over newly plastered walls, paint a coat of size on the plaster first. Plaster patches made before painting and wallpapering should be covered with size first, too. This will seal and prevent the absorption of water from the paint or wallpaper glue.

Primer is a sealing substance; its purpose is to seal the pores in wood. It comes ready to use like a can of paint, and may be called priming paint. Primer should always be used before painting wood, because without it the wood will absorb too much of the oil from the paint. When you replace panes of glass in windows, you should paint a coat of primer over the areas where the putty will be applied. Putty is very oily, and if too much of the oil is lost the putty will dry up and crumble.

Memorize: *Size plaster; prime wood.*

WALLPAPERING

There seem to be two kinds of people—those who hate to wallpaper and those who prefer it to painting. I'm sure the choice is related to the wallpaper process. (I'm a painter.) The process involves much in the way of equipment, measuring, cutting, smoothing, matching and possibly recutting, rematching and resmoothing. Wall preparation before wallpapering is for the most part similar to prepainting. Because of its washability, wallpaper probably has a longer life than paint, however. Here goes, if you want to do it.

The equipment:

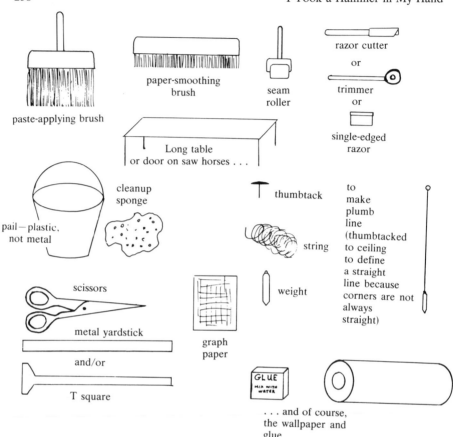

paste-applying brush

paper-smoothing brush

seam roller

razor cutter

or

trimmer

or

single-edged razor

Long table or door on saw horses . . .

pail—plastic, not metal

cleanup sponge

thumbtack

string

weight

to make plumb line (thumbtacked to ceiling to define a straight line because corners are not always straight)

scissors

metal yardstick

and/or

T square

graph paper

GLUE
MIX WITH WATER

. . . and of course, the wallpaper and glue

Preparation of walls: New plaster: size. Painted walls: none. Wallpapered walls: you have a choice (maybe). If you want to remove the old wallpaper, rent a steamer, a piece of equipment which directs steam to small sections at a time, loosening it so that it may be pulled off. This process is slow and may take a day or so for a big room. If the wallpaper is still firmly attached to the wall, leave it up. Remove any loose edges and sand the area smooth.

Measuring for and selecting the wallpaper: Here is my advice. Forget you have windows and doors and measure the whole room. Measure the width of each of the four walls and then the height of the room. (Adjust these suggestions if you are doing just one or two sides.) Use a piece of graph paper and lay the walls side by side on the paper.

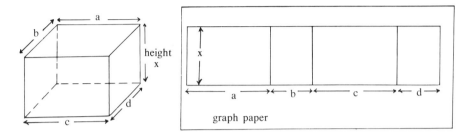

graph paper

With this piece of paper in hand, go browsing through the wallpaper books. Wallpaper comes in different widths. Your pattern selection will determine how much length to buy, based on width. With your graph paper you will quickly be able to calculate the length, once you are given the width. Another concern is how often the pattern repeats, for example, every 12 inches, or every 18 inches or every 24 inches. You may not want to select a pattern that repeats so infrequently (like a 24-inch one) because there will be too much wastage. For example, a 7-foot height means you could lose a foot for each panel.

Unless you have an excess of windows and doors, don't worry about the extra amount too much. If you are a novice, it provides you with a safety margin. The extra paper can also be used to give you a coordinated room. It can be used to cover wastepaper baskets, lampshades, valance and all sorts of boxes.

Wallpaper is available with either paper backing or material backing. My very strong recommendation is to get material-backed wallpaper, even though there is a larger selection in paper-backed patterns. When removing the paper-backed type, you will find that the paper backing remains on the wall—only the outside comes off. It is then necessary to apply hot rags to the paper and wipe it off (little shreds all over the floor!). Another disadvantage is that paper-backed wallpaper may rip if you move it around too much while positioning it on the wall. Material-backed wallpaper easily rips off the wall during removal and is also sturdy enough to take much repositioning.

Buy pretrimmed paper, not untrimmed, unless cost is a serious matter. The edges must be cut off both sides of untrimmed paper before you put it up. Why is this a problem? Wallpaper panels only meet, do not overlap. (How straight can you cut?)

Outer surfaces available are plain paper, vinyl-treated paper, textured (burlap, for example), flocked (the velvet look) and foil. Aside from the fact that vinyl-treated paper is preferable to untreated paper, the only other recommendation I have is this: You may be concerned about hiding flaws in the wall, in which case outer surface selection is important. Textured and flocked patterns and busy paper patterns will hide flaws well. Striped patterns will not, nor will shiny vinyl ("the wet look"). Old wallpaper seams or bumps will be visible, particularly in the wet look, which especially highlights these flaws.

The glue comes in a box as powder and is mixed in water before use. My sister, the paperhanger in the family, tells me her favorite brand is Metylan—because it is mildew-proof, and doesn't discolor (some glues turn brownish, which is undesirable under light-colored patterns, she says); and also because the mixed glue will stay in good shape for about two weeks (just add a bit of water).

An economy tip: Wallpaper comes in single rolls, double rolls and triple rolls. (A double roll is a continuous roll of paper twice as long as a single roll.) For a very big project, get triple rolls. Less wastage.

One final piece of advice for novices: Select a striped pattern for your first attempt so that you don't have to learn all the techniques at once. Save pattern matching for the next job.

Hanging the wallpaper: Measure away from the corner, horizontally, the width of the paper, minus one or two inches. Hang the plumb line from the ceiling edge. Corners aren't always straight. Use this plumb line to pencil or chalk a guideline for your first piece, which should go around the corner a bit, for those one or two inches. Pick

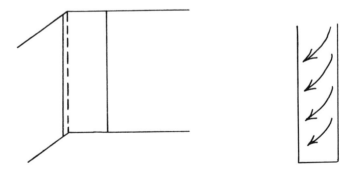

a corner you care about. God knows how you'll be ending up. Maybe you'll only have half or less of a width at the end. Measure, adding an inch or so, and cut the first piece. Apply the glue with the glue brush . . . not too thick . . . and put the paper up on the wall. Position it carefully along the guideline; it should move easily. Next, you must smooth it, removing all the bubbles. Use the smoothing brush (bristle side for flocked and foil, wood-handle side for paper or flat textures) and start at the top, moving in a sweeping arc downward, not straight down. Never go back up, either arced or straight. The extra inch, which should end up on the bottom, is extra margin. (Some papers shrink with glue.) The lower margin can all be cut off at the end of the job, and it can be more easily trimmed after the glue dries a bit. If the placement goes badly, pull it off, put it right back up and smooth it into position again.

Next, cut all the pieces for the wall, or at least enough to reach a door or window. Use a metal yardstick to draw the line for cutting. (Wooden yardsticks warp.) Cut the paper with scissors, or cut with a razor guided by the metal yardstick. (I am told that the circular-disk trimmers are not a very good investment because they are not effective on flocked or textured papers.) You may want to draw the cutting line using a T square to guarantee a perpendicular-to-the-edge line.

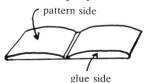

pattern side

glue side

Glue each piece. Fold them over, glue to glue and lay them on the floor. Folding them keeps the glue from drying out. You save time by doing similar jobs in bulk.

The panels are not supposed to overlap, just meet exactly. Therefore, place the panel up, leaving some leeway between it and the one already up, maybe an eighth of an inch or so, and smooth it in arcs toward the meeting edge in order to position it. You will quickly learn how much to leave between when you grapple with the problem. For a final debubbling on each panel, the second smoothing effort, after correct placement is attained, should be a vertical smoothing, down only.

Bubbles discovered later can be removed by pricking the paper with a pin. Or, if it's a big bubble, slit the paper with a razor and insert some glue with a toothpick.

After smoothing is completed, run the seam roller down along the seam to press it together. Remove any sqwooshed-out glue with a sponge as soon as you finish a panel.

Around windows, doors and outlets: Cut less off, so that you have an excess, an overhang, and cut it off after the wallpaper is up on the wall. It's much too tricky trying to cut out the exact dimension. Remove the plates covering electric outlets for a finished look. (Don't if you don't care.) Perhaps you might also feel safe cutting off the electricity while the plates are off. (That limits you to daytime or candlelight[?], so you decide about that.)

Washing wallpaper: Use a very mild soap, not a harsh detergent, or you will eventually wash away the pattern . . . on some papers.

PLASTERING

Prepainting preparations include sealing cracks. The crack is a crack in plaster, if you have plaster walls, so you must fill the crack with plaster. For very thin cracks, take a pin, or something else thin, and scrape around the edges of the crack to remove any loose plaster particles and dust. You may then use a premixed, ready-to-use, vinyl plaster, like Dap, which comes in a can and can be applied to the crack with a knife or a trowel. Dap, my favorite, dries within an hour, then can be sanded and painted over. Or you might prefer to use plaster to which you add water—follow the mixing directions carefully to get the right consistency. This is probably a cheaper way. I think it might take longer to dry. Check the box. The brand of this most familiar to me, and maybe to you, is Spackle.

For larger holes, you may have to stuff some newspaper in the hole first, to give some backing and to save on plaster. The trick to making the plaster adhere well in these larger cracks is to wet down both the paper and the edges of the plaster edges of the crack. Plaster adheres best to wet surfaces. A good tool for this purpose is a water pistol. That will wet the edges well. The paper can be wetted before it is inserted.

For very large holes, plaster is not the best idea. The kind of holes the plumber leaves in your ceiling after he fixes a pipe are huge, and often the lath behind the plaster he broke into is also gone. The answer here is a piece of Sheetrock cut to fit. However, the Sheetrock won't just sit up there against nothing. You first have to nail some wood backing to the beams; yes, you may have to make the hole larger to accomplish this. Then cut a piece of Sheetrock to fit (see earlier instructions on cutting Sheetrock). Nail the Sheetrock up to the backing. Next. fill the edges, at which the Sheetrock meets the plaster ceiling, with plaster. Lay perforated tape over the seam and press it, allowing the plaster to sqwoosh through. (If it doesn't, put some on a trowel and apply it on the tape outside.) Give it the once-over with the trowel to even it, scraping off the excess. After it dries, it can be sanded and painted. (See pages 64–65 for illustrations of Sheetrock, trowels and perforated tape.)

Here are two other approaches to that hole:
1) Make the hole square. Cut a square of Sheetrock to fit, but let the paper on one side be bigger, an overhang. Make a hole in the center and push a piece of coat hanger wire through, bending it in the back. Leave enough coming out from the front to hold it. Dab some plaster on the wall edges and Sheetrock edges where they will meet. Also dab some plaster on the outer wall to meet the paper overhang. Place the piece in position, holding the wire as an aid, press the paper against the plaster and the wall behind, smoothing the excess plaster with a trowel to hide the edges of the paper. Push the wire through to the inside wall, or cut it off, and dab some plaster over that little hole in the middle of the patch.

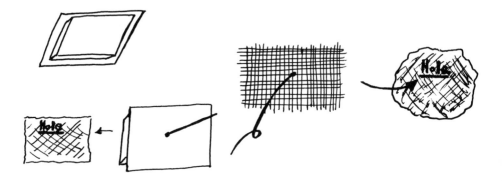

2) A piece of wire mesh, cut larger than the hole, and with a piece of string tied to its center, can be pushed through the hole and held against the inside of the hole with the string while a layer of plaster is applied. (Apply not-too-thick layers, one at a time, after the previous one is completely dry.)

DOORS

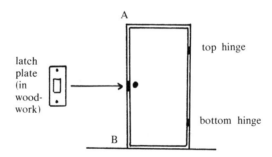

latch
plate
(in
wood-
work)

A

top hinge

bottom hinge

B

CORNER A STICKS

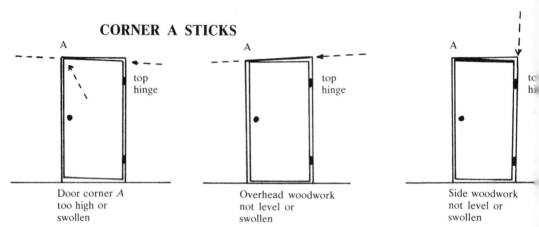

A

top
hinge

Door corner *A*
too high or
swollen

A

top
hinge

Overhead woodwork
not level or
swollen

A

to
hi

Side woodwork
not level or
swollen

These exaggerated pictures may give you some idea of the kinds of things that can cause problems with doors.

Often the simplest solution is to widen the space between the side of the door and the side woodwork, in the above case at the top hinge. If you look at the illustrations above, you will see (in your head) that more space at the top-hinge area will bring the corner of the door at the top *A* down and away from the top woodwork. Most of the time this works, but not always. Let it be the first thing you try.

1) Cut a piece of cardboard (cut two or three in order to be prepared) the same size as one side of the hinge so that the cardboard will fit behind it. Unscrew the hinge (top) of the woodwork side, place the piece of cardboard behind that hinge and screw the hinge back on. Try the extras if one isn't enough. This piece of cardboard now has a name: a shim. The process is "shimming."

CORNER B STICKS

If the corner sticking is the bottom corner *(B)*, shim the bottom hinge (top sticks—top hinge; bottom sticks—bottom hinge).

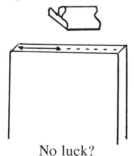

No luck?

2) Now you will have to try sanding the corner, or the whole top if it looks as though the top is flushly a smidgen tight. Use a sandpaper block or an electric sander on the top of the door, the part facing the sky. With a ladder or high chair you should be able to accomplish this without removing the door.

No luck?

3) Sorry, but the next option is to plane the top to remove more wood than a sanding will. Not too much at a time—a plane is not a saw. If you can't see the grain of the wood because of paint, you will soon know whether you're planing in the right direction, because the plane will keep getting stuck. Turn it and plane in the opposite direction. (This is probably the *best first approach* if the door is actually *hitting the woodwork* and not going within it at all.) If you would prefer to remove the door to do the planing, look first at the hinges to see if

they have pins holding the two parts together. If so, aim from under *(a)* with a fat nail and a hammer if the paint has made the hinge pins stuck. If the pins are nice and loose, you can insert a screwdriver tip at the top *(b)* and pull the pin out. Remove the *bottom hinge pin first,* maybe sticking a thin piece of wood under the hinge side of the door to help brace it, and then remove the top hinge pin. (If no pins, unscrew the screws from the hinges in the woodwork, not from the door. This I recommend because screwing them back in is easier, the woodwork is stationary, the door too wobbly when rescrewing.)

Determine how much to plane off by marking the side of the door top before you take the door down. If the amount that has to be removed is really a lot, perhaps you would be better off moving the hinges in the door and woodwork. This has to be done in both, unless the difference is tremendous, or you will be making the new screw holes too close to or even partially in the previous ones. (Sorry, this is a real dog of a job, or at least it is one to me, especially if I must chisel new spaces for the hinges . . . which I must if the vertical fit is tight.)

DOOR WON'T STAY CLOSED

This is an easy one. Shim the latch plate in the woodwork (and shim both hinges, too, to gain tighter fit if you need to). Cut some cardboard to fit behind the latch plate, remove the latch plate, put the cardboard behind and screw it back on. A thin piece of wood is an alternate to the cardboard.

Screws also loose? Use some matchsticks jammed into the screw hole, not protruding. The matchsticks fall down in a hole? I have the same problem, but only with one hole, so I live with it. The other screw sits there OK, because the screw that fits tightly holds the plate well. What would I do if I were you, with two holes? If you are more ambitious than I (there are lots of jobs I'm lazy about) you could take off the woodwork and replace it if it's not repairable, or nail a piece of wood in the back to stop the hole exit. Or you could try epoxy-gluing the matches into the holes and screwing after the glue is dry.

P.S. I tried something and it worked . . . and it may be the best method! I jammed wood putty into the hole, let it dry for two days, then drilled a tiny hole and replaced the screw. This method was also used where screws had come loose from hinges for a very heavy door . . . and the door is still up.

SIDE OF DOOR STICKS

Sand, plane, saw (on hinge side, not lock side) or buy a new door. Or you could try mortise hinges. They look like this. They occupy the space of only one side of the hinge, because one part is cut out to fit into the other.

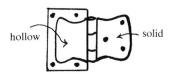

hollow   solid

This type of hinge is also a neat way of eliminating the chiseling out of hinge space, one side at least, both if you have the leeway for the hinge, without making the door fit too snugly. (Less work is less work! You learn to live with your own ways.)

LATCH-PLATE HOLE TOO LOW OR TOO HIGH TO RECEIVE LOCK

Move the plate up or down accordingly. Fill the prior holes tightly with matchsticks. This type of thing is not like a hinge hole, where strength is required and going into old holes partially is bad. Here the job really requires only that the plate sit there relatively secured.

SCREEN DOORS

Let's make one, and the answer to some of your problems may be obvious.

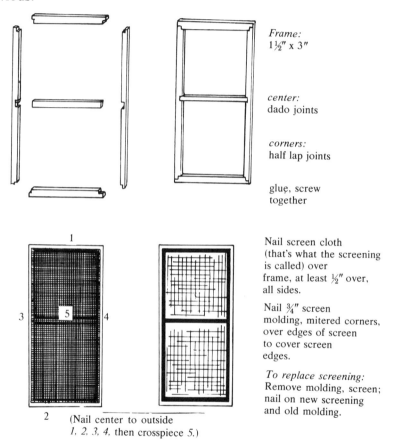

Frame:
1½" x 3"

center:
dado joints

corners:
half lap joints

glue, screw
together

Nail screen cloth
(that's what the screening
is called) over
frame, at least ½" over,
all sides.

Nail ¾" screen
molding, mitered corners,
over edges of screen
to cover screen
edges.

To replace screening:
Remove molding, screen;
nail on new screening
and old molding.

(Nail center to outside
1, 2, 3, 4, then crosspiece *5.*)

Screen patch: Save leftover pieces for patching. Pull off some outside strands, 4 sides, bend edge strands, stick through screening, bend back. Secure by threading some previously removed strands in and out.

DOORKNOBS, LOCKS

AND SECURITY

DOORKNOB

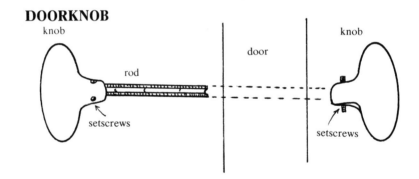

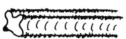

Many doorknobs (old-fashioned ones) are connected by a square threaded rod that passes through a square hole in the latch mechanism within the door. The rod, threaded at the square points, screws into the knobs at each end. The setscrews are tightened against the rod after the knobs are in place. The rod will go quite a way into the knobs. Set one side into a knob, push it through the hole and then screw it into the other knob. Be sure the setscrews in that other knob are loose, and not in the way of the rod entering, for the rod must go in as far as necessary. It is because of the square rod and square hole that the latch is withdrawn when the knob is turned, so the door may be opened or held closed. Get a tiny-tip screwdriver and take a door-knob apart to look at. You'll see what I mean.

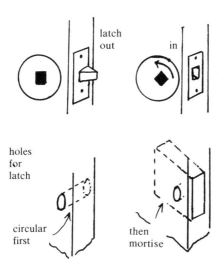

LOCK

A typical spring lock is one with all the housing attached outside the door. The lock is screwed on, with a hole drilled through the door for the actual lock mechanism to pass through and sit in. There is usually a template guide with a new lock for where the hole should be drilled in the box.

First, let's look at the parts.

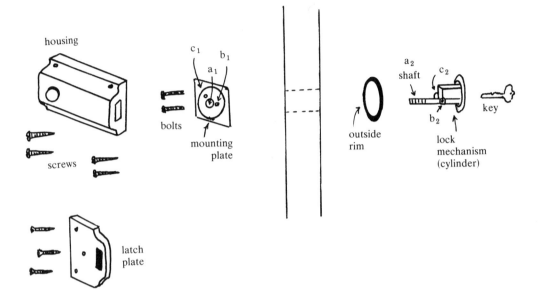

After the hole is drilled in the door, place the lock mechanism (slipped through the rim) through the hole from the outside of the door. Place the mounting plate against the inside of the door so that the shaft (a_2) passes through the large hole in the plate (a_1). Bolts passed through holes c_1 and b_1 will now screw into the holes in the lock mechanism $(b_2$ and $c_2)$. The mechanism is now held rigid on the door. The shaft may be too long for the housing to fit tightly against the door; and if this happens, snap some of the shaft off. Those little ridged lines on the shaft are partial guide cuts to facilitate shortening the shaft. Next, screw the housing over the mounting plate, in the proper place. The template should indicate where the screws are to go in relation to the drilled hole. If you have no template, take a thin piece of paper and lay it over the back of the housing. Mark the outline of the housing and the places where the screws go. There is also a space behind there where the mounting plate fits, a rectangular space; mark that too. The mounting plate is not flat, but has a circular indentation so that it sits well in the drilled hole. Lay the plate under the paper and pencil the circle within the rectangular space already drawn. This should complete the template.

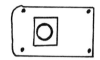

In order to set the latch plate snugly into the woodwork so that it may receive the lock, it is necessary to chisel a bit of the wood away from the woodwork, just the thickness of the plate where the screws go to hold it to the woodwork. After that's done, hold the plate there, close the door (with the lock attached) and test to see if the latch (or bolt, if that's the kind you have) fits into the hole in the latch plate when locked. If not, but the vertical height of the plate is OK, chisel some of the front of the woodwork away. If all of this works out smoothly (and it doesn't always the first time), you can screw in the latch plate and you have a new lock!

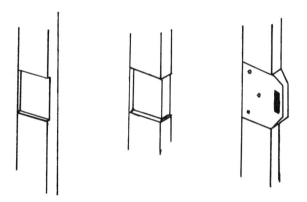

Other types of outside-housing locks are similar. New locks should come with fairly good instructions. (If they don't, write and complain to the manufacturer. Locks are expensive; the cost of a locksmith about doubles the cost of some locks.)

SECURITY

I wonder how much of our lives is spent worrying about our security. I wonder what percentage of our money has been spent making veritable fortresses of our homes. For those of us who live in cities, where fortresses are the only way to guard our property and our lives, the worry is always with us . . . the money always "well spent" . . . but too often the alleviated worry after the purchase of some new security device is short-lived. I have often felt one step behind, not ahead of, the latest break-and-entry method. I devise security after I've heard of a new way, but I'm always worrying what will come next. . . .

When I was young and single and living in an area popular with burglars because most of the population worked during the day, I was burgled often. The loss was not great, as I look back now, because I didn't really have much. One time the most important loss was a radio, an old one. And actually, as I look around my house now, I still don't have "valuables"—no rare paintings, no expensive jewelry. But I do have the pawnables—TV, phonograph, a couple of radios— and it would be an expense to replace them. Those of us with small children usually have someone home in the daytime, if not ourselves, our babysitters; thus the likelihood of daytime burglary is not great. Those of us who work and leave our houses empty during the day need more security measures. And for the nighttime, we all must be protected adequately so we can sleep.

A policeman once told me, after one of those early burglaries, that there is almost no way to be sure of your security. "If a burglar wants to get in, he'll get in!" he said. "However," he added, "the trick is to make it very hard and time-consuming. They want to be in and out swiftly." This is surely the best security philosophy and one I have tried to employ. In its simplest form it means that two locks are better than one, three better than two, etc. I heard an ingenious idea about lots of locks that I'd like to pass on to you. A woman had *ten* locks on her door! Every day she locked only five of them and noted down which locks were locked. What would happen if the burglar came . . . passkeys, picks and all? Simple. He'd unlock some and lock others, and I doubt if he'd ever figure out the combination, don't you? Yes, each type of lock turns a particular direction to open, and surely many burglars know this, if they know the brand, but then it depends upon which side of the door the lock is on; and besides, it would take a long time before he was on to exactly what was happening. I think he'd give up. I like that invention, particularly for the daytime, but I think one has to be pretty organized to use this plan. What if you lost the code?

For the nighttime, besides whatever locks-with-keys you have, extra devices should be used. Chains, even those with key locks, are good, but I never feel too secure about them. If the burglar got the locks opened, I feel certain he could break the chain. Here's one of the measures I've taken with chain locks: A screw, screwed into the woodwork under the woodwork plate of the chain, allows you to hook a link of the chain over it. The chain is then held tight. (Use a long screw, so that it is well into the woodwork.)

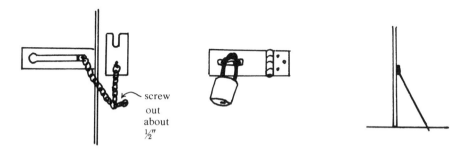

A couple of hasps and padlocks help. The padlocks do not have to be locked but should be kept hanging on to hold the hasp closed. The key(s) should hang on the woodwork nearby in case you need to get out quickly.

One other door device which could be employed is an adaptation of the police lock (a bar from the door into the floor; the bar is removable from the outside with a key, but it inhibits forcing the door). Place a thick rod flush against the door and let it sit in a hole in the floor, a hole drilled at least 1 inch down. A type of rod that could be used is a ½-inch-diameter threaded rod 3 feet long. It can be held against the door by the part of the hasp-lock device that holds the lock. Perhaps these parts can be bought separately.

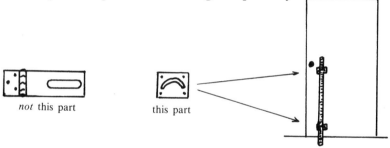

Actually, you could use the other part, too, under the rod as extra security. The device should be of a size that the rod slips in and out of comfortably. And maybe for ultra comfort-of-security you could add some kind of gadget that would sit on top of the rod to hold it down, but movable so that the rod could be pulled out.

Among the other locks, the regular one on your door should be a type in which a key is needed on both sides, especially if there is glass in the door.

Any combination of all these gadgets should give the burglar a long, hard time . . . and an overhead light will make him more nervous.

Windows are a more worrisome proposition. Glass breaks easily . . . but not soundlessly. However, a thought to remember: it must be forcibly banged to break. Glass cutters don't work, my glass-cutting man tells me. If you will recall, when you cut glass, you sear it, and then you press one side of it down; underneath is empty. The other side of glass is braced up higher from underneath. So a glass cutter isn't what a burglar uses to get in. A lot of good this knowledge about there-must-be-noise does you if you are a sound sleeper or out at the time. Again, the tactic to employ is to make the job hard and time consuming.

One of the window-security techniques I have employed resulted from putting up a store-bought device wrong, and then realizing the security advantage of leaving the mistake as it was. Available is this device, which, properly placed, keeps the window from being opened from the outside. It is supposed to be attached on the top surface of the bottom window and screwed into the wood of the upper window.

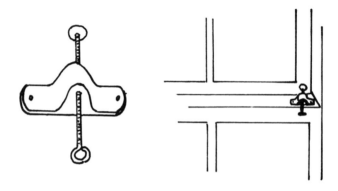

The pressure from screwing it tight prevents the top window from moving. However, it has always seemed to me that if the burglar managed to break a small enough section so that his hand would fit through, he could simply untwist the device and gain entry.

This device, along with many other things we occasionally pick up in hardware stores, was a "loosie," one of many, unpackaged and lying in a bin. Without instructions, I put it up this way, on the top window:

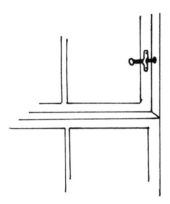

I screwed the bolt tightly against the window frame.

A few days later I realized that I couldn't open the window past the device; the bottom window hit it and there wasn't enough room between windows for the device. So, I quickly told myself, if I can't open the window, neither can the burglar. And if he breaks the glass, he will have to remove the screws and take the device off. That will take longer than just twisting the bolt around, as in the case of the "properly placed" one. I measured the window opening allowed by the device. No, a body couldn't fit through! I put one on the other side, just to make the screw-unscrewing job longer for a persistent burglar, and have been happy about that invention for years. A screwdriver is kept nearby in case of emergency and the kids are trained. This is not good to use on fire-escape windows. We don't have that problem, but you might.

A friend told me of an invention of his for the fire-escape window. I think it's an excellent one. Get some 1-by-1-inch wood, cut in lengths equal to the distance between the top of the bottom window and the top of the frame *(X)*. Place these lengths in the corners, above the bot-

tom window. The bottom can't be forced up because it hits the wood. Paint the wood the same color as the woodwork and it is almost invisible to a burglar. It should be fitted snugly so that it can't easily fall out. However, you should be able to pull it out from inside. Screw a little screw eye near the bottom, into the side of the wood facing you, so that it's less visible, and attach a piece of string or wire to it. You or the children could pull on this string or wire to get the wood out in an emergency.

Now that I've given away all my security inventions, I have to get busy inventing others. What if the burglar read this book? He'd know how to get into my house!

WINDOWS

REPLACING A PANE OF GLASS

Glass is held in the frame against a framework of triangular mold-ing on one side and putty on the other side. The side to work from is the putty side. The putty side is fairly easy to spot—it's not even, like a piece of wood. (It's "thumb-evened.")

Remove the broken glass first, pulling out whatever will come out without too much effort. If the window is located in a hazardous spot, where some glass could accidentally fall on someone below, tape it, on the outside if you can, or, even better, put a piece of Con-Tact paper on it to hold it together, wherever necessary; and then work away at removing the rest. Save the little glazier points as they come out.

Next remove the putty, using a strong knife or a chisel.

The replacing glass should be cut slightly smaller than the space . . . a smidgen, maybe $\frac{1}{16}$ inch less all around, at least, to allow for swelling of the wood on moist days, or the frame might sqwunch the glass.

Roll a thin strip of glazier putty ($\frac{1}{4}$ inch) and line the frame with it.

Place the glass into the frame against the puttied molding. Insert glazier points every 6 inches or so, or wherever they were before.*

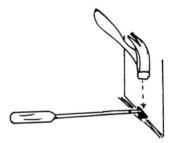

Finally, line the outside of the glass edges with rolled putty, again about $\frac{1}{4}$ inch or more in diameter, and press it triangularly into the corners, as the putty was before. The putty will take about four days to dry well enough to paint.

DOUBLE WINDOWS WITH WEIGHTS

Words, words, words! How do some things get their names? For years I have not been able to understand how to remove my windows because of one word: *sash*. I have read and read (but probably not looked too carefully at the illustrations), and I never got past the line ". . . then remove the sash." In my head the sash always meant the chain holding the weight in the framework of the window. This mystery was recently cleared up for me. "The sash *is* the window, it is the wooden framework that holds the glass and which slides up and down." I went back to the books and all is clear now. And all the sections of that wooden framework have names.

---

*Lay edge of screwdriver or chisel horizontally on top of glazier side (point going into wood); let hammer slide down along glass to edge of screwdriver or chisel.

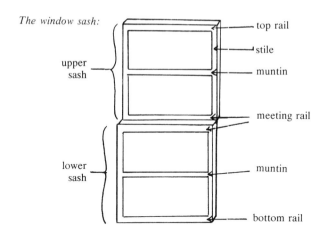

The window sash:

upper sash

lower sash

top rail

stile

muntin

meeting rail

muntin

bottom rail

The upper and lower sashes sit in the window frame and move up and down in tracks. The tracks are made by nailing strips of wood to the frame.

Since they are usually only nailed in, they may easily be pried out with a chisel.

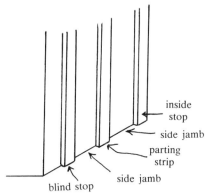

inside stop

side jamb

parting strip

side jamb

blind stop

Remove the blind stop to remove the bottom sash (bottom window). Next, push the upper sash down so that it rests on the bottom. Pry off the parting strip to remove the upper sash.

Actually, you can't remove the window yet without removing the weights attached to the side of the sash.

The open-window positions are maintained because a weight, sitting in a hollow behind the side jamb, is attached to the side of the

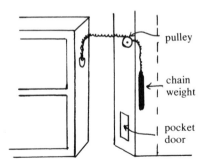

sash by a chain. The chain passes over a pulley as it comes out of the hollow. This provides ease of movement. In the illustration, I have pulled the units apart for viewing.

The pulleys for both the upper and lower sashes are at the top of the frame. Before you pull out the sashes, put a nail through a link of each chain, near the pulley, to keep the weight and chain from falling into the hollow. Then pull out the sash and unhook the chain from the side.

If you should lose the chain down the hole, don't fret. There is an access door on the side, low. It may be only barely visible because of many layers of paint, but it is there. The door is not hinged and may easily be pried off with the tip of a screwdriver or chisel. The blind stop and parting strip will have to be removed to get at that door.

My guess is that the weight of the sash is equal to the weight of the sash weight and this is why the window will sit in any position. Therefore, if you replace a sash you will have to replace the weight.

If the window is loose and it rattles, it may need a repositioning of the stop and/or parting strips. Or it may be too far from the jamb. A thin piece of wood can be nailed against the jamb filling the space; or if the space is less than ⅜ inch, use a piece of felt strip against the jamb.

If the windows are too tight and they stick, it may only be necessary to remove some layers of paint with paint remover. You might also be able to solve this problem by moving the stop and parting strips, giving the window moving room.

If you suspect that dampness is the culprit, it would be wise to plane down one side of the sash. New windows should be given a coat of priming paint to seal the wood, and dampness problems will be avoided.

HANGING CURTAIN AND DRAPERY RODS

There is almost nothing to say. As you have probably realized after all these pages, the trick is in knowing what the walls are made of and that the woodwork is wood. The hardware may be as simple as a screw, or it may have to be more complicated—a toggle, molly, plaster plug or even a lead plug, depending on the design of the rod device.

One additional suggestion for the seeming disaster cases in which nothing seems to work: Epoxy-glue some wood to the wall. Yes, it works beautifully and the hold is very durable. Then you have wood to work with . . . Nature's gift.

SHADES WON'T WORK, WON'T STAY UP?

In one side of the rod holding the shade is a little spring. If it isn't broken, it may just need to be wound tighter. Get up on a ladder, pull out the side from the holding device which has a slit for removing it. The other end of the rod has a flat piece projecting from it. This is attached to the spring. With this side in, wind the shade rod around. You should feel the spring tightening . . . not too tight, or it will keep flying up again. (This may be an easier task if you first wind the shade up all around the rod. Take the shade down, wind it up, then put the flat end in the elongated slot and wind up the spring.)

Have a look at how that shade is attached to the rod. It's stapled on. You may want to replace the shade someday with some lively material . . . an easy job. Use sturdy material.

UNFINISHING, FINISHING AND FIXING FURNITURE

This is one heck of a topic for a cellar constructionist like me to attempt. I'm not there yet! As much as I would like to know everything in the world, I don't . . . and that's as it should be. Besides, what fun would it be if there was nothing new to learn, to try, and to make mistakes with?

I'll tell you about my shutters. The brownstone house I bought is one of a string of duplicates, about six or so. A good friend of mine owned one two doors away, and she had completely renovated the house, restoring it to its original Victorian quality. Among the assets of this beautiful house were the parlor-floor shutters, which were pure walnut, and a magnificent staircase, also walnut. These had been restored beautifully. My house at purchase was almost entirely different. It had been converted into four apartments, all the molding and fireplace mantels had been removed and the fireplaces plastered up (they are now freed); and new walls had been put up to facilitate apartment dwelling, with a kitchen and bath on each floor. As I said earlier, my lack of money meant that I had to live with much of it.

However, one of the first things I looked at, when I was examining the house before purchase, was the parlor-floor shutters. They were there, nailed closed . . . no problem, I'd get them open, and I did. It was the first thing I did after I moved in. A scratch in a hidden place revealed that they were walnut! If I had nothing else, I would have

286

beautiful shutters in my front window . . . someday . . . when I got all
the paint off and sanded and waxed them. HA! The following summer
I set about the task. (Four years ago, and I'm not even half-finished
yet!)

STRIPPING

Stripping is the process of removing the paint. You just paint on
some paint remover (Zip Strip is my favorite), let it set about twenty
minutes and wipe it off. You can gently scrape off the flat areas with
a thin putty knife. Then use rags and Q-tips in the tiny areas. (That's
the story I got.)

I set myself all up in the backyard. Got some old tin cans so that
I could push the gunk off the edge into the cans, and heaps of rags,
and a box of Q-tips, and rubber gloves. It is not recommended that
you let this substance get on your skin; it's like acid. However, just
some cold water will wash it off. So . . . I painted the paint remover
all over the top surface of one of the shutters . . . and I sat out in the
sun for the waiting time, feeling smug. (In a couple of weeks, no one
would be able to imagine what a disaster area the inside of my house
had been, because of the lovely . . . handsome . . . walnut shutters
outside. Another restored house, people would comment as they
passed. Dreams like this I had out there in the sun. Well, it was a good
dream, anyhow.)

The twenty minutes were up. I leaped to the task. I started,
gently(!) to push the gunk (paint mixed with the remover) along the
outside of the panel. Oh, God! It's beautiful . . . it's walnut . . . not
many layers of paint . . . a breeze! But as I pushed the gunk along, it
grew in thickness and spilled over into the center, lower panels and
all the grooves of the wood. I went into the house for the massive
Sunday papers and placed them all around under all sides of the shutter, which was up on two milk boxes. This time I pushed the stuff over
the side, swiftly, so that not too much would dribble onto the center.
I remember that I was hurrying a lot, pushing all that mush over the
side, and I was running around a lot.

OK, the edges were done, now the flat center, and I'd do the shutter strips last. I started to scrape the center panel. Where can I push

this stuff? Up over the edge . . . oh, no, not that again! I grabbed some rags and tried wiping some off but the rags didn't absorb too well. Perseverance. Three hours later, at least, I was ready to tackle the shutter strips. The paint remover had loosened them. I figured I'd just scrape them and let it fall to the ground. Take a look at a shutter some time. The gunk sat in the corner ends; it seeped around to the other side (which I hadn't put remover on) . . . the putty knife would do only half a strip (the strips touch each other when closed), so then I had to turn the whole damn shutter over onto the other side to get at the rest of the strip. . . .

What a job! It was night before I was satisfied that I had finished, that all the gunk was off . . . off one side of one shutter. There are eight sections, two sides to each, fifteen more sides to go! And they all had to be sanded and waxed or varnished.

The end to this story is that the uppers are still under the paint. The lowers were six-eighths finished by this summer . . . I did one or two sides each summer.

A new family moved in next door this summer and one of the tasks they decided to do was to strip the shutters, or, rather, have it done. They were carrying all the shutters to the car and I inquired where they were taking them. "To a fabulous place where they dip them and remove the paint," they responded.

"Oh, I don't think you should do that," I cautioned. "I've heard that that process can ruin the shutters, lye is too strong for the walnut." Me, I knew from nothing, but I'd heard that.

"No problem," they said, "we asked about that. They said they never lost a shutter."

"Listen," I said, "would you take mine with you?"

"Sure."

I raced upstairs, took down the bottoms—even the sides I had done could use some additional work. The tops, still untouched, wouldn't come loose. The screws were all painted over and there was at least an hour's work ahead if I was to get them out. "Take these with you today. I'll send the tops with you when you go to get the others. . . . And thanks, you're saving me ten years of work!"

Two weeks later I was not home when they left for the pickup, so the tops didn't go . . . thank God! The bottoms came home warped, cracked, just about ruined but not quite. "The man said that the chemical reacted with what you had used to remove the paint, perhaps. Sorry. And he said to let them dry thoroughly for two weeks before sanding them." (The wood was all mushy and thick.) That isn't all that was wrong, but the story is too long already. Don't dip your good woods, unless you are in control.

Being in control means a vat of lye in your cellar. You have to use it all up, or how do you get rid of it? You can't throw it down the pipe; it will eat the pipe away.

No, I'm not going to paint the whole mess. I'm just waiting for another sunny day.

SANDING

On fine furniture, be careful not to use a coarse sandpaper. It will leave deep ridges. Use fine sandpaper and move with the grain of wood, so the result is smooth and invisible. How do you get into those tiny areas? Use steel wool on the softened paint in those crevices. Push it through with your finger. And you can use this on any little spots that didn't quite come off in the scraping-wiping procedure.

VARNISH OR SHELLAC? OR WHAT?

Varnish should be used on furniture on which a durable finish is required, like a table top. Because of the strength of the finish, it is most resistant to water marks and heat marks from hot dishes. However, for this there is a price. The varnish must be applied very carefully. More than one coat is necessary. It should be allowed to dry overnight before a second coat is put on. If there are any little bubble marks, use fine steel wool or very fine sandpaper, rubbed lightly over the surface. The thinner for varnish is turpentine.

Shellac in comparison to varnish leaves much to be desired, in almost all areas except that of applying it. It dries almost within a half hour and you can debubble with fine sandpaper or steel wool and get on to the second coat. That coat should be allowed to dry for at least two hours. However, shellac is marked by water, hot dishes and spilled alcohol—and worse than that, it gets sticky on damp days. Don't use it on chair seats or anything else on which this stickiness would be unpleasant. (I wonder why people use shellac.) The thinner for shellac is denatured alcohol.

A word about *thinners.* They are noted because it is useful to know how to thin a material, especially if the substance is a bit old and needs some thinning. More important, they are mentioned because they are the ingredient to use for removal of that substance. If you want to remove varnish, you use turpentine and plenty of muscle, similarly for shellac and denatured alcohol. In addition, these thinners are the thinning device to cut the substance with if you are using it to seal the wood after staining, to prevent the stain from bleeding into the finish coat. The formula for making the sealer is 4 to 1. Four parts of thinner to one part of the finish: i.e., 4 parts of denatured alcohol to 1 part of shellac; 4 parts of turpentine to 1 part of varnish.

Lacquer is much like varnish in its strong and resistant surface. However it dries *very, very* fast, almost immediately. This means your workmanship—brushwork!—must be careful, or you will end up applying many corrective coats. Debubble between coats. Lacquer is a good thing to apply to hardware to keep it from tarnishing. The thinning agent is lacquer thinner. (That's what to ask for.)

Linseed oil will give a duller finish than varnish, shellac or lacquer. For this dull finish, much desired these days, prepare yourself. It could take months! First, you brush on boiled linseed oil thinned with turpentine, 2 to 1 (2 parts of linseed, 1 part turpentine). The application is easy; just brush it on freely (each time). After the first application rub the oil into the wood for about a half hour. Use a coarse rag for rubbing. Let this application set for about two or three days while the oil sinks into the wood. If it's still damp, leave it longer. No, you are not finished yet, you've barely begun. You will need about five applications of oil, and much, much rubbing after each coat of oil, as long as you can stand it. And you should space the additional coats each no closer together than a week. I make that about six weeks, six very tired rubbing weeks, six weeks without a table, or whatever. But it will look beautiful, positively! And you will have a long-tired-rubbing story to tell in gatherings of do-it-yourselfers. Finally, you can easily restore vitality to the surface by giving it ONE MORE COAT . . . AND MUCH RUBBING . . . when it wears.

Wax is a shining agent and can be applied to most finished surfaces, oiled ones included. I didn't say "sheening" agent—shining agent, a dull shine.

Now, do you want to know what I do? I build everything (or leave it as I found it in the street—for a rainy day of fixing, restoring, etc., but that rainy day never comes). I build with pine because it is the cheapest wood. I sand here and there, over the very rough and visible places only, careful not to destroy my cellar-construction mystique, and then I apply one coat of walnut Minwax, a combination of stain and wax. No, I don't shine the wax because the wood is usually too rough from being unsanded. To each her own!

FLOORS—LINOLEUM, TILES, SCRAPING, SANDING AND FINISHING

SANDING

Pure wood floors are truly the most handsome kind of floors to have, if you can. This is how I feel. This is one of those things easier said than done, however.

If you have a bit of money, "to have some things done," this is a very good place to invest some and get in a professional to scrape the floors. I have heard complaints from the best of the do-it-yourselfers who have tried scraping their own floors. No one seems quite prepared for this mechanical gadget, the floor scraper, which at times seems more like a robot with a mind of its own. The most difficult part is trying not to gouge the floors away or making big dents, by going over a section too often. Starting from painted floors makes the job ten times worse, which I conclude by watching people at the task.

If you still want to try it, and are prepared to breathe in all that sawdust, here's the scoop: (1) Rent a sander. (2) Hammer down all protruding nails. (3) As soon as you turn the sander on, get going across the floor. Travel with the long lengths of wood, don't go across them. As soon as you reach the other side of the room, turn off the scraper, turn the scraper around and cross the floor again, scraping a new section. I think this would be better than turning with the machine on, for you may leave tracks. This will take care of most of

292

the floor, but not the edges near the wall. For this task you must also rent the edger scraper, and then get down on your hands and knees and crawl around the room in order to finish the job. (I think I simply don't like this job because of the sawdust-ingestion potential, just as I don't like spray painting . . . or is it just the work?)

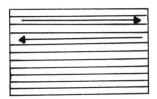

That one little paragraph above in no way does justice to the enormity of the job, nor does it give you any indication of how sorry you may be if you try it, and are miserable as a result. Do it, by all means, if you are so inclined . . . what I might hate, you may enjoy, I know that. I'm really just giving you some of my impressions (don't-say-I-didn't-tell-you-so stuff). Buy plenty of sandpaper for the sander when you rent it, and change it as frequently as you feel comfortable about. I do want to recommend that you economy-shop about this decision to do or to have done (scraping only). Check on the cost of renting all the equipment and the purchase of the sandpaper. Then get an estimate for a scraping-only job from someone a neighbor can recommend. Compare the prices. The difference could be small enough to have a professional do it and could also mean even floors. But be sure to use people highly recommended and look at their work first.

FINISHING

I haven't suggested having the floors professionally varnished or shellacked or whatever, because I think this is a safe project to try.

After the floors are scraped, vacuum over and over again until all dust is gone. Then wet-mop the floor so that the surface is really dust free. Let it dry thoroughly.

Varnish and shellac properties have just been discussed. My recommendation is neither for the floor. Rather, I suggest polyurethane. This finish will give you a hard, almost undentable surface, water-

proof, with a dull sheen and fantastic resistance even to scratches.
It's like a miracle. And the best brand I have found so far is FMB.

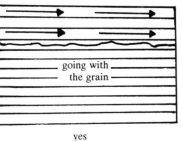
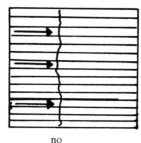
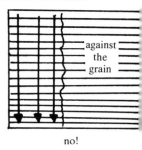

yes   no   no!

Again, paint this across the floor, traveling with the wood strips
in the floor. This is my method, rather than doing half the floor, stopping in the middle and going back to the wall again. I guess I think that
it is easier to blend at natural lines than take a chance that I'd have
any kind of visible blending across the middle of the floor, as in the
"no" picture.

Let the first coat dry overnight at least. It may take longer, particularly if the weather is damp. The second coat can be applied after
the first is completely dry. Yes, if you want all the properties of this
miracle that are mentioned above, do at least two coats. It's the same
as covering your floor with plastic.

STAINING

If you prefer a floor darker than the natural light color, stain before
finishing. (Floors are usually a light color because most frequently
the wood used is oak, a hard wood, appropriate for the tough job of
being a floor.) Buy a good-quality oil stain. Apply to the floor with a
2- or 3-inch brush and travel with the grain. Wipe the excess off with
a dry rag before the stain gets too settled. When is that? Well, for a
small floor, I'd do half and then wipe, then do the other half. You
have to let the last bit you brush on get set a little in order to match
the set of the beginning, so guide yourself accordingly to get an even
stain. Just don't wait too long. Do a big floor in patches. Stain takes
at least one to two days to dry, before you can apply a finish. If you
opt for shellac or varnish, seal the stain by brushing on a coat of the
appropriate sealer. (See the earlier paragraph on thinners for sealer
proportions.)

LINOLEUM

Laying down linoleum is another one of those tasks best done by a professional. (How do you unroll it if it's too wide for the room? That's my hangup.) However, because linoleum is sometimes cheaper than floor tiles, that savings could be shot on the expense of having it laid. The clue is to measure *very* carefully, and have it cut so that it can be unrolled—at least over most of the floor, if the room is not a perfect rectangle or square.

Remove all the wall-floor molding first. This will give you some margin for not meeting the edges everywhere. Start at the side where the cutouts for the radiator and/or pipes have to be made first. Save the pieces from cutouts for later patching . . . or in case your cut is wrong. A flat surface is a must if the linoleum is to last. Cover a bumpy, uneven wood floor with some sheets of ¼-inch Masonite, nailed in, before laying the linoleum. Make sure all the nails are hammered down well. Felt underlayers help preserve linoleum. The pieces of

felt underlayer should be placed across the boards, not traveling with them. The process for both the underlayer and the linoleum is to lay out, cut and trim to fit, then roll up and glue. Get the linoleum out of the way. Apply linoleum paste (glue) to the floor and roll the felt down onto it. The felt can be smoothed with a rolling pin. Next, position the rolled linoleum, apply the linoleum glue and roll the linoleum on as you go. Use the rolling pin again where the seams of the linoleum meet, to press them together.

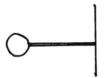

Cutouts for radiator legs and pipes are accomplished by cutting a line to the place where the circle must come out, rather than by just gouging out a circle. A good knife, the only kind to use for the trimming and cutting, looks like this:

FLOOR TILES

Years ago, before all the niceties of today, I heard of an ingenious way of putting down floor tiles. Double sticky tape! That approach appealed to me—no messy tile cement. It never dawned on me until just this minute to consider the task of cutting all those little pieces of tape! Now life is easier, for those of us who want it to be. There are self-sticking tiles available, and of good quality, both the tiles and the glue underneath. Yes, of course that's the route I took with a floor that needed covering when I didn't feel up to scraping. The quality is excellent and none of the tiles have loosened; the job was done at least a year and a half ago. The pattern selection in this type of tile leaves something to be desired, but I found an imitation wood grain (which I thought would look terrible, but turned out surprisingly good and fooled many of my finicky-renovation friends). The areas that were covered were two rooms, 15 by 15 feet each, and the job took about four hours . . . my kind of job! My floors were nice and even, so I just laid the tiles directly on the wood, which was well washed and dried earlier. These tiles are thin, thus the job of cutting at the edges, where there's never enough room for a whole tile, can be done with scissors.

For the more elegant(?) tile, asphalt or vinyl, a cement must be applied to the floor. Buy the proper kind for the type of tile you select. Go to a reliable store, buy a good-quality tile and ask for the proper good-quality cement. Use a ridged trowel to apply the cement, enough for only one or two tiles at a time. Keep a wet rag nearby to wipe off any ooze at the tile joins. If the ooze is too much, you're applying too much cement.

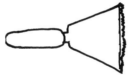

Where to start? One book recommends drawing a cross in the room and starting at the middle, working toward the four corners. No, thanks! To me, that means four wall edges of cutting and that is *work!*

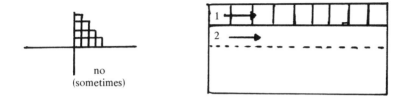

no
(sometimes)

I recommend starting across the longest wall (don't forget to remove all the molding). Do row by row. If the room is crooked, the last tiles won't line up. You decide where to start. That's really the best advice I can give you. Look at the room layout and decide which way you want to go so that the room doesn't look lopsided when the tiles are on. Yes, you may have to measure a cross and start from the middle after all.

CERAMIC TILING—
BATHROOMS
(AND WHEREVER ELSE
YOU WANT TO DO IT)

I have not tiled a bathroom, only done repair jobs with ceramic tiles. Looking at my bathroom walls, I notice that the whole tiles were started down (across?) from the most visible corner. That appears to be a good rule to follow.

This is the technique I would recommend: Draw a level line down, or use the woodwork as the edge if you have determined it to be level. Then draw a level line across, or use the floor as that bottom line. Yes, I would start at the bottom, and work up, row by row, constantly checking for the level of the row. Adjustment to nonlevel rows can be made by leaving bigger spaces between the tiles, starting from the end that has to come up a bit.

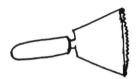

Using a ridged trowel, apply tile cement to the wall, enough for about four tiles at a time. Put a thin layer on the back of the tile and place it against the wall, twisting it, as you place it, to sqwoosh the adhesive into contact (wall to tile). The space between tiles should be about ⅛ inch or a bit less. (Remember this spacing when measuring the wall and calculating how many tiles to buy.)

Grout is the name of the substance used to seal the job. It is a mixture of cement, lime, sand and water, and it is pasty when applied. You can use your fingers to squeeze it into the spaces.

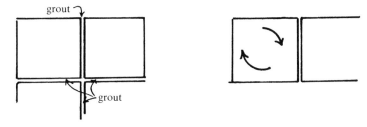

To Remove a Ceramic Tile

Use a glass cutter to score an X on it. Tap it lightly (but hard enough to accomplish something) at the center. This should loosen it and/or crack enough of it off to give you working space. Dig the rest out with a chisel.

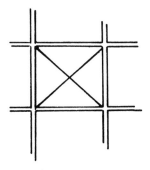

ALL THE OTHER WONDERFUL INFORMATION THAT ISN'T HERE

If this is the first time you have seriously read a book like this . . . if you are beginning to feel that tingling excitement of wanting to try . . . if you know, if only philosophically at this point, that there is much you are able to do that you never thought you could before . . . then nothing has really been left out. The information is there, waiting for you to discover it with the same enthusiasm you are currently experiencing. In fact, I don't want to rob you of much more of that joy of discovery. There are books devoted to subjects that are just chapter subjects here—in some cases, just short paragraphs here. Whatever you read now will be read with more ease, with at least a background of general information. Although some words may still be mysterious, many concepts will not be. You have more than just an educated eye now; you have an educated head and educated ears, and the education of your hands will happen as you progress, as you attack each new project, regardless of whether it is completed or not, a success or a failure.

I said I didn't want to rob you of the joy of discovery. That is true. It is also true that there simply isn't space here to include everything I know, the little tips I remember as I start a project (some of which are elusive because they come to one's mind only as the task is in

300

progress). A last-minute look at my notes reveals many tips and interesting tidbits to be passed on to you, enough for another book. However, as I study the contents, almost none of it is essential information at the start. Also, many of the techniques are of such a nature that you might even invent them yourself, if you don't already know them. Finally, some are on the list because they excited me when I discovered them . . . there's still so much I don't know. What I do know is that I feel OK about some of what isn't here, because in my imagination I see you discovering many of the "left-outs" yourself.

I would like to give you a quick sampling of what you're in for, and where to find these goodies. (The place is magazines.)

1) This one solved my problem with adjustable wrenches and never getting good results because of slipping:

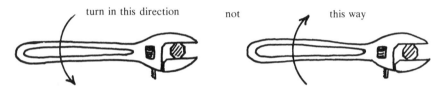

My guess is that going in the suggested direction prevents the lower, adjustable jaw from loosening, because as you push down and around with your hand, the lower jaw is the pushing, forcing jaw, thus perhaps being locked into position better. Try your finger between the claws and you will immediately feel the difference, turning one way, then the other.

—*Home Repairs* (magazine), spring edition, 1969

2) "A bit of steel wool or a tiny roll of sandpaper inside a worn-out screw hole holds the screw tightly."

— *Woman's Day,* May, 1970

3) Metal anchor plates, with a nail attached, may be glued (with black adhesive) to those horror walls. The little perforations in the metal are for the glue to sqwoosh through. These hold very well and are available, I have noticed, with more than one nail. You can put

these in a row down the wall and hammer a piece of furring strip to them, as a wooden basis for a cabinet, bookcase or whatever.

—*The New Carpentry Handbook* (magazine-type format), Fawcett Publications, Inc., 1968

4) Tie a stick (or tape the stick) to a paintbrush, before setting it in a paint-remover solvent. This will keep the bristles from getting bent while sitting.

—Science & Mechanics' magazine *1001 How-To Ideas,* 1970 edition

5) "When brads, tacks or very small nails must be driven into places where it is difficult to hold them with the fingers, the nail may be inserted in the open end of a bobby pin." (Does anyone use bobby pins anymore? Also, I'd suggest that you could use tweezers, the kind for the eyebrows or the jewelry tool that looks like tweezer, or any other improvisation you may come up with.)

—*1001 How-To Ideas* (again)

6) "Mending Linoleum Holes—You can mend small holes in linoleum by filling them with a thick paste made of finely chopped cork and shellac. Allow the paste to harden, then sandpaper the surface smooth and touch up with matching paint."

—*1001 How-To Ideas* (again!)

7) "Filling Cracks in Woodwork— . . . use a mixture of [fine] saw-dust and resin glue." They further recommend that you overfill the hole, for the mixture has a tendency to shrink. Also, the mixture should be of the consistency of putty.

—1001 How-To Ideas (yeah, again)

8) Here's a tip I've seen in probably every book and magazine that refers to furniture repair, and I definitely want to include it in this book. Chair-leg joint keeps coming out, too loose for glue to hold well and long. Hammer a small wedge into the dowel. As the dowel is forced into the hole, the wedge will sink into the dowel and widen it, thus making it hold better. Glue, of course, is always a necessity for a joint like this.

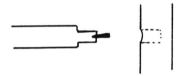

AN APPROACH TO
BROKEN APPLIANCES

The first point in the philosophy is that if the appliance is already broken, fiddling around is OK. The result of the fiddling will be that it will be fixed . . . or still broken . . . or more broken. Fine if it's fixed. If it's still or more broken, so what? "More broken," in most cases, will only mean a few more minutes of a repair person's time, if you have to go that route eventually, so the cost of the repair won't sky-rocket because of the fiddling. "Still broken" means that at least you've gotten some experience in the insides. Thus you can ask the repair person what is wrong—"Would you mind showing me?" Don't be afraid to ask. This will add even more to your experience, and the information you gain may be applicable to other appliances. Also, you are accumulating tidbits which can be shared with your neighbors.

Let me add that manufacturer's care-and-maintenance instructions are usually included with newly purchased appliances. Suggestions such as "Oil frequently" are designed to help you avert some of the "broken" conditions.

CARS

HORSEPOWER VERSUS
COLOR POWER

When my ex-husband and I went to turn in our used car for a brand-new one, his list of priorities was very different from mine. In fact, I actually had only one requirement, that the car be RED. My reason at the time was very logical. I had a friend who had had a red car, and she told me about the interesting discovery she had made as the driver of a red car. It seemed to her that she got a great deal of watch-out-for-the-red-car-ism, which she compared to the angry respect that we give to taxis. Here in the city, at least, one often defers to taxis in right-of-way situations, because we know they'll take it anyway! My friend began to suspect that the reason she was often deferred to was that other drivers thought the owner of a red car was a "wild one" and didn't want to mess with her. That made a lot of sense to me, my knowing that I was not the best driver in the world (though certainly not the worst); red could provide an extra margin of safety. It was like buying more insurance. I do believe that if our purchase had been a sports car, this philosophy might have proved to be a sound one. However, we bought a conservative nonspeedster—red—and I can't be sure I got my color's worth.

Naturally, my ex-husband's priorities related to performance. We've all heard those *importance* words: horsepower, cylinders, transmission, etc. At that time in my life, seven years ago, I was totally unconcerned about these features of a car. I was still role-playing—the car is the man's domain. Besides, how often would I be driving it—in his head, anyway? (Do men have any idea how many hours a day are involved in getting kids to school, the dentist, or their friends, or doing chores like marketing and picking up the shirts?)

Now this little red car is all mine, and I am not only The Driver, but also the one who has to pay the repair bills, so I am now dealing with a *horse* of a different *color!*

What I did first was to go to the library to read about the principles of a car's movement. I needed to know the Words. I had to have at least Word Power! You certainly can't fix everything that goes wrong in your car without a great deal of specialized equipment, but knowing the words and having some idea about the principles is a step in the right direction. And the list of words is longer than the list of principles. (My list of abuses at the garage, however, is the longest list!)

The Words are as follows (don't stop yet; it never occurred to me either that a battery was a battery, or that a generator was a generator, or that a filter was a filter!): starter, battery, generator, coil, distributor, spark plug, piston, cylinder, air, fuel, choke, carburetor, throttle, fan, crankshaft, camshaft, radiator, fan belt, air filter, fuel pump, friction plate, drive plate, clutch, transmission, gasket, gears, universal joints, differential gears, axles, brake drums, wheels, brake shoes, tires, brake fluid, oil filter, fuel filter, muffler, water pump, fuel reservoir, oil dipstick, drum lining, drive shaft, clutch shaft, eccentric, lights, windshield wiper, horn, oil gauge, ammeter, speedometer, gas pedal, brake pedal, parking brake, fuse box, heat-control unit, thermostat, bearings, exhaust pipe . . . oh, God, what else? There must be many I've forgotten . . . Oh, yes . . . pollution! (I guess that last thought really unveils my true feelings—that I'd rather say, Get rid of the car and we'll talk about repairing bikes, but unless enough of us gang up on the world, we're stuck with cars!)

And now for the principles—a picture is worth a thousand words, it is said. Well, that list was no thousand words, and I'm going to have to do it in more than one picture, but I hope that the pictures will swiftly diminish the fearfulness of that long list of words.

Let's start with the hardest part, the engine, and how a car moves . . . . Mull over the diagram a while, then you can read the Words again, with feeling. . . .

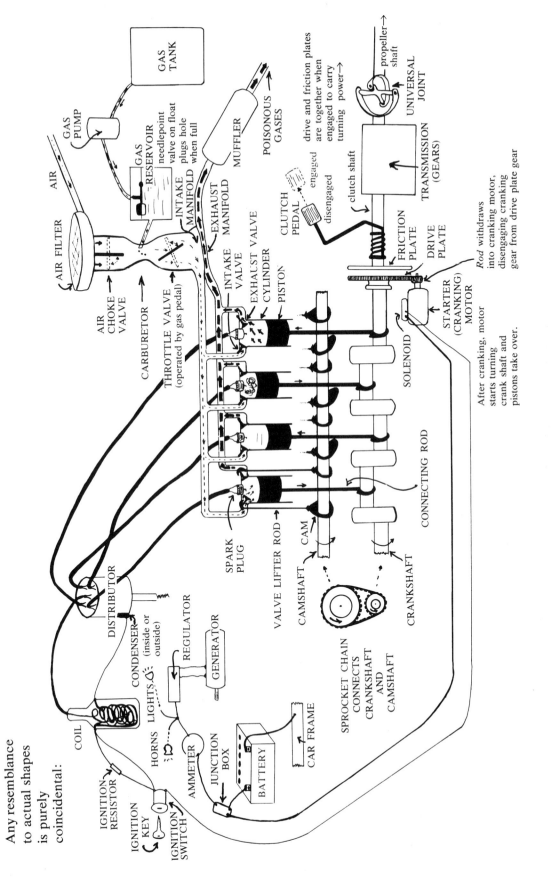

The Engine

(*1*) When you put your key into the *ignition switch* and turn it, the turn is like flicking a flashlight switch—the stored electricity in the *battery* comes forth. It travels out along a wire, through a *junction box,* to the *cranking motor.* The cranking motor, electrically driven, has a rod that slides in and out, and at the end of this rod is a gear. At start time the rod and gear come out and the gear meshes with the gear of the *drive plate* (or flywheel) at the end of the *crankshaft.* This starts the crankshaft revolving and keeps it up until the crankshaft is turning fast enough to allow the combustion in the cylinders to force the pistons up and down to turn the crankshaft. What does that mean? OK, let's go back to the almost-beginning and see what moves the car.

(*2*) Electricity is also emitted from the battery through the ignition switch to the *coil.* Usually, the battery is a 12-volt battery, which means that 12 volts are emitted. The coil is a mechanism which increases this voltage many thousands of times—to 10,000 volts or so. This high voltage is carried to the *distributor.* A *rotor* which is geared to the crankshaft is inside the distributor. Think of the rotor as a metal clock hand which can conduct electricity. Electricity comes from the coil along a wire which is connected to the axis of this clock hand. As the rotor turns, the end contacts the spark-plug wires, which are arranged around the circumference of the distributor like the numbers on the face of a clock. Each time the tip of the rotor touches one of the spark-plug wires, electricity flows along this wire to a spark plug that is screwed into the cylinder.

The action that takes place within a cylinder is a cycle of four events. (Look at the diagram, at the first four cylinders from the left, as I explain. Leftmost is *1.*)

(1) The *piston* is going down and the *intake* valve is open, allowing the air/fuel mixture into the cylinder.

(2) The intake valve closes the opening when the cylinder is full, and the piston moves up, compressing the air/fuel mixture.

(3) The spark from the sparkplug comes into the cylinder and ignites the fuel, which explodes—*combustion*—and the force of this, many tons of pressure, pushes the piston down, providing the *power* to turn the crankshaft forcefully.

(4) As the piston comes up again (because it's attached to the crankshaft), the *exhaust valve* (closed during the other cycles) opens and the poisonous gases left from the explosion are forced out of the cylinder.

Then, as the piston goes down and the intake valve opens (exhaust valve closed), more fuel comes into the cylinder—cycle (1) again, etc. Thus the four cycles are: intake, compression, power and exhaust.

This system of cylinders, pistons and crankshaft, etc., is the engine. Perhaps you can see now that the engine has to be cranked until the shaft is turning around fast enough so that the pistons move up and down fast enough to effect proper compression and thus power. When the action in the cylinders takes over, the rod in the cranking motor withdraws into the motor, pulling the crank gears away from the drive plate, which now turns solely because it's attached to the crankshaft. Before we take our foot off the clutch and deliver the turning motion to the drive shaft, let's look at the fuel intake.

③ The *carburetor* is the place where air, drawn in by the engine vacuum, and fuel mix and pass together through the *intake manifold* (a pipe!) to the cylinders. The *choke valve* (the "choke") opens and closes to determine how much air can enter. (When the engine is starting, a "rich mix" is better, which means a higher ratio of fuel than usual; so the choke valve should be closed instead of open, to let only a little air in.) Fuel, from the *fuel tank,* is drawn into a *reservoir* near the carburetor by the fuel pump. As air passes through the narrow part of the carburetor, a vacuum is created, which draws fuel from the reservoir into the carburetor. Actually, it's lots of little vacuums, thus the gas enters in droplets. These droplets quickly evaporate in the air, and it is a vapor that is sent to the cylinder. The *throttle valve,* which is operated by the gas pedal, lets out much or little vapor, depending on the position of the gas pedal—down is more.

④ Another set of pipes, or tubes to a pipe, the *exhaust manifold* (did you ever think that "the manifold" was just a pipe?), allows the poisonous gases to get out of the car. Because lots of sounds are made by the combustion in the cylinders, thousands per minute, the exhaust, in put-puts, passes through a *muffler,* which is simply a container designed to muffle the sounds. The exhaust then is let out of the car through the exhaust pipe.

(5) There is one final mechanism to mention before we get on to moving the wheels. The *camshaft* is a rod situated somewhere below the spark plugs and above the crankshaft. (As you might have guessed by now, the diagram is a picture of only some of the parts; and those have been spread out all over the page, unrelated to where they are actually positioned under the hood, all neatly packed together or screwed in place, but accessible.) The camshaft is a rod with cams on it, positioned so that as the rod rotates the cams perform their function. The function of the cams is to open and close the valves. As the tip—the pointed end of the cam—comes up, it pushes up a rod which is eventually connected to either an intake valve or an exhaust valve in the cylinder. The rod opens the valve so that fuel can come in or exhaust fumes may get out. One eccentric cam on the shaft operates the fuel pump. The camshaft, linked to the crankshaft by a sprocket chain, is turning half as fast . . . see diagram.

At this point I want to mention that we are talking about the type of car with standard transmission, not automatic, because the principles seem easier that way.

(6) Looking at the diagram, you will see that the *friction plate* and the *drive plate* are not touching. This is because the *clutch pedal* is down and the clutch spring is holding them apart. When the clutch pedal is let up, the plates meet and the turning motion from the crankshaft is carried through to the *clutch shaft.* (Think about a phonograph record and the turntable and you can understand what happens when the plates meet.) The clutch shaft ends in the *transmission,* which consists of the gears designed to deliver power (at low speeds) or speed (faster turning). The transmission is a fascinating yet simple setup of gears, and I've included a set of diagrams so that you may share my fascination. Have a look.

The Transmission

This is the gearbox. The gears combine in various patterns for low, medium or high speed, or reverse, or for no movement. The pattern is determined by the position of the shift stick (in the car without automatic transmission). The turning motion of the clutch shaft is delivered to the propeller, or drive, shaft through the meshing of a pair of gears. Pictures are better than words. (Automatic transmission means a fluid clutch.)

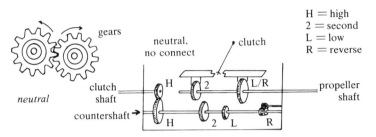

The high gears are always meshed, thus connecting the clutch shaft with the countershaft. The propeller shaft, with upper gears *2* and *L/R,* has grooves in it so that these gears may slide back and forth, and the end is grooved so that it will fit into the hole of the *H* gear in the clutch shaft. Note that in neutral position there is no connection of the clutch and propeller shafts, thus no turning motion is brought to the propeller shaft.

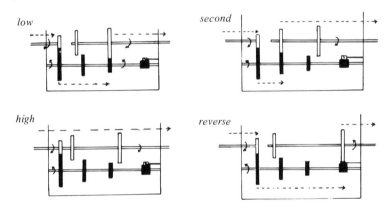

Out of neutral into low . . . let's go. . . .

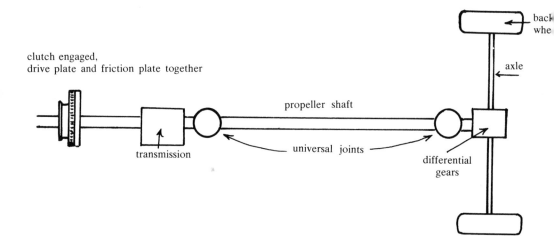

The Universal

The *universal joints* are necessary to keep the propeller shaft from cracking during the jouncing a car does while moving. They're like springs for the shaft.

The Differential Gears

The differential gears ("the differential") are another interesting combination of gears, which are necessary because the wheels must be

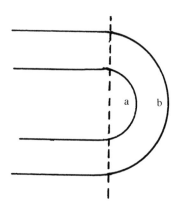

allowed to turn independently of one another when the car makes turns. Think about a horse race. The horses are at the turn . . . the horse on the outside has to run faster than the horse on the inside to keep up . . . distance *a* is less than distance *b*. So it is with wheels; the inside wheel must turn more times than the outside wheel to complete the turn, or the car will skid.

The differential gears are designed to allow this, and I'd like to illustrate how they work.

First of all, the differential gears are all gears that are angled; the diameter of one side is larger than the diameter of the other. These kinds of gears are called bevel gears. (A bevel is any angle other than a right angle.)

Let's put the differential together, to illustrate best how it works.

At the end of each wheel axle is a bevel gear—or at least, picture it that way.

These gears connect with a third gear attached to the differential housing, as is the left gear. The top gear is connected to the housing by a rod. Imagine this box revolving. The top gear turns the left and right gears, and the wheels turn.

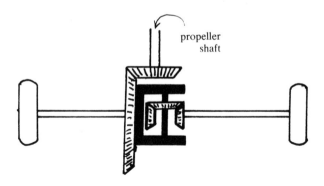

Attached to the outside of the housing is a larger gear, and this gear is driven by a gear at the end of the propeller shaft; thus the housing and the gears within rotate as the propeller-shaft gear drives the outer differential gear.

Cooling the Engine

The cylinder arrangement is held together by a housing called the *block*. This block is actually more than just a steel housing; it is more like a jacket with passageways in it through which either water or air flow. (Most cars are water-cooled; the Volkswagen is air-cooled.) The action within the cylinders creates a tremendous amount of heat; thus a cooling process is required.

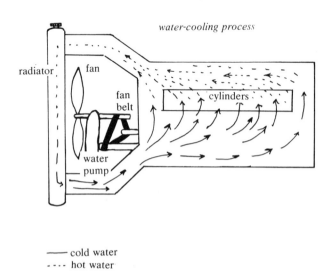

Water is circulated from the radiator through the block and back to the radiator by the water pump, which is operated by the fan belt. The water, which starts out cool, is quickly heated in its travels and must be cooled when it returns to the radiator before its next trip. This is done by the fan behind the radiator. The fan is driven by the fan belt, which is connected to the crankshaft.

Two important facts about water: it expands when freezing, and it evaporates when heated. Thus in cold weather, the water within the radiator and the block can freeze and "crack the block"! (That was something I heard about for years and never knew the meaning of.) In times of temperatures lower than 32° F. (at which water freezes), an additive is necessary to stall the freezing process. Alcohol is an antifreeze additive. But alcohol isn't a permanent antifreeze because while it freezes at a lower temperature, thus stalling the freezing, it also boils at a lower temperature and will evaporate faster than the water; it will therefore have to be replaced. The additive which is permanent is ethylene glycol, which doesn't boil away. Permanent antifreeze does not have to be replaced as frequently, maybe only once a year. It is more expensive but perhaps worth it. There is a gadget available for a couple of dollars which will measure your level of safety—how low the temperature can get for you to be safe with the amount of antifreeze that is presently in your car. (The test should be made after you've driven the car about a half hour.)

When the engine is running the water is hot, about 170° F., but when the water reaches 200° there is great danger that it may boil. When the temperature gauge on the dashboard registers that danger, stop and sit for a while, maybe half an hour or so, to let the water cool off.

In air-cooled systems, air is circulated through the block and it is cooled by fans, thus there are no freezing or boiling problems.

A thermostat controls the flow of water from the radiator. On very cold days, for example, the valve allowing water from the radiator is kept closed—controlled by the thermostat—until the water is a safe temperature. Defective valves, sticking, etc., can cause overheating and other problems.

Oiling the Engine

Metal—steel—does not actually have a perfectly smooth surface; microscopic investigation would reveal it to be rough and dented.

Interaction between two surfaces further corrodes them. To prevent this, the moving parts must be lubricated, or greased, to provide smooth interaction. An elaborate oiling system is built into the design of the engine, so that oil may be delivered to all moving parts. The oil reservoir (the *oil pan*) is located under the crankshaft, in what is called the lower part of the *crankcase*. The oil is delivered to the parts by a *pump* and is cleansed by passing through an *oil filter*.

The crankshaft is perhaps one of the most vital moving mechanisms in the car, and the oil passageways are illustrated here.

oil passageways in the crankshaft

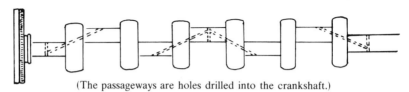

(The passageways are holes drilled into the crankshaft.)

The lower part of the piston's connecting rod is wrapped around the horizontal rod of the crankshaft and must pass around it smoothly, so the rod must be lubricated. (The lower parts of the connecting rod are bolted together.)

Oil must not slip up the connecting rod into the upper part of the cylinder. The piston actually has a set of *rings* around it, two of which prevent this. (There's another mystery word—"RINGS"!) The piston moves up and down within the cylinder, but no exhaust may pass down and out with it, nor may oil get up with it. The compression rings prevent the escape of exhaust and the oil rings prevent the passage of oil. The rings sit in cavities around the piston and are not attached to the piston, but provide the "plugging" necessary.

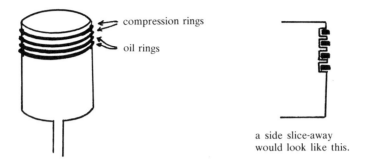

compression rings

oil rings

a side slice-away
would look like this.

Two Important Features of the Engine

Before we leave the engine and talk about the brakes and the electrical setup, two features within the engine must be discussed. The first big diagram illustrated neither, because they each need special attention.

THE IDLE SCREW   Another look at the *carburetor*—what it really looks like: The throttle valve is operated by the gas pedal; it opens as the pedal is pushed down. When you start the car and it's warming up, the throttle is closed. However, some fuel vapor must reach the cylinders, so an extra passageway exists to allow some air and gas to pass through, bypassing the throttle valve, into the intake manifold.

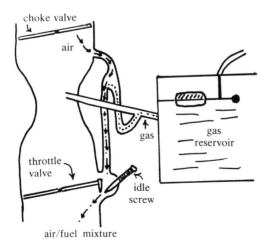

choke valve

air

gas   gas
             reservoir

throttle
valve   idle
               screw

air/fuel mixture

The *idle screw,* screwed into the side of the carburetor, determines how much vapor is permitted through. It is adjustable and visible. Besides a screwdriver, the only other thing you need for making this kind of adjustment is a trained ear! (You can tell if it's idling right if it sounds right! If you don't have any idling problems now, lift your hood, start the car, letting it idle, and bend over and listen—once a day or so, until you've tuned your ear. Listen to the fastness-slowness quality of the idle. The fastness-slowness quality relates to the number of explosions in the cylinders.)

In the course of reading all of this information about a car, you may be getting awed by the many things that can go wrong with it. My ultimate purpose in explaining the principles of a car are to provide you, first, with the overall relationships of the different components to one other; second, to give you a kind of mental checklist of what may be causing the problem when one occurs; third, the knowledge to deal with some of the problems yourself; and lastly, the words to go into the garage with, if you don't have the special tools and/or if you are unable to pinpoint the malfunction.

THE HEAT-CONTROL VALVE IN THE MANIFOLD   The second thing I feel it is important to know about is the thermostatically controlled *heat-control valve* in the manifold. I use the word "manifold," not "intake manifold" or "exhaust manifold," because the valve has to do with both.

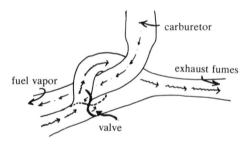

There is an alternate passage for the exhaust to pass through. This passage is used when the intake is cold. This alternate passage is a pipe that wraps around the intake pipe. The exhaust, which is warm, may then warm the intake as it passes through. The heat-control valve is regulated by a thermostat to allow the warm exhaust either through the regular pipe or the alternate pipe. The value position shown in the diagram permits the exhaust to pass through the alternate pipe. (It is one more thing that can malfunction!)

Don't stop! We can't talk about brakes yet—the car is still moving, and the next principle involves the electrical system. . . .

The Battery . . . the Generator . . . Charging and Discharging

The *battery* is the source of electricity in the car. No, that's not quite true . . . it's almost like the old question "What came first, the chicken or the egg?" In a brand-new car the battery is the "first source." What am I talking about? you wonder.

The battery is a container for stored electrical energy in chemical form. (We've talked about gas reservoirs and oil reservoirs; here is the electricity reservoir.) As electricity is required for use in the car—starting, lights, windshield wipers, radio, etc.—the supply in the battery is depleted. The battery is *discharging* its electricity for these functions. When you get to the point when there's no supply left, the battery is dead! This should not happen for a long time—years—if related parts are working and if you don't abuse the battery.

The mechanism most important to the battery and its supply of electricity is the *generator*. The generator is a unit which converts mechanical energy into electrical energy. This converted energy is then sent to the battery for storage and "charges the battery," or replenishes the electrical supply in the battery. The mechanical energy is created by the rotation of the crankshaft and is transferred to the generator in this way: The rotation energy of the crankshaft is transferred to a rotating rod in the generator by the fan belt, and some-how, inside the generator, this energy is converted to electricity.

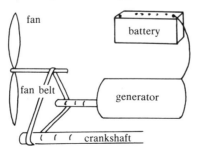

This rotation energy is not delivered at a constant rate, because it's coming from the crankshaft, which is turning variably, according to driving needs. Thus this converted energy must be evened out, made to flow at a fixed rate; so on its way back to the battery it passes through a *regulator,* which regulates, or evens out, the voltage, for a constant flow. Instead of a generator and regulator, you might have an *alternator* and *voltage regulator.* Together these two perform the same function as the generator and regulator, but their individual functions vary. (No, I can't explain the difference yet. You don't really want to know, do you? You're only getting your feet wet. There are libraries full of books to read after this, if you have to know.)

Thus, the only time the battery can be charged is when the crankshaft is rotating powerfully—when the car is going. In theory, you should be discharging only at the start of the car, at which time you shouldn't have lights, radio, etc., on because they put an additional strain on the battery. The gauge that registers the condition of charging-discharging is called the *ammeter* and is on the dashboard. A prolonged condition of discharging indicates trouble and should be tended to swiftly. Already you may be able to guess about some of the things that could be wrong—faulty wire or connection from the generator to the battery, for example—see the repairs section following for more detailed suggestions.

The Brakes

All right, we've had a nice long ride, recharged the battery, and haven't had any problems (they all happen in the repairs section), so let's stop the car and talk about the braking system.

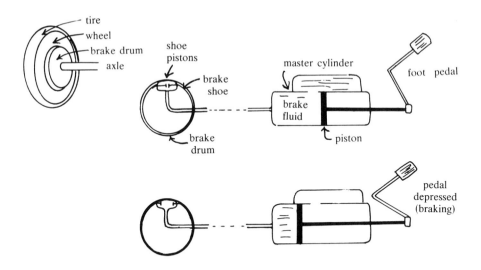

As the brake pedal is depressed, the piston in the master cylinder pushes the brake fluid through the tubes to the brake drums. The shoe pistons in the drum cylinders are forced apart by the entrance of the fluid and the brake shoes are forced out against the walls of the brake drum, causing friction; this eventually slows the wheels' motion to a stop.

The emergency brake, separate, is operated by wires and tensions.

The Front Wheels

Not totally insignificant, if you want to get where you're going, the front wheels come last anyway, because they're not really connected to anything we've talked about. The wheels, on axles, are actually just attached to the frame of the car and are pushed along by the action of the back wheels. (In four-wheel drive, this is not true—you've got a double dose of troubles and/or controls, whichever way you want to look at it.)

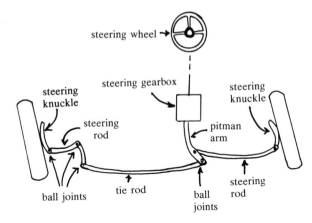

Suspension

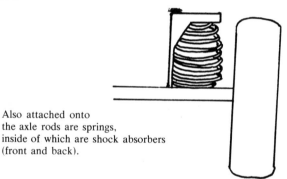

Also attached onto
the axle rods are springs,
inside of which are shock absorbers
(front and back).

There you have it, not quite in a nutshell, but much of the mystery has been explored—surely not everything. I notice, as I look back at that original list of words, that I haven't mentioned "gasket" at all. I will now, and perhaps you will have the same reaction as mine when I found out what it was. "Blowing a gasket" has always sounded like such a major catastrophe, involving a large and significant component. Here are some of the many, many gaskets that are all over the engine:

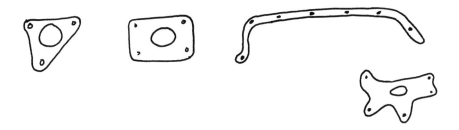

Do you believe it? They're pieces of thin steel—of many shapes—that act as seals between units attached together; their function is to prevent leakage of oil, water and fuel. Imagine, "blowing a gasket" is just an expression for a worn-down gasket (thus a leak)!

Oil, water and fuel are pumped and air is vacuumed in; everything is filtered; and there are shoes, belts and drums! And somehow, when all of this is squashed together under the hood or strung out under the body, the car works . . . sometimes. . . .

WORDS IN SYSTEMS

Before I leave the principles, I'd like to reorder the Words—most of them, at least—into orderly combinations, referring to their relationships (just to give this an inkling of a textbook).

The Start, or crank, system: key, ignition switch, junction box, battery, cranking motor (start motor), drive wheel and wiring.

The Ignition system: battery, coil distributor, spark plugs, cylinders, pistons and valves.

The Electric system: battery, generator, regulator, distributor, coil, junction box, lights, horn, windshield wipers, gauge, fuses, thermostats, radio and wiring.

The Cooling system: water, radiator, water pump, thermostat, fan, fan belt, block.

The Fuel system: gas, fuel tank, fuel pump, hoses, carburetor, pedal manifold, gas gauge, choke, throttle, reservoir, air, filter.

The Lubricating system: oil, oil pump, oil filter, oil pan (reservoir), hoses, gaskets.

The Braking system: brake fluid, master cylinder, hoses, brake shoes, brake drums, brake lining, brake pedal, parking brake.

The Revolution system (I just made that up because there seems to be a lot left out like): crankshaft, camshaft, drive plate, friction plate, clutch, clutch shaft, transmission, universal joints, propeller shaft, differential gears, axles and wheels . . . and tires.

Now this is all very good, and (except for the Revolution system) may be the way the textbooks have it; but I think it is necessary to talk about other systems when we're concerned with problems and repairs.

Therefore I propose some new systems: *The Noise system* (what's a ping-ping and what's a put-put?), and *the Leak system* (water? oil? where?), and *the Stall system* (how to relax and hum a song, when you stall on the busiest streetcorner in town, and go through the checklist), and *The No-Start system* (summer and winter, the checklist is a beauty!) and finally *the Do-It-Yourself-Beforehand! system* (antifreeze *before* you crack the block, water *before* you overheat, oil *before* you grind to a halt, spark plugs *before* you don't explode—in the cylinders, that is, and that's called "backfiring"—and checking and charging the battery *before* it's all discharged).

UNDER THE HOOD

There you have it—the whole picture, the concepts. You do not have the *picture,* though. All that information swimming through my head, after I learned it all. . . . I ran out to the car, lifted the hood, and could identify almost nothing! The battery . . . that was about it . . . then as I looked and looked, I spotted . . . was it? yes, it had to be! . . . the distributor! Gradually, my eyes walked around under the hood and I was eventually able to determine what the visible things were, most of them. For the mysteries, I grabbed the car manual. Then I got down on the ground to look underneath to see what was there that I could identify. (Yes, naturally, at that point, some male neighbors gathered and wanted to know what was wrong and could they help: Naturally, they were dumbfounded when I said I was simply trying to become more acquainted with the parts of a car, that I was learning about cars . . . and they walked away . . . not needed and baffled. None of these nice men continued their offer to help at this point . . . and I could have used it. Many mysteries still needed to be unfolded.)

What follows next is a walking tour for your eyes and hands— under the hood and under the car. Take the book now and go out to your car. (Good luck with the street scene if you live in the city.)

Bring a screwdriver and a flashlight. . . .

Let's use, as our jumping-off place, the *distributor,* a unit with thin

328

hoses coming out of the top. (Look back at the master drawing in the beginning for the clues.) See it? OK, now let's work back from the distributor. Follow the one hose ("secondary wire") that goes in a different direction from the others (and there may be four, six, or eight others). That hose goes to another unit: the *coil*. From that coil should be a thin, electrical-looking wire ("primary wire") going to the *condenser*, the component responsible for building the high electrical voltage, and also related to spark timing. The condenser is on the side of the distributor (or inside in some cars) and is very tiny. (See it?) Another wire should be coming out of the coil, going to the ignition switch and eventually to the *battery*. (I can't see my wire, so it may be behind the metal framework under the dashboard.) (You don't have the battery?! Yes, you do, you have a VW . . . look under the back seat.) Look at the battery. One wire, coming out of "Negative" (look through the grease, you'll see — or NEG), is attached to the frame of the car. That's the grounding. Now that you've read the electricity chapter—you have, haven't you?—you know what that's all about.

All right, go back to the distributor. Follow those other wires (four, six or eight). They all lead to a big metal case . . . the *block!* The car *must* be *off* to do the next thing: Pull one of the wires off, at the end near the block. They're not screwed on or anything, just pull it off . . . just one! This is the wire the electricity travels along to get to the spark plug. What you just pulled the wire off was the top of a *spark plug*. A spark plug is screwed into a cylinder (see the master drawing). You can't see the cylinders, pistons, crankshaft, etc., because they are sealed into the block. (Not permanently; you could spend a day or so and take the block apart . . . no! don't do it! For that you need special tools and expertise—the kind we wish garages had!) However, what you can know now is what kind of a car you have, in terms of that cliché "How many cylinders?" Count the number of spark plugs (or wires from the distributor to the block). That's how many cylinders you have. Four spark plugs, you have a four-cylinder car; six if you have a six-cylinder car, etc. Now, in case you don't have one in front of you, I'll tell you what a V-8 engine is: eight cylinders, four on each side of a block which is shaped like a V! How about that?

In the middle of this tour, I'd like to stop for a minute and explain why I said to remove only one spark-plug wire. Take a look at how they're set onto the plugs. Not in the sequence as they come out of the distributor, not like this:

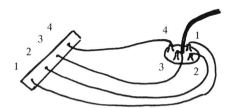

Think a minute about that crankshaft under the cylinders. It's like a paper clip that you bend this way: ⌐_⌐_⌐ and as you twist it around with your fingertips, the two "up" parts come down and the "down" parts go up: ⌐_⌐_⌐ up/down → _⌐_⌐_

This is the way the crankshaft works, almost; the ups and downs aren't level at the same place as the paper clip, but are at different stages of turning. The way the wires are attached to the plugs determines the firing sequence of the sparks. Mine is like this:

1, 3, 4, 2 . . .   1⌐3⌐4⌐2   down, up, down, up.
. . . Now you can see how the turning is accomplished. If it's still unclear, try the concept on a paper clip, pushing tops around to the bottom, etc., instead of twisting it at the ends with your fingertips. Now is the best time to make a diagram and keep it in your glove compartment—call the first spark plug, nearest the front of the car, #1; the next #2; etc. Make a picture like mine . . . just in case you ever need it. (You could have a sloppy mechanic . . . a robot without a computer to remind him of the sequence.) This sequence should be in your car manual.

Well, you can't see anything in the block (the house of the engine), but you know what's there: *cylinders, pistons, oil,* the *oil pan* underneath (the *crankcase*), *crankshaft, camshaft, gaskets, cams* . . . and various other vital components.

You will see, in my kind of car anyway, another shaped housing, behind the fan and attached to the engine housing, and this covers the *chain gear* connecting the camshaft and the crankshaft. From this area, a rod protrudes with a disklike thing on which part of the *fan belt* sits. The rod is the end of the crankshaft and that disk thing is called a *belt pulley*. Another *belt pulley* within the belt is delivering rotation power to the *generator* at crankshaft speed. The other belt pulley operates the *water pump*. In front of the *fan,* also driven by the belt, is the *radiator*. (You don't have a radiator? . . . that's you again, with your VW . . . right, your car is air-cooled.)

Follow the wires from the generator and you should see them pass into the regulator. Instead of a generator and regulator, you could have an *alternator* and *voltage regulator*.

Back to the block. Besides the spark, we need gasoline vapor and air coming into the cylinders. Out of the block should be coming a *hose,* or hoses, to the *carburetor(s).* . . . My God! I have two! . . . It may not be too visible, because often the *air filter* is attached on top of it. Try to follow the hose out of the block to something that looks somewhat like a cylinder or goes under what looks like a filter. Yes, yes, I know, what does a filter look like? Like it's ventilated? Like you could blow through it . . . airy . . . ! OK. Got it.

Look at how the carburetor is attached . . . or remove the air filter (unscrew it) and try to find a screw that doesn't look as if it's performing a hold-together, attaching, function. Check the position in the manual. That screw is the *idle screw.* This is the screw you adjust to get faster or slower idling . . . more or less gas through the carburetor during idling time. Start the car and try moving the screw . . . remember where you started from, so that you can put it back in the same position . . . just turn it a bit . . . you will hear a change in the motor hum . . . faster or slower. You don't have to turn it much at all to hear a difference. (Hear it? . . . If you don't, stop. That's not the idle screw. You are taking the carburetor apart! Get out your manual.) Sometimes that little screw is the difference between stalling and not stalling. More gas may be needed to keep you from stalling a lot . . . you may simply need an adjustment of the idle screw.

And *now*—you can at last try to see if that's the problem . . . *yourself!* (Keep some learning $$$ in a can, in case you need to call the garage after a mistake, but do try some of the simple things.)

Turn off the car. Look around behind, beside, under the carburetor to find the *gas reservoir,* then the *hose* to the *gas tank;* the hose disappears under the car. No, don't get under the car yet; we're not finished identifying everything under the hood.

There is a *hose* from out of the radiator to the block, locate that, so that if you have a leak some time, or if all of a sudden you have overheating problems, you can check it for holes.

To get some indication of where the oil is, try to remember what the mechanic does (always if you live in the country, sometimes if you live in the city) when you buy gas. He checks the water and oil. He unscrews the cap on the radiator to check the level of the water—should be to the top. (If you do this, wrap a rag around the cap. It will be hot if the car has just been running.) Perhaps you remember where he goes to pull out the rod to check the oil. That rod has a little finger hold at the top. Look for it, sticking out on the side of the block, low maybe. I thought I remembered . . . or, rather, I thought there would only be one of these little gismos, but I sighted two! One was surely for the oil, but what was the other? What else would have a rod accessible for checking its contents? The brake fluid? No good guessing. I opened the car manual. Wrong! The transmission fluid. And the manual indicated which was which. If I had given more thought to it, I would have realized which had to be the oil, because the direction it indicated was toward the bottom of the block, where the crankcase is. (Of course, you can use the manual to do all of this observation. That's part of the reason they gave you one with the car. But you've tried that already, haven't you? And you know what that scene is like. Yeah, so do I.) As for the *oil pump,* it's down there underneath, too. Mine, according to the manual, is connected to a rod under the distributor. That rod, the distributor part of it, has a gear end, probably part of the rotor function.

What else? The windshield wipers are driven by a motor under the dash. If you have a windshield-washing feature, there's a motor near, under(?) the container of water. And there are wires running all over the place to operate these, and the lights, and the horn, and the radio, and—did I forget the *starter motor?* . . . yes, that, too. That's an important one to trace back to the battery. Look way down beside the block for a case that's near where you'd guess the *drive plate* is (look back at the master drawing to get your bearings) . . . near the back of the block. (I'm sorry, VW, I know you are standing in the back of the car because your engine is in the back . . . under the back seat?) That's the *starter motor*. Also, besides the wires for all the electrically operated things, there are *fuses*.

The purpose of fuses, as you will remember from the electricity chapter, is for protection of the electrical system. They blow during electric-fault situations, and I guess they can also wear out. If one continues to blow, it indicates a problem—faulty wiring, perhaps—and should be checked into. You could be without brights only, and it would be because of that fuse. Look in your manual to locate where they all are.

That's about it for under the hood. Yes, I've surely not mentioned everything . . . do you care? Now is the time to get down and look under the car. You really can't see too much unless you are directly underneath, but you can start at the exhaust *tailpipe* and work back. You'll see, next, the *muffler.*

As for the rest, I have a suggestion. Go over to your friendly garage someday, when it's not too busy there, and ask them to put the car up on the lift so you can have a look. You're laughing! Sure, it's an absurd suggestion, but you might just luck out and have a generous mechanic. . . . And it could be the start of some real training . . . you might be able to hang around to watch sometimes.

All right, now that you've spent an hour or so under the hood, you should feel better and more knowledgeable. You know what some of those too many things are. If something falls off, or leaks, or makes strange sounds, you could possibly identify it. This ability not only to identify what it is but also to understand its function would be helpful, in times of crisis, in determining whether to abandon the car and go for help, or to crawl the car to a gas station, or to make an emergency repair.

For example, suppose the fan belt broke—what to do? Well, let's see, one purpose is to transfer the engine power to the generator for conversion of the electricity stored in the battery. But it also drives the water pump, which forces the water through the block to cool it; and it drives the fan which cools the returning water. I don't know, that's iffy. A very short distance might not be a disaster, the engine might not get too hot, but that short a distance could be walked. I think my choice would be abandon. However, if you found a leak in the water hose from radiator to block . . . and if you had some tape or something else waterproof, or reasonably so, to wrap around the hole, then you could drive on to a gas station . . . provided you haven't lost all the water in your radiator. If you should smell gas fumes and trace them to a hole in the fuel line . . . remember, first, that gas is highly flammable. Don't light a cigarette near the motor; turn off the car, immediately; and only if you have a surely-no-leak patch of some sort to cover the hole should you proceed. And if you're too nervous, leave it.

One other example: a hole in your exhaust pipe before it reaches the muffler, or a hole in the muffler, or a fallen-off muffler means two things: noise, OK to drive with to the garage; and fumes (poisonous carbon monoxide) seeping up from underneath into the car, OK to drive with if you're ventilated well—open all the windows.

So you see, you may now be qualified to make some judgments you couldn't before. A rule: When in doubt, abandon and walk. A *warning:* This may be the beginning of husband-wife arguments in the car. You have information now!

WOMEN AND CARS, MEN AND CARS, AND NEVER THE TWAIN SHALL MEET

MEN AND CARS

Before I get into simple repairs of cars, I want to get something out of my system about men and "their" cars—in a one-car family, it's his car; in a two-car family, the jalopy is yours, right? I suppose that some of the importance to men of the appearance of the car can be compared to some women's feeling about clean floors; maybe it's as simple as that. Maybe it isn't, though, because—well, we have all been called "a hysterical female" at some time in our lives, but how often have we heard the cliché "hysterical male" used? However, there is no phrase that better describes the condition of a man when he discovers a scratch or dent in "his" car, resulting from either unknown causes or—worse—the actions of that woman driver—his wife! (Generalities, I'm speaking in generalities only. I know there are exceptions.) My dictionary defines *hysteria* as "a nervous disorder marked especially by defective emotional control," and *defective* as "faulty, deficient." I've never liked it when the cliché has been applied to me; I like it not at all now that I've read the dictionary, because it's applied so freely. However, it is the most absolutely perfect and correct way to describe that usual and expected condition of man and his newly scratched car, worse a hundredfold if the car is brand-new!

One of the assets of our marriage that I retained after my ex-husband and I split was the car. In the early months of our separation, before I had established with him my philosophy about cars, I got a lot of flak from him about the condition of the car. "Why don't you have the car washed?" he'd ask. Another time he noticed a scratch on the door of the car. "How did that happen and why don't you have that taken care of?"

"So what?" I'd respond, or, "Why should I? It still runs OK." He told me all about what happens when the paint is scratched off and the body can rust and get holes, and all of that. I would reply, "So, it will get holes, so, it'll still run, won't it? This Volvo is supposed to last me eleven years, and it's doing all right so far. Then it will have a junk price anyway, because of that 'blue book' scene, so what difference do a few holes make?"

An even better example of the hysterical business happened over the jelly beans. One evening after he brought the children home, he really lost his cool. "That car is a mess, why don't you clean it out? There are jelly beans all over the floor!"

"Listen," I said calmly, "that's by design. When they spilled last week, I deliberately left them there. When I'm alone in the car with the boys, I like them to have something to do, and looking for jelly beans is a better occupation for them than bugging me!"

And a word about the contortions men go through for the appearance of that car. . . . The other evening, as I was coming home from work, I passed a friend, a normally happy guy, cursing and swearing, trying to pull out a dent in his car with a bathroom plunger! After all the "What are you doings?" and such (and I could see it wasn't working, because it was kind of a double dent, and he'd get one part out, push the plunger at the other side to pull it out, too, and the first part would get pushed back in), I said, "Listen, Bob, your car still rolls, doesn't it? Why don't you just leave the dent. In fact, why don't you add a few, and maybe it won't get stolen."

He looked at me, got a wild smile across his whole face, tossed the plunger high into the air and said, "Yeah, what the hell am I knocking myself out for?" And he was his normally happy self again.

WOMEN AND CARS

This section is included because the car is an almost universal for all of us. So much so that when a friend told a group of us, all women, that she read that the YWCA had a course in auto mechanics and repair for women, we all responded, "When?" We've had it, all that stuff about the "woman driver," and all that macho bull from the gas-station mechanics, or from the other men we know—"Well, of course you hear noise, the muffler is gone!"—and stuff like that. (What's a muffler?)

Recently, I had to be pushed—no gas! It happens to all of us humans, I think, at least once. I always expend more energy getting the boys to fasten their seat belts than I do checking the dashboard dials— or at least I used to. The man who was nice enough to offer to give me a push was also generous enough (at the outset) to pay me the compliment of assuming I knew what to do when being pushed, and gave me no instruction. I sat there, happy in my good fortune to get help, with my gear in drive, and he pushed and pushed—nothing! He finally jumped out of his car, looked through my window and screamed, "Lady, what the #**Z# are you doing? Disengage the #*ZZ#* clutch!"

"How?"

"Put the car in neutral! Jesus, women drivers!"

Yes, true, I probably should have known, but why the awful abusiveness? Why can't men remember that teen-age girls don't spend their time taking apart and putting together old jalopies? Why do they even assume that knowledge about cars is instinctive to them, after they have labored for many hours, learning about this mechanical mess, the car? That last pushing scene decided it for me. No man was ever going to say that to me again! And so I went about gathering information about my car, about cars in general, about driving, about emergencies . . . and I changed a tire; many years with AAA had made me lazy and kept me totally inexperienced.

For what they're worth, these are the things that I think are important. . . .

THE GARAGE—HOW TO
MAKE THEM LISTEN
TO YOU

OK, you've just pored over all those words and concepts about cars. Although you're probably no expert yet—I'm certainly not—you are better informed now than before you read it, I hope. All, not just some, of that information will eventually be helpful to you, but I have to warn you right now. You may now know more than the mechanic at the garage who fixes your car! Did you ever hear of a car mechanic's license? Do they have to apprentice, as plumbers and electricians do, for years and years, before being let loose—out on their own—with your car, a potentially deadly weapon? No, and I herewith make a serious suggestion for immediate change. Come on, world, let's get some sense.

Here is a glorious example. One day a few weeks ago, my tail pipe cracked and was dragging along the ground. I stopped the car immediately. I had seen other drivers pass me with cars in the same condition, and I had seen the sparks the pipe made against the ground. Somewhere I had read that a spark like this could ignite the gas tank and—BOOM! Good old worrywart, me, didn't stop to figure out how that could happen—isn't the gas tank pretty well sealed? . . . No, I take no chances. I got out and pulled the tail pipe off and threw it in the trunk. This meant that some fumes (poisonous carbon monoxide) might come up into the back of the car, but, well ventilated, we could make it until I could get the car to a garage in a few days. ("Keep your windows open, boys," I told my sons.) That weekend we went away on vacation, and I lent my car to a friend for the time. She had the pipe—and the muffler—replaced. A couple of days after the car was returned to me, I started the car and *ZOOM!* . . . I was sitting in a hot rod! (But my little old Volvo isn't supposed to be a hot rod!) I cursed a lot.—Damn the fool that fixed the muffler! The sound wasn't being *muffled!* That I knew. The next morning the garage mechanic put the car up on the lift. "You need a new muffler, lady."

"But I just had a new muffler put in, two weeks ago. See it? There it is," I said, pointing to the tail pipe and the round, ball-like attachment. (And thinking, as I saw it for the first time, My God, is that plastic? Fantastic . . . no sparks.) I also noticed another unit farther in on the pipe.

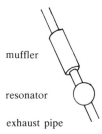

muffler

resonator

exhaust pipe

"No, lady, you have a new resonator. See, you have a crack in the pipe leading into the muffler," he said, pointing to the inside end of the muffler.

"What's a resonator?" (You may be asking the same question yourself, because it's not in that list of words earlier.)

"Well, it muffles the sound of the exhaust."

"No!" I said, my voice rising, "that's what the muffler does! What does the resonator do? What's the purpose?"

"Leave the car, lady, I'll have it ready for you this evening. I got a lot of work to do," he said, and walked away.

Thanks a lot, buddy! . . . and this guy was not young; he must have been fixing cars for twenty or thirty years. Did they just invent the resonator? I wondered. That same day I spent the lunch hour at the library. My dictionary was absolutely useless. RESONATOR: *something that resounds or exhibits resonance.* RESONANCE: *the quality or state of being resonant.* RESONANT: *continuing to sound; resounding.* Do you believe that? I thought you weren't supposed to define a word by the same word. And . . . if my car resounded, wouldn't I get a noise ticket?

From the car books, the best definition I get is that this gadget helps you have "quality" muffled sound. I suppose all it does is further muffle the sound. But to call it a "resonator"? Well, I guess the labelers in Detroit don't have word licenses, or dictionaries . . . not that my dictionary is too hot . . . but it did say "resounding," boys. How about "supplemental muffler"? Or how about simply improving the muffler?

There are pages and pages of stories. Now that you have some of the vocabulary, you'll have your own stories to write. And you'll find out how dangerous a little knowledge is! It will lead you directly to the truth, that some of these mechanics don't know what they're doing! They're robots! Let's all lobby for some necessary qualifications for car mechanics. I'd feel safer, wouldn't you?

There is, I must add, some glimmer of hope that we may see more women in this field. This summer, the gas tank of my rented vacation car was filled by a woman! I did not hesitate to question her. (I felt the same excitement I felt when I came across my first woman taxi driver.) "Wow, great . . . do you like it? Are there any others like you that you know of? [No] Do they let you learn the mechanical end?"

"Yes, the owners are very good about letting me watch and learn, and say I'm quite good. But it's the car owners who object."

REPAIRS—AN APPROACH

Now that you have all this information—some picture of what it's all about—what good is it? Well, you can't fix most things yourself without a garage full of tools, testing meters or a hydraulic pump to lift the car up.

What you *are* equipped to do now is to troubleshoot the problems. Even if you can't fix it yourself, you will be able to direct the mechanic, more clearly describe the symptoms and know if the car is fixed when returned to you.

Let me illustrate the approach with common problems:

NO-START SYSTEM

Go back to the principles and the words: key, battery, starter motor cranks the crankshaft (cranking sound), air/fuel vapors to cylinders, combustion (kickover sound), the pistons take over turning the crankshaft (motor-running sound). What didn't happen?

1. Absolutely nothing happened when you turned the key: Ignition switch? Battery? Starter motor? Wires connected? You have to try to look into every possibility before you assume the battery is dead and recharge it . . . with jump cables. Is generator functioning?

2. Cranking but no kickover: Out of gas? Cranking too slow for the combustion to take over? The battery could be too low to supply enough power for a good kickover. Try again with the lights inside the car or radio on. If they dim a lot when you turn the key, your battery is low. Starting motor out of whack? No sparks to the cylinders? Take off one wire from the distributor where it attaches to a spark plug, hold the tip of the wire against the block (which is grounded) and have someone start the car. Watch for the spark to come out . . . no spark? distributor bad? coil? *Warning:* If *anything* is wrong with your wiring, you'll get a hell of a jolt doing this. Yes, a spark—spark plugs could be saturated, need drying. Unscrew one at a time (for which you will need a socket wrench) and dry the inside part off with a rag. Oil leaking through into the cylinders because of worn rings could be causing this saturation. Another thing that might have "flooded the motor" (too much gas vapor in the cylinder not used up because of too slow cranking). You can smell the gas when this happens. Wait at least a full minute or two—time it—and try it again with full throttle, foot down on the pedal, to get more air into the cylinders to clean them out. Also, you need a rich mix for good starting combustion (a rich mix is heavy on gas)—maybe the choke valve isn't working properly. Open up the carburetor and check it; you could try closing it manually to get started if that's the trouble. (Cold air can have a corrosive effect on the thermostatic coil which controls the choke valve.) You may simply find nothing, and after looking at the choke and replacing the air filter, you may discover that the car will start. That might be because the air filter had gotten stuck in a bad position and thus jammed the choke valve. To continue, there could be a problem with the fuel pump . . . ice blocking fuel flow. In cold weather you could cover the motor with a blanket at night (don't forget it's there in the morning!) to keep it warmer. Also recommended is keeping the fluid level lower in the battery in cold weather . . . ad infinitum. . . . What I have really said is that it could be almost anything along the way . . . and we've mentioned plenty of parts already! I think perhaps that first master drawing is the best checklist. Keep a copy in your car.

LEAK SYSTEM

Anything that carries a fluid can spring a leak . . . get a hole . . . water lines, oil lines, pipes, gas hoses and pipes. Gas leaks could lead to an explosion, and your nose will tell you if the leak is gas. Abandon a turned-off car, unless you can repair the hole . . . pipe tape, hose tape, impenetrable. In many cases of leaks you will be able to determine what type of fluid is leaking and where it is coming from. Your decision to make emergency repairs or go for help will be based on the type of condition and/or the supplies you have stashed in the trunk for emergencies.

NOISE SYSTEM

1. Resounding noise: Your car is suddenly a hot rod! This is muffler trouble . . . the explosions in the cylinder and the noise from them traveling out through the exhaust pipe, are not being quieted . . . muffled. Hole in the muffler? Hole in the exhaust pipe leading to the muffler? Get to a garage and hope you don't cross the path of a cop who wants to give you an "excessive noise traffic ticket." And don't let yourself be talked into being towed for this one, ticket or not—it's a hype. Your intentions are to get to the gas station. Tell the cop to save his tickets for the real offenders, the real hot-rodders.

2. Backfires: This is an inside the cylinder to outside problem; the explosions are escaping the wrong way . . . valves? piston rings? timing? bad connections? Is oil getting up into cylinders (rings)?

3. Clanking noises: Parts need more oil? Part fallen off or loose? Determine where the noise is coming from and when it happens. And check the oil level. Pull out the dipstick, wipe it off with a rag, insert it again and pull it out. Oil is dense and will cling to the dipstick. It should be up to the lowest marker at least, and that's low. (Normal and OK are between the marks.)

4. Knocking noises: This could indicate that you need to use a higher-quality gas. (I used to think the high-test premium gasolines were for the big, powerful cars, until one time a gas station attendant recommended that I use it for my little Volvo. . . . I thought my ex-husband had said, as he turned the car over to me, "Regular gas, special oil." My manual couldn't straighten me out on the gas—yes, special oil—so I followed the mechanic's advice.) Knocking could also be due to carbon trapped in one of the cylinders—a fast drive up a long hill is a recommended cure. It could also indicate the need for a timing adjustment—timing relates to the sparking sequence.

5. Buzzing: Could mean low oil in the transmission, causing it to overheat and not be smooth.

6. Clunking and thumping: Fan-belt pulleys out of line? Worn or ungreased universal joints. If it happens when you switch gears, it could be at the propeller-shaft connection where a lubrication is needed. Any number of other parts may be out of line and need adjusting.

7. Growling: Cold oil? If so, will go away after you drive awhile, slowly.

8. The horn . . . won't stop! The contact points could be stuck. Bang the horn box. No luck? Disconnect the wires.

9. Shudders when turned off: Idle too fast?

NOT-MOVING-RIGHT SYSTEM

1. Shimmy: Slight or not-so-slight fluttery movement. Uneven tire pressure in one or more tires? Front or back (or all) wheels must be properly lined up . . . facing exactly the same direction. . . . Not necessarily front and back together facing the same direction, but rather both fronts going the same place, and both backs going the same place . . . exactly. Springs or shock absorbers out of whack?

2. Wobbles and big wiggles: Stop! A tire could be coming off, or be loose enough to cause you an accident because of less maneuverability.

3. Pulling to one side: During braking it means that you need adjustment of brake drums and/or shoes and/or wheel cylinders, etc. something within the braking mechanism . . . the disks if you have disk brakes . . . have them attended to immediately. *During driving* it indicates the need for wheel realignment.

OVERHEATING SYSTEM

(Skip this, all you VW owners)

1. Serious overheating with steam visible: This means water-distribution problems. Do nothing until you think the car has cooled off considerably, because whatever is happening, the water is boiling, scalding . . . dangerous. Open the hood slowly and carefully, standing away a bit. A leak in the in or out hose could spew you with hot, *hot* water. Thermostat valve stuck? The water pump functioning? Fan belt broken (thus, no water pumping)? Fan belt loose and sluggish? (Could be slit and about to snap, or could mean an adjustment of one of the belt pulleys to tighten up the scene.) Water level? Release the pressure first before removing the cap, if you have a pressure-release cap. . . . No, not with your finger; that's *hot* steam coming out . . . but with a tool, screwdriver maybe. The water level should not be kept higher than 2 inches from the top and it mustn't get too much lower. If you can't see any, you've lost some or all. Look for a leak . . . and abandon! Go for help if you don't have enough spare water with you. If you refill, turn the car on as you do, so that it heats up a bit. Sounds kooky, I know, but it's recommended. You can also speed up the cooling-down time—if you have enough spare water to do this—by pouring some on the radiator. As it drips past the fan, the fan will distribute it all over the radiator. This means the car is on. (You will have to determine the safety of doing this.) Oil is also part of the engine-cooling process, so the overheating could be due to clogged or faulty oil distribution . . . any number of places.

   2. Minor overheating, no steam visible from under the hood: Heavy traffic? Stop, start . . . and you can't get off. Stay back; give yourself room to move forward every so often. Close your ears to the horns . . . they're in the same traffic mess . . . and they won't go through you, they'll just crawl up close to your bumpers, so that they feel they're going somewhere. Do yourself and them a favor: Don't start when everyone else starts. Wait a minute. Another thing you can do while you're stopped those times: Switch over into neutral and gun the motor to move things around a bit, get the water pump going (no cranking, no pumping). One final suggestion for this problem, when nothing serious is indicated, and nothing obvious is wrong—and yes, this will be the hottest day of the year when you decide to try it: Turn on the heater. The heater works because it draws off heat from the motor and delivers it into the car. (A trick my ex-husband related to me as he stripped off his wet clothes after a trip with a friend who tried this. It worked . . . it got them home and to a garage.)

BRAKE PROBLEMS

I've probably barely touched the surface of common problems, but you have the idea. It's an iffy, guesstimation diagnosis . . . many components come into the analysis, and the list is very long almost every time. Sometimes you'll be lucky, sometimes you won't. That is surely obvious by now.

It is also obvious that I haven't mentioned the *brake problems.* I was talking about *common* problems. Braking problems should *never* be a common problem, nor are they often a repeated problem if unattended for too long (a minute is too long). They can be the cause of a very severe, possibly fatal wreck for the car—and you! Anything funny at all—pull over and abandon! Be towed; don't try to get to the gas station, even slowly. The complete failure of the brakes (presaged by the unusual behavior) could happen on the way . . . and there could be a child, animal or another car in front of you when this happens.

The warning signs of *impending brake failure* are:

1. Having to push the brake pedal *all the way to the floor* before getting any action. (Low on brake fluid? Drums or shoes need adjustment?) It should hold at 2 inches above the floor, any closer means danger.

2. *Pedal sticks* to the floor. (Mechanism needs lubrication?)

3. *Mushy* feeling or *hard* feeling. This means trouble that must be checked.

4. *Not holding,* not locking, slipping: Bad, bad, bad.

5. *Pulling* to the side. (Drum linings worn? or shoes? Trouble with distribution of brake fluid from the master cylinder?)

6. Any kind of *noise* that occurs during braking.

All of these spell problems which need immediate attention . . . and abandonment. (Leave your husband and take the children with you if he insists on doing a macho scene!)

Occasional, non-repetitive problems (disaster may not be imminent):

1. Wet brakes: The brakes can become wet while you are driving in a rainstorm. After the storm they will dry out and function normally. During the storm, while you are driving, you should test them frequently. Don't drive long stretches without doing this. Gently push on the brakes. This will help them dry out for one thing and will tell you if you are in trouble.

2. Pumping the brakes to get better action sometimes gives a sort of adjustment to the workings, but frequent need of this . . . more than once . . . means trouble. Get thee to a garage!

PERIODIC SERVICE CHECKS

As you certainly know by now—always knew—parts wear out. The purpose of the periodic tests suggested by the manufacturer is to prevent the danger of parts going bad and creating emergencies. The suggested times for these tests are surely based on the life-expectancy of whatever is included in each test, and are surely scheduled before the life-expectancy is up. They are not just for the metal parts, but for the fluids as well. Thus, every time you buy gas, the water in the radiator, the battery fluid and the oil level should be checked. This is a habit suggested by the manufacturer. (Pity that all the gas-station attendants don't know more about cars!)

There are "2 months and/or 2,000 and 4,000 miles" checks (every 2 months and/or every 2,000 miles, every 4,000 miles). There are "6 month and/or 5,000 and 6,000 miles" checks, "12 months and/or 10,000 and 12,000 miles" checks . . . "24 months or 24,000 miles," "36 months or 36,000 miles," etc. These mean whichever is first. For example, every 2,000 miles it is necessary to lubricate the distributor cup, generator cup and water pump (if greased). Universal joints should be lubricated every 6,000 miles if they have grease fittings, every 24,000 miles if they are without grease fittings. Tires should be rotated every 6,000 miles. I won't give the long list because it is spelled out in your owner's manual. These periodic tests are usually done in the garage—unless you become qualified and have the thousands of tools and meters to do it—and they know what's included in each type of test.

I discovered recently that garages also have manuals detailing each type of test for each make of car and for many years of models. Thus you don't have to lend them your manual. Also, if you don't have a manual, and you have no luck getting one from the manufacturer (first make a big stink, as public as possible!), then ask to look at the garage copy if you need to know a part number or fuse number or whatever.

BE PREPARED—IN THE TRUNK

First, let us assume—let us know!—that the emergencies will come, no matter what good practices we employ, doing the 1,000-mile, 3,000-mile, etc., inspection checks. There will come times, if they haven't already, when you could have used some preparation. Get a cardboard box and begin to fill it with these preparations. This is a little like buying insurance. Once you've done it you probably won't need it. It'll be what you (and I) forgot! But do it anyway.

In the *spare parts area,* I would recommend a few that could be important; buy when you can afford or buy right away, depending on how you feel:

1. Spare gas-tank cap (if you live anywhere where they are stolen or if you've ever experienced the mechanic who forgot to put it back. Both have happened to me. One match tossed into the hole and *boom!*).
2. Spare fan belt—you know why.
3. Extra fuses, necessary for your lights.
4. Radiator cap with a pressure-relief valve. This allows you first to let out the pressure from a boiling radiator before you remove the cap. You could get badly scalded removing the cap too soon.
5. Spare tire, if you know that the one you have would get you only to the gas station in its condition . . . maybe all new tires if they are really worn.
6. Can of oil.
7. Gallon container of water.

Tools and temporary devices:

1. Screwdrivers. Look at any screws you think you might have to tighten or replace, and have a proper-sized screwdriver for each.
2. Socket wrenches. Particularly one that fits the nuts on the tires, this kind not this so that you have better leverage when turning it. Sometimes, (always?) they are very difficult to start turning. You could also carry a hammer to hit the end of the wrench with to get it started;

or a piece of hollow pipe big enough to slip the end of the wrench into, which will give you added leverage.

3. A good jack. We all differ in our likes and dislikes, abilities, strengths . . . you may like one too hard for somebody else to operate. If you're satisfied with yours, so be it. If you're not, look at all the kinds your friends have and try them. Look at what is available in the auto-parts stores, and have them demonstrated. Then select.

4. A bucket of sand or ashes, if you live in a temperature sometimes or always snowy or icy . . . for the tire going nowhere.

5. A couple of boards, if you live in a muddy area or will be traveling to one. The boards should be long enough to deliver you from the mush.

6. A roll of waterproof, leakproof tape, about 2 inches thick, for the holey hoses.

7. Jump cables, so that if your battery is dead, you can siphon off some electricity from somebody else's battery. Connect positive to positive, negative to negative, from car to car, but be sure to use a car that has the same battery voltage as yours. (*Safety note:* Attach the two positives, car to car, *then* the two negatives. Very serious is the possibility that if the positive and negative are attached to one car's battery, giving juice, the yet unattached positive and negative ends will touch each other on the way to the other car . . . DANGER!!! So do it the other way.) Regular passenger cars usually have 12-volt batteries, but check your manual to be positive. This is a bit scary the first couple of times. Connect the cables first, before you turn your car on. The car with the juice can be on, and you may see sparks as the connection is made. Then you can turn your car on. After the car kicks over, let it just sit for five or ten minutes to get a decent charge. Don't give it the gas during this time. Remember that the reason you need a charge may not be simply that you need a new battery; it could be the generator, the connections, etc. Search for the problem or have the car checked at the garage.

8. Flashlights, which must be tested periodically, and spare bulbs for them. Spare batteries are a waste, for they go bad as fast as the ones inside. One flashlight—or more, in case you and the family are stranded and have to walk after you've used one to

check for the malfunction. Another with a red blinker, to place behind the car five or ten car lengths back to give plenty of advance warning to oncoming cars. Or you could also get flares and light-sensitive signs telling of your trouble. These types of things are available in emergency kits for cars—a good investment. In any case, if you have to remain with the car and it's not in too safe a place—and even if you've got warning lights, etc.— get out of the car and go back behind the car, many feet to be safe. You've surely read about all the people killed while standing by their disabled cars. If you have no warning lights, put on your back blinkers, or anything else if it's working, day or night. Also, standing back several feet from your car, you can wave to cars, by hand or flashlight, to warn of danger.

9. Wedges of wood or bricks, for stabilizing the car during a tire change.

OTHER TYPES OF CAR
PROPULSION

The electric engine, which we hear much about these days during the war on pollution, is simply an electrically operated motor used to turn the shaft propelling the car. There are no cylinders, sparks, or pistons. Acutally, the motor is probably just a more powerful motor than the starter motor, and it functions similarly. However, a huge battery of great weight is required to store enough electrical energy for only about 60 miles, limiting the car to local trips. Thought has been and is being given to making it possible to recharge the battery at "gas" stations so that the car could be used for longer trips, but the ideas are still on the drawing table. Perhaps some breakthrough battery invention will make electric cars a viable alternative. Besides, isn't the world's gas supply diminishing?

The Wankel engine is a revolutionary departure from the "reciprocating" engine, with its piston-up-and-down-turning-the-shaft procedure. The internal-combustion property of the engine discussed earlier is still a feature of the Wankel, but the Wankel engine is termed a "rotor engine."

Here is a simplified version of how it works (we are still dealing with the four phases of internal combustion: intake, compression, power and exhaust):

The engine exterior is shaped like an ellipse. The chamber within is shaped like an 8. (That shape is called epitrochoidal . . . in case you didn't know. I didn't.) Within the chamber, a rotor (shaped like a triangle) rotates around a fixed gear. The fit is very tight in each position of the rotor, providing three separate chambers in which various phases of the internal combustion take place.

Look at the first illustration. In chamber *a* the fuel mixture has just been taken in.

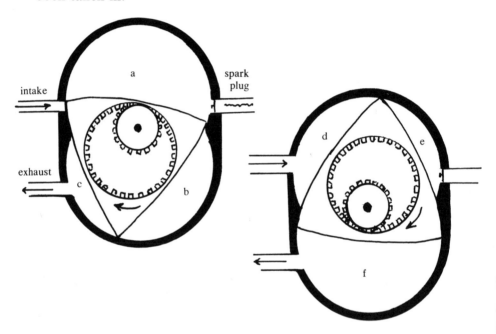

Now look at the second illustration. The rotor has turned; the chamber *d* is smaller than *a* was, thus the fuel is compressed. At the right time, the spark will fire and cause combustion, creating the power to continue turning the rotor.

In chamber *b* exhaust is on its way out. In chamber *f,* the exhaust from a previous cycle is being sucked out. In chamber *c* it's out, or almost out. In chamber *d,* the fuel is coming in. Many things are going on as the rotor turns.

The advantages of the Wankel are that the size of the motor is about two-thirds that of the reciprocating engine, and the ride is smoother and quieter because there is less vibration.

The disadvantages are that it consumes more fuel than the reciprocating engine, thus polluting more; and there is current concern about the wear and tear on the points of the rotor, where seal is critical.

However, the advantage of the smaller motor size enhances the possibility of reducing the polluting disadvantages somewhat. For more effective antipollution devices can be designed to fit in all that extra space.

APPENDIX

THE MATH OF BUILDING

IS NOT "NEW MATH,"

THANK GOD

There is one factor contributing to this myth of man's which sometimes impedes us, and it dates from grammar school. Arithmetic! Yes, that subject forbidden to girls—all those "mental blocks" we had were encouraged! Math was the boys' thing. Only their minds could absorb its complexity, right?! (But it was OK if they weren't such good spellers!) As we got older, the myth was perpetuated even further—what do girls need math for? Engineers, architects, and physicists all are men, right? Did anyone ever stop to realize the monumental level of higher math required every day of women in supermarkets all over the world? And how many times did we shrink back in school when we knew the math answer because we might seem smarter than the boys (and not get dates)? That, perhaps, was the ultimate success of the myth making the cliché "mental block" acceptable for girls—the bigger the block, the more dates you had.

I want to reveal something now which may cause some of you to say, "No wonder she can build." (Don't say it, it is really not true.) Anyway, I was good at arithmetic and math (the high-school word then). It seems that I've spent a good part of my forty years justifying it, too. And I've spent another good part of those years in awe of people who could analyze literature, or even a movie; because, as an infrequent reader during school years, I didn't get the kind of training to accept variable thoughts.

357

Arithmetic, on the other hand, is an unvarying progression of facts, concepts, which can be memorized, which will never change . . . $1 + 1 = 2$ . . . 12 inches $= 1$ foot.

FRACTIONS: THE WORDS AND THE RULES

"And" means plus $(+)$, add.
"Less" means minus $(-)$, subtract.
"Of" means times $(\times)$, multiply.
"Over"/"into" means $\div$, divide.

Add Fractions

a) Change all fractions to fractions with the same number on bottom, the common denominator.
b) Add the tops.
c) Reduce the fraction by dividing the same number into both top and bottom if possible.

Example: $\dfrac{1}{2} + \dfrac{1}{3} = \dfrac{3}{6} + \dfrac{2}{6} = \dfrac{5}{6}$ *or* $\dfrac{3+2}{6} = \dfrac{5}{6}$

⅚ is the smallest fraction and cannot be reduced further because there is no number that will divide into both 5 and 6.

Subtract Fractions

Change fractions to those with the same denominators, as in addition. (Multiply top and bottom of fraction by same number to get desired bottom number.)

Example: $\dfrac{1}{2} - \dfrac{1}{3} = \dfrac{3}{6} - \dfrac{2}{6} = \dfrac{3-2=1}{6}$

Getting the common denominator: $\dfrac{1 \times 3}{2 \times 3} = \dfrac{3}{6}$ $\dfrac{1 \times 2}{3 \times 2} = \dfrac{2}{6}$

Multiply Fractions

a) Multiply tops; multiply bottoms.
b) Reduce fraction.

Example: $\dfrac{3}{4} \times \dfrac{2}{5} = \dfrac{3 \times 2}{4 \times 5} = \dfrac{6}{20} = \dfrac{3}{10}$

Reduce fraction: $\dfrac{6}{20}$ $\dfrac{6 \div 2}{20 \div 2} = \dfrac{3}{10}$

Divide Fractions

a) Reverse divisor (fraction to right of ÷).
b) Multiply fractions (follow multiply steps).

Example: $\dfrac{3}{4} \div \dfrac{2}{5} = \dfrac{3}{4} \times \dfrac{5}{2} = \dfrac{3 \times 5}{4 \times 2} = \dfrac{15}{8} = 1\dfrac{7}{8}$

$\dfrac{15}{8} = \dfrac{8}{8} + \dfrac{7}{8} = \dfrac{1}{1} + \dfrac{7}{8} = 1 + \dfrac{7}{8} = 1\dfrac{7}{8}$

In Tips on Using Tools and Materials (page 76), it was recommended that the screw or nail connecting two pieces of wood at a joint be 1⅔ longer than the first piece of wood's thickness, which was ¾″ in the example.

$$1\dfrac{2}{3} \times \dfrac{3}{4} = \left[\dfrac{3}{3} + \dfrac{2}{3}\right] \times \dfrac{3}{4} = \dfrac{5}{3} \times \dfrac{3}{4} = \dfrac{15}{12} = \dfrac{5}{4} = 1\dfrac{1}{4}$$ $$\dfrac{15 \div 3}{12 \div 3} = \dfrac{5}{4}$$

or

$$1 \times \dfrac{3}{4} + \dfrac{2}{3} \times \dfrac{3}{4} = \dfrac{3}{4} + \dfrac{6}{12} = \dfrac{3}{4} + \dfrac{2}{4} = \dfrac{5}{4} = 1\dfrac{1}{4}$$

or

In ¾ there are 3 quarters; ⅔ of 3 quarters is 2 quarters. So the original ¾ plus ¾ more is 1¼.

HOW TO BUY

HOW-TO-DO-IT BOOKS

Yes, there are some very good books. I particularly like the Sunset soft-cover books for building-project ideas. However, I must warn you that the plans for all the ideas mentioned are not included and you will need your educated eye for many things in the books.

Some books, however, the fat "everything" books in particular, are not conveniently organized; most assume some previous knowledge of the vocabulary and methods; and many are a compilation of magazine articles, some ten or more years old.

Some books assume that you know how to do the step before the one they are discussing at a particular point . . . and nowhere is this previous step described. Some suggest sophisticated methods when simple ones would do. Others simply do not start at the beginning. (I can't tell you in how many books I searched for a clear description of just exactly what *short circuit* means, in terms of what is happening in relation to what should be happening. And nowhere could I find *how* poisonous was poisonous sewer gas!)

1) Try a library first, one big enough to have a good variety.
2) Have a specific need in mind, or use a test word or project. Look in the alphabetical index for it. If it's not there, look for other words it might be listed under. If it's not there, go on to another book.

3) If you do find the subject you are looking for, read the information carefully. If you find it confusing, close the book and put it back on the shelf. Other things may be confusing.

4) You do find the subject clear and understandable. Try a few other basic subjects to be sure it isn't a fluke, subjects you understand well enough to be critical. With luck you may find one book for all, but it is more likely that you will have to live with specialized books—one for plumbing, one for electricity, etc. That's OK, there are some good ones: Sears has a great book on wiring a house . . . and Audel's books, organized by topic, are also clear and basic. Audel's books are in many libraries, have a look at them. And the Sunset books, large paperbacks, have great building ideas. And if you want to explore the subject of refinishing furniture, and have some laughs at the same time, get a copy of Grotz's *The Furniture Doctor.* In the automobile area, the best series I've seen are the Chilton books. You will find one devoted to your own specific make of car. They are quite clear and well illustrated.

BIBLIOGRAPHY

Audel, Theodore, & Co., Publisher, *Carpenters and Builders Library* series; *Plumbers and Pipefitters Library* series.

Crouse, William, *Automotive Engines* (McGraw-Hill, 1966).

Daniels, George, *1001 Ways to Repair and Improve Your Home* (Hawthorne Books, Inc., 1955).

Day, Richard, *The Practical Handbook of Plumbing and Heating* (Fawcett Publications, Inc., 1969).

Frankl, Lee (Training-Thru-Sight Associates), *Home Repairs Made Easy* (Nelson Doubleday, Inc., 1949).

Hyde, Margaret Oldoroyd, *Driving Today and Tomorrow,* illustrated by Clifford N. Geary (McGraw-Hill, 1965).

Richter, H. P., *Wiring Simplified* (Park Publishing, Inc., 1971).

Simplified Electrical Wiring (Sears Roebuck and Co., 1969).

INDEX